Principles
in Practice

MW01154722

The Principles in Practice imprint offers teachers concrete illustrations of effective classroom practices based in NCTE research briefs and policy statements. Each book discusses the research on a specific topic, links the research to an NCTE brief or policy statement, and then demonstrates how those principles come alive in practice: by showcasing actual classroom practices that demonstrate the policies in action; by talking about research in practical, teacher-friendly language; and by offering teachers possibilities for rethinking their own practices in light of the ideas presented in the books. Books within the imprint are grouped in strands, each strand focused on a significant topic of interest.

Adolescent Literacy Strand

Adolescent Literacy at Risk? The Impact of Standards (2009) Rebecca Bowers Sipe

Adolescents and Digital Literacies: Learning Alongside Our Students (2010) Sara Kajder

Adolescent Literacy and the Teaching of Reading: Lessons for Teachers of Literature (2010) Deborah Appleman

Rethinking the "Adolescent" in Adolescent Literacy (2017) Sophia Tatiana Sarigianides, Robert Petrone, and Mark A. Lewis

Restorative Justice in the English Language Arts Classroom (2019) Maisha T. Winn, Hannah Graham, and Rita Renjitham Alfred

Writing in Today's Classrooms Strand

Writing in the Dialogical Classroom: Students and Teachers Responding to the Texts of Their Lives (2011) Bob Fecho

Becoming Writers in the Elementary Classroom: Visions and Decisions (2011) Katie Van Sluys

Writing Instruction in the Culturally Relevant Classroom (2011) Maisha T. Winn and Latrise P. Johnson

Writing Can Change Everything: Middle Level Kids Writing Themselves into the World (2020) Shelbie Witte, editor

Literacy Assessment Strand

Our Better Judgment: Teacher Leadership for Writing Assessment (2012) Chris W. Gallagher and Eric D. Turley

Beyond Standardized Truth: Improving Teaching and Learning through Inquiry-Based Reading Assessment (2012) Scott Filkins

Reading Assessment: Artful Teachers, Successful Students (2013) Diane Stephens, editor

Going Public with Assessment: A Community Practice Approach (2018) Kathryn Mitchell Pierce and Rosario Ordoñez-Jasis

Literacies of the Disciplines Strand

Entering the Conversations: Practicing Literacy in the Disciplines (2014) Patricia Lambert Stock, Trace Schillinger, and Andrew Stock

Real-World Literacies: Disciplinary Teaching in the High School Classroom (2014) Heather Lattimer

Doing and Making Authentic Literacies (2014) Linda Denstaedt, Laura Jane Roop, and Stephen Best

Reading in Today's Classrooms Strand

Connected Reading: Teaching Adolescent Readers in a Digital World (2015) Kristen Hawley Turner and Troy Hicks

Digital Reading: What's Essential in Grades 3–8 (2015) William L. Bass II and Franki Sibberson

Teaching Reading with YA Literature: Complex Texts, Complex Lives (2016) Jennifer Buehler

Teaching English Language Learners Strand

Beyond "Teaching to the Test": Rethinking Accountability and Assessment for English Language Learners (2017) Betsy Gilliland and Shannon Pella

Community Literacies en Confianza: *Learning from Bilingual After-School Programs* (2017) Steven Alvarez

Understanding Language: Supporting ELL Students in Responsive ELA Classrooms (2017) Melinda J. McBee Orzulak

Writing across Culture and Language: Inclusive Strategies for Working with ELL Writers in the ELA Classroom (2017) Christina Ortmeier-Hooper

Students' Rights to Read and Write Strand

Adventurous Thinking: Fostering Students' Rights to Read and Write in Secondary ELA Classrooms (2019) Mollie V. Blackburn, editor

In the Pursuit of Justice: Students' Rights to Read and Write in Elementary School (2020) Mariana Souto-Manning, editor

Already Readers and Writers: Honoring Students' Rights to Read and Write in the Middle Grade Classroom (2020) Jennifer Ochoa, editor

Already Readers and Writers

Honoring Students' Rights to Read and Write in the Middle Grade Classroom

Edited by

Jennifer Ochoa
MS 324, The Patria Mirabel School, New York City
Lehman College, City University of New York

National Council of Teachers of English
340 N. Neil St., Suite #104, Champaign, Illinois 61820
www.ncte.org

Staff Editor: Bonny Graham
Imprint Editor: Cathy Fleischer
Interior Design: Victoria Pohlmann
Cover Design: Pat Mayer
Cover Image: Pam Hinden

NCTE Stock Number: 01155; eStock Number: 01179
ISBN 978-0-8141-0115-5; eISBN 978-0-8141-0117-9

Library of Congress Cataloging-in-Publication Data

Names: Ochoa, Jennifer, 1970- editor.

Title: Already readers and writers : honoring students' rights to read and write in the middle grade classroom / [edited by]Jennifer Ochoa.

Description: Champaign, Illinois : National Council of Teachers of English, 2020. | Series: Principles in practice | Includes bibliographical references and index. | Summary: "Middle school teachers and others examine current middle school literacy practices that support students' rights to read and write authentically"—Provided by publisher.

Identifiers: LCCN 2020019869 (print) | LCCN 2020019870 (ebook) | ISBN 9780814101155 (trade paperback) | ISBN 9780814101179 (adobe pdf)

Subjects: LCSH: Language arts (Middle school)—United States.

Classification: LCC LB1631.A46 2020 (print) | LCC LB1631 (ebook) | DDC 428.0071/2—dc23

LC record available at https://lccn.loc.gov/2020019869

LC ebook record available at https://lccn.loc.gov/2020019870

For Franki, our lovely little reader.

My wish for your school life is that every teacher you learn with honors that you have been a reader since your very first days.

Contents

Acknowledgments

The first meeting I ever had with Principles in Practice Imprint Editor Cathy Fleischer was ten days after the 2016 presidential election. Everyone that year at the National Council of Teachers of English (NCTE) Annual Convention, it seemed, was reeling. And after Cathy and I hugged and stared at each other meaningfully—because at that point, there just were no words—she said, wisely, "Well, let's talk about your book; it's going to be really important for it to be in the world now." As with many people, that election went beyond stunning me; it paralyzed me. The results gripped me in a vise that made productivity difficult. During the writing of this book, I often sat staring at the screen and thinking, What can I possibly say when everything feels so impossibly out of control? And throughout it all, Cathy kept saying, "Jen, we need this book! Just keep writing!" For that, I am forever thankful. What a kind, generous editor, who got this book and its author through the writing so patiently.

Similarly, I thank the Books crew at NCTE, Kurt Austin and Bonny Graham, who waited and continued to wait for a book well past the time we'd thought a book would be born. I so appreciate that you were still there, ready to publish when I finally finished.

I'd also like to extend my most heartfelt thanks to all the teachers and other contributors who shared your classrooms, your kids, and your teaching life through your vignettes. As other middle school teachers read your words, I know they will feel the special kinship that only people who spend all day being the grownups in middle school classrooms completely understand.

Personally, I have to start with my teacher moms. When I was a baby teacher in Lansing, Michigan, in 1992, Diana Mitchell opened her classroom and her career to me. She stood next to me as I took the reins, coached from the sidelines, and then became my colleague. Luckily, she brought my other teacher moms, Janet Swenson and Toby Kahn-Loftus, into my life. Thank you, Moms; I am the teacher I am today because of all of you. You didn't tell me what to do or even show me what to do; you all said, "Come stand next to us. Do this with us." And that has made all the difference.

I could not have written a book without my Flock: Priscilla Thomas, Alie Stumpf, Kate Seltzer, Tom Venker, and our additional flock member, Christy Kingham. A person could never have better cheerleaders than all of you. Thank you for just deciding it was a fact I would write a book. I never thought that I would, but you all always knew it would happen. Thank you for our teaching family.

I want to extend love and appreciation to the four amazing teachers I have shared a classroom with as a co-teacher: Ann George, Blake Kastle, Sarah Merchelwitz Kuhner, and Meagan Hammerbacher. Folks who co-teach say it's like a good marriage or a bad marriage. Our relationships have been the kind of teaching marriages that feel like a home. There is something extraordinary about having another adult in the classroom; in all the moments that are charged with adolescent electricity, it's good to have a partner to bear witness with; . . . thank you for bearing witness with me.

In addition, these pages are filled with ideas and strategies and lessons born not just from my own thinking, but from the deep collaboration a grade team can achieve together. I want to thank my amazing eighth-grade co-planners: thank you Gina Salerno, Lindsey Stoddard, Jon Cabrera, Thelma Dolmo, and Judith Myrthil Singleton. When my ideas get loopy and too big, you all have helped me bring them down, added your own ideas, and together we've made a really fine curriculum for our MS 324 kids to live and learn through.

When you are in your classroom teaching, you don't think that what you do is work others could easily learn from. I'd like to thank Kylene Beers and Bob Probst for visiting Room A205 and telling me, and then the world, the work we were doing was something worth knowing about.

Of course I have to thank my brothers, Ian and Jon(athan). Before I was a teacher, before I read books every day with students, before I read drafts of kid writing that I needed to grade, I read books with you and edited your poetry and essays and papers. I have loved being your big sister, and I thank you for letting me practice being an English teacher on you two.

Mom and Dad, you both showed me what it meant to honor a person's rights to read and write from the time I was a tiny person. You let me pick whatever books I wanted, never limiting how many stories you read and reread to me or censoring what books I was reading. You were the first readers of my writing when I was writing plays and stories and poems and reports because I was bored and had stuff to say. You always told me that my words mattered in the world. Without you two and the literacy ground you planted me in, I would not be the reader, writer, or teacher I've come to be. I am so lucky I got to be your kid.

And finally, thank you to my beloved Pam. Everything just got better when you came along. Thank you for knowing we belonged to each other. Your encouragement and support through the process of writing this book has made the whole thing possible. Even now, as I type, you are calling down that you've made dinner and I should come up and have some. I'm done now, and I can come back to joining you in our happy, happy life.

The Students' Right to Read

The NCTE Executive Committee reaffirmed this guideline in November 2012.

This statement was originally developed in 1981, revised April 2009 to adhere to NCTE's Policy on Involvement of People of Color, and revised again in September 2018.

Overview: The Students' Right to Read provides resources that can be used to help discuss and ensure students' free access to all texts. The genesis of the Students' Right to Read was an original Council statement, "Request for Reconsideration of a Work," prepared by the Committee on the Right to Read of the National Council of Teachers of English and revised by Ken Donelson. The current Students' Right to Read statement represents an updated second edition that builds on the work of Council members dedicated to ensuring students the freedom to choose to read any text and opposing "efforts of individuals or groups to limit the freedom of choice of others." Supported through references from text challenges and links to resources, this statement discusses the history and dangers of text censorship which highlight the breadth and significance of the Students' Right to Read. The statement then culminates in processes that can be followed with different stakeholders when students' reading rights are infringed.

The Right to Read and the Teacher of English

For many years, American schools have been pressured to restrict or deny students access to texts deemed objectionable by some individual or group. These pressures have mounted in recent years, and English teachers have no reason to believe they will diminish. The fight against censorship is a continuing series of skirmishes, not a pitched battle leading to a final victory over censorship.

We can safely make two statements about censorship: first, any text is potentially open to attack by someone, somewhere, sometime, for some reason; second, censorship is often arbitrary and irrational. For example, classics traditionally used in English classrooms have been accused of containing obscene, heretical, or subversive elements such as the following:

- Plato's *Republic*: "the book is un-Christian"
- Jules Verne's *Around the World in Eighty Days*: "very unfavorable to Mormons"
- Nathaniel Hawthorne's *The Scarlet Letter*: "a filthy book"
- Shakespeare's *Macbeth*: "too violent for children today"
- Fyodor Dostoevsky's *Crime and Punishment*: "a poor model for young people"
- Herman Melville's *Moby-Dick*: "contains homosexuality"

Modern works, even more than the classics, are criticized with terms such as "filthy," "un-American," "overly realistic," and "anti-war." Some books have been attacked merely for being "controversial," suggesting that for some people the purpose of education is not the investigation of ideas but rather the indoctrination of a certain set of beliefs and standards. Referencing multiple years of research completed by the American Library Association

The Students' Right to Read

(ALA), the following statements represent complaints typical of those made against modern works of literature:

- J. D. Salinger's *The Catcher in the Rye*: "profanity, lurid passages about sex, and statements defamatory to minorities, God, women, and the disabled"
- John Steinbeck's *The Grapes of Wrath*: "uses the name of God and Jesus in a vain and profane manner"
- Peter Parnell and Justin Richardson's *And Tango Makes Three*: "anti-ethnic, anti-family, homosexuality, religious viewpoint, unsuited to age group"
- Harper Lee's *To Kill a Mockingbird*: "promotes racial hatred, racial division, racial separation, and promotes white supremacy"
- Katherine Paterson's *Bridge to Terabithia*: "occult/Satanism, offensive language, violence"
- Toni Morrison's *The Bluest Eye*: "offensive language, sexually explicit, unsuited to age group"
- Jessica Herthel and Jazz Jennings's *I Am Jazz*: "inaccurate, homosexuality, sex education, religious viewpoint, and unsuited for age group"

Some groups and individuals have also raised objections to literature written specifically for young people. As long as novels intended for young people stayed at the intellectual and emotional level of *A Date for Marcy* or *A Touchdown for Thunderbird High*, censors could forego criticism. But many contemporary novels for adolescents focus on the real world of young people—drugs, premarital sex, alcoholism, divorce, gangs, school dropouts, racism, violence, and sensuality. English teachers willing to defend classics and modern literature must be prepared to give equally spirited defense to serious and worthwhile children's and young adult novels.

Literature about minoritized ethnic or racial groups remains "controversial" or "objectionable" to many adults. As long as groups such as African Americans, Pacific Islanders, American Indians, Asian Americans, and Latinxs "kept their proper place"—awarded them by a White society—censors rarely raised their voices. But attacks have increased in frequency as minoritized groups have refused to observe their assigned "place." Though nominally, the criticisms of literature about minoritized racial or ethnic groups have usually been directed at "bad language," "suggestive situations," "questionable literary merit," or "ungrammatical English" (usually oblique complaints about the different dialect or culture of a group), the underlying motive for some attacks has unquestionably been discriminatory. Typical of censors' criticisms of ethnic works are the following comments:

- Maya Angelou's *I Know Why the Caged Bird Sings*: "homosexuality, offensive language, racism, sexually explicit, unsuited to age group"
- Rudolfo Anaya's *Bless Me, Ultima*: "occult/Satanism, offensive language, religious viewpoint, sexually explicit, violence"
- Khaled Hosseini's *The Kite Runner*: "sexual violence, religious themes, 'may lead to terrorism'"

- Sherman Alexie's *The Absolutely True Diary of a Part-Time Indian*: "anti-family, cultural insensitivity, drugs/alcohol/smoking, gambling, offensive language, sex education, sexually explicit, unsuited for age group, violence, depictions of bullying"

Books are not alone in being subject to censorship. Magazines or newspapers used, recommended, or referred to in English classes have increasingly drawn the censor's fire. Few libraries would regard their periodical collection as worthwhile or representative without some or all of the following publications, but all of them have been the target of censors on occasion:

- *National Geographic*: "Nudity and sensationalism, especially in stories on barbaric foreign people."
- *Scholastic Magazine*: "Doctrines opposing the beliefs of the majority, socialistic programs; promotes racial unrest and contains very detailed geography of foreign countries, especially those inhabited by dark people."
- *National Observer*: "Right-wing trash with badly reported news."
- *New York Times*: "That thing should be outlawed after printing the Pentagon Papers and helping our country's enemies."

The immediate results of demands to censor books or periodicals vary. At times, school boards and administrators have supported and defended their teachers, their use of materials under fire, and the student's right of access to the materials. At other times, however, special committees have been formed to cull out "objectionable works" or "modern trash" or "controversial literature." Some teachers have been summarily reprimanded for assigning certain works, even to mature students. Others have been able to retain their positions only after initiating court action.

Not as sensational, but perhaps more important, are the long range effects of censoring the rights of educators and students to self-select what they read and engage with. Schools have removed texts from libraries and classrooms and curricula have been changed when English teachers have avoided using or recommending works which might make some members of the community uncomfortable or angry. Over the course of their schooling, many students are consequently "educated" in a system that is hostile to critical inquiry and dialogue. And many teachers and other school staff learn to emphasize their own sense of comfort and safety rather than their students' needs.

The problem of censorship does not derive solely from the small anti-intellectual, ultra-moral, or ultra-patriotic groups which will typically function in a society that guarantees freedom of speech and freedom of the press. The present concern is rather with the frequency and force of attacks by others, often people of good will and the best intentions, some from within the teaching profession. The National Council of Teachers of English, the National Education Association, the American Federation of Teachers, and the American Library Association, as well as the publishing industry and writers themselves agree: pressures for censorship are great throughout our society.

The material that follows is divided into two sections. The first on "The Right to Read" is addressed to parents and the community at large. The other section, "A Program of

The Students' Right to Read

Action," lists Council recommendations for establishing professional committees in every school to set up procedures for book selection, to work for community support, and to review complaints against texts.

Where suspicion fills the air and holds scholars in line for fear of their jobs, there can be no exercise of the free intellect. . . . A problem can no longer be pursued with impunity to its edges. Fear stalks the classroom. The teacher is no longer a stimulant to adventurous thinking; she [sic] becomes instead a pipe line for safe and sound information. A deadening dogma takes the place of free inquiry. Instruction tends to become sterile; pursuit of knowledge is discouraged; discussion often leaves off where it should begin.

—Justice William O. Douglas, United States Supreme Court:
Adler v. Board of Education, 1951

The Right to Read

An open letter to our country from the National Council of Teachers of English:

The right to read, like all rights guaranteed or implied within our constitutional tradition, can be used wisely or foolishly. In many ways, education is an effort to improve the quality of choices open to all students. But to deny the freedom of choice in fear that it may be unwisely used is to destroy the freedom itself. For this reason, we respect the right of individuals to be selective in their own reading. But for the same reason, we oppose efforts of individuals or groups to limit the freedom of choice of others or to impose their own standards or tastes upon the community at large.

One of the foundations of a democratic society is the individual's right to read, and also the individual's right to freely choose what they would like to read. This right is based on an assumption that the educated possess judgment and understanding and can be trusted with the determination of their own actions. In effect, the reader is freed from the bonds of chance. The reader is not limited by birth, geographic location, or time, since reading allows meeting people, debating philosophies, and experiencing events far beyond the narrow confines of an individual's own existence.

In selecting texts to read by young people, English teachers consider the contribution each work may make to the education of the reader, its aesthetic value, its honesty, its readability for a particular group of students, and its appeal to young children and adolescents. English teachers, however, may use different texts for different purposes. The criteria for choosing a text to be read by an entire class are somewhat different from the criteria for choosing texts to be read by small groups.

For example, a teacher might select John Knowles's *A Separate Peace* for reading by an entire class, partly because the book has received wide critical recognition, partly because it is relatively short and will keep the attention of many slower readers, and partly because it has proved popular with many students of widely differing skill sets. The same teacher, faced with the responsibility of choosing or recommending books for several small groups of students, might select or recommend books as different as Nathaniel Hawthorne's *The Scarlet Letter*, Alexander Solzhenitsyn's *One Day in the Life of Ivan Denisovitch*, Marjane Satrapi[1]'s *Persepolis*, Malcolm X's *The Autobiography of Malcolm X*, Charles Dickens's *Great*

Expectations, Carlos Bulosan's *America Is in the Heart*, or Paul Zindel's *The Pigman*, depending upon the skills and interests of the students in each group.

And the criteria for suggesting books to individuals or for recommending something worth reading for a student who casually stops by after class are different from selecting material for a class or group. As opposed to censoring, the teacher selects texts, and also helps guide students to self-select them. Selection implies that one is free to choose a text, depending upon the purpose to be achieved and the students or class in question, but a book selected this year may be ignored next year, and the reverse. Censorship implies that certain works are not open to selection, this year or any year.

Wallace Stevens once wrote, "Literature is the better part of life. To this it seems inevitably necessary to add / provided life is the better part of literature" (1957). Students and parents have the right to demand that education today keep students in touch with the reality of the world outside the classroom. Many of our best literary works ask questions as valid and significant today as when the literature first appeared, questions like "What is the nature of humanity?" "Why do people praise individuality and practice conformity?" "What do people need for a good life?" and "What is the nature of a good person?" English teachers must be free to employ books, classic or contemporary, which do not hide, or lie to the young, about the perilous but wondrous times we live in, books which talk of the fears, hopes, joys, and frustrations people experience, books about people not only as they are but as they can be. English teachers forced through the pressures of censorship to use only safe or antiseptic works are placed in the morally and intellectually untenable position of lying to their students about the nature and condition of humanity.

The teacher must exercise care to select or recommend works for class reading and group discussion. One of the most important responsibilities of the English teacher is developing rapport and respect among students. Respect for the uniqueness and potential of the individual, an important facet of the study of literature, should be emphasized in the English class. One way rapport and respect can be developed is through encouraging the students themselves to explore and engage with texts of their own selection. Also, English classes should reflect the cultural contributions of minoritized groups in the United States, just as they should acquaint students with diverse contributions by the many peoples of the world. Finally, the teacher should be prepared to support and defend their classroom and students' process in selecting and engaging with diverse texts against potential censorship and controversy.

The Threat to Education

Censorship leaves students with an inadequate and distorted picture of the ideals, values, and problems of their culture. Writers may often represent their culture, or they may stand to the side and describe and evaluate that culture. Yet partly because of censorship or the fear of censorship, many writers are ignored or inadequately represented in the public schools, and many are represented in anthologies not by their best work but by their "safest" or "least offensive" work.

The censorship pressures receiving the greatest publicity are those of small groups who protest the use of a limited number of books with some "objectionable" realistic elements,

The Students' Right to Read

such as *Brave New World*, *Lord of the Flies*, *George*, *The Joy Luck Club*, *Catch-22*, *Their Eyes Were Watching God*, or *A Day No Pigs Would Die*. The most obvious and immediate victims are often found among our best and most creative English teachers, those who have ventured outside the narrow boundaries of conventional texts. Ultimately, however, the real victims are the students, denied the freedom to explore ideas and pursue truth wherever and however they wish.

Great damage may be done by book committees appointed by national or local organizations to pore over anthologies, texts, library books, and paperbacks to find passages which advocate, or seem to advocate, causes or concepts or practices these organizations condemn. As a result, some publishers, sensitive to possible objections, carefully exclude sentences or selections that might conceivably offend some group, somehow, sometime, somewhere.

The Community's Responsibility

Individuals who care about the improvement of education are urged to join students, teachers, librarians, administrators, boards of education, and professional and scholarly organizations in support of the students' right to read. Widespread and informed support in and across communities can assure that

- enough residents are interested in the development and maintenance of a rigorous school system to guarantee its achievement;
- malicious gossip, ignorant rumors, internet posts, and deceptive letters to the editor will not be circulated without challenge and correction;
- news media will observe that the public sincerely desires objective reporting about education, free from slanting or editorial comment which destroys confidence in and support for schools;
- the community will not permit its resources and energies to be dissipated in conflicts created by special interest groups striving to advance their ideologies or biases; and
- faith in democratic processes will be promoted and maintained.

A Program of Action

Censorship in schools is a widespread problem. Teachers of English, librarians, and school administrators can best serve students, literature, and the profession today if they prepare now to face pressures sensibly, demonstrating on the one hand a willingness to consider the merits of any complaint and on the other the courage to defend their literacy program with intelligence and vigor. The Council therefore recommends that schools undertake the following two-step program to protect the students' right to read:

- establish a diverse committee that is representative of the local school community to consider book selection procedures and to screen complaints; and
- promote a community atmosphere in which local residents may be enlisted to support the freedom to read.

Procedures for Text Selection

Although one may defend the freedom to read without reservation as one of the hallmarks of a free society, there is no substitute for informed, professional, and qualified book selection. English teachers are typically better qualified to choose and recommend texts for their classes than persons not prepared in the field. Nevertheless, administrators have certain legal and professional responsibilities. For these reasons and as a matter of professional courtesy, they should be kept informed about the criteria and the procedures used by English teachers in selecting books and the titles of the texts used.

In each school, the English department should develop its own statement explaining why literature is taught and how books are chosen for each class. This statement should be on file with the administration before any complaints are received. The statement should also support the teacher's right to choose supplementary materials, to build a diverse classroom library, and to discuss controversial issues insofar as they are relevant. In addition, students should be allowed the right to self-select books to read from classroom and school library shelves.

Operating within such a policy, the English department should take the following steps:

- Establish a committee to support English teachers in finding exciting and challenging texts of potential value to students at a specific school. Schools without departments or small schools with a few English teachers should organize a permanent committee charged with the responsibility of alerting other teachers to new texts just published, or old texts now forgotten which might prove valuable in the literacy program. Students should be encouraged to participate in the greatest degree that their development and skill sets allow.

- Devote time at each department or grade-level meeting to reviews and comments by the above committee or plan special meetings for this purpose. Free and open discussions on texts of potential value to students would seem both reasonable and normal for any English department. Teachers should be encouraged to challenge any texts recommended or to suggest titles hitherto ignored. Require that each English teacher give a rationale for any text to be read by an entire class. Written rationales for all texts read by an entire class would serve the department well if censorship should strike. A file of rationales should serve as impressive evidence to the administration and the community that English teachers have not chosen their texts lightly or haphazardly.

- Report to the administration the texts that will be used for class reading by each English teacher.

A procedure such as this gives each teacher the right to expect support from fellow teachers and administrators whenever someone objects to a text.

The Legal Problem

Apart from the professional and moral issues involved in censorship, there are legal matters about which NCTE cannot give advice. The Council is not a legal authority. Across the nation, moreover, conditions vary so much that no one general principle applies. In some

The Students' Right to Read

states, for example, textbooks are purchased from public funds and supplied free to students; in others, students must rent or buy their own texts.

The legal status of textbook adoption lists also varies. Some lists include only those books which must be taught and allow teachers and sometimes students the freedom to select additional titles; other lists are restrictive, containing only books which may be required for all students.

As a part of sensible preparations for handling attacks on books, each school should ascertain what laws apply to it.

Preparing the Community

To respond to complaints about texts, every school should have a committee of teachers (and possibly students, parents, and other representatives from the local community) organized to

- inform the community about text selection procedures;
- enlist the support of residents, possibly by explaining the place of literacy and relevant texts in the educational process or by discussing at meetings of parents and other community groups the texts used at that school; and
- consider any complaints against any work. No community is so small that it lacks concerned people who care about their children and the educational program of the schools, and will support English teachers in defending books when complaints are received. Unfortunately, English teachers too often are unaware or do not seek out these people and cultivate their goodwill and support before censorship strikes.

Defending the Texts

Despite the care taken to select worthwhile texts for student reading and the qualifications of teachers selecting and recommending books, occasional objections to a work will undoubtedly be made. All texts are potentially open to criticism in one or more general areas: the treatment of ideologies, of minorities, of gender identities, of love and sex; the use of language not acceptable to some people; the type of illustrations; the private life or political affiliations of the author or the illustrator.

Some attacks are made by groups or individuals frankly hostile to free inquiry and open discussion; others are made by misinformed or misguided people who, acting on emotion or rumor, simply do not understand how the texts are to be used. Others are also made by well-intentioned and conscientious people who fear that harm will come to some segment of the community if a particular text is read or recommended.

What should be done upon receipt of a complaint?

- If the complainant telephones, listen courteously and refer them to the teacher involved. That teacher should be the first person to discuss the text with the person objecting to its use.
- If the complainant is not satisfied, invite them to file the complaint in writing, but make no commitments, admissions of guilt, or threats.

- If the complainant writes, contact the teacher involved and have the teacher call the complainant.
- For any of the situations above, the teacher is advised to be aware of local contractual and policy stipulations regarding such situations, and keep a written record of what transpired during the complaint process.

An additional option is to contact the NCTE Intellectual Freedom Center to report incidents and seek further resources (http://www2.ncte.org/resources/ncte-intellectual-freedom-center/ [2]).

Request for Reconsideration of a Text

Author _____

Paperback_____ Hardcover _____ Online _____

Title _____

Publisher (if known) _____

Website URL (if applicable) _____

Request initiated by _____

Telephone _____

Address _____

City / State / Zip _____

Complainant represents

____ (Name of individual) _____

____ (Name of organization) _____

1. Have you been able to discuss this work with the teacher or librarian who ordered it or who used it?

    ___ Yes ___ No

2. What do you understand to be the general purpose for using this work?

    - Provide support for a unit in the curriculum?

        ___ Yes ___ No

    - Provide a learning experience for the reader in one kind of literature?

        ___ Yes ___ No

    - Provide opportunities for students' self-selected reading experiences?

        ___ Yes ___ No

    - Other _____

3. Did the general purpose for the use of the work, as described by the teacher or librarian, seem a suitable one to you?

    ___ Yes ___ No

If not, please explain.

_____

_____

4. What do you think is the author's general purpose for this book?

_____

_____

The Students' Right to Read

5. In what ways do you think a work of this nature is not suitable for the use the teacher or librarian wishes to carry out?

_____
_____

6. Have students responded to this work?
___ Yes ___ No
If yes, what responses did the students make?

_____
_____

7. Have you been able to learn what qualified reviewers or other students have written about this work?
___ Yes ___ No
If yes, what are those responses?

_____
_____

8. Would you like the teacher or librarian to give you a written summary of what qualified reviewers and other students have written about this book or film?
___ Yes ___ No

9. Do you have negative reviews of the book?
___ Yes ___ No

10. Where were they published?

_____

11. Would you be willing to provide summaries of their views you have collected?
___ Yes ___ No

12. How would you like your library/school to respond to this request for reconsideration?
____ Do not assign/lend it to my child.
____ Return it to the staff selection committee/department for reevaluation.
____ Other—Please explain

_____
_____

13. In its place, what work would you recommend that would convey as valuable a perspective as presented in the challenged text?

_____
_____

Signature _____
Date_____

At first, the English teacher should politely acknowledge the complaint and explain the established procedures. The success of much censorship depends upon frightening an unprepared school or English department into some precipitous action. A standardized procedure will take the sting from the first outburst of criticism and place the burden of proof on the objector. When the reasonable objector learns that they will be given a fair hearing through

The Students' Right to Read

following the proper channels, they are more likely to be satisfied. The idle censor, on the other hand, may well be discouraged from taking further action. A number of advantages will be provided by the form, which will

- formalize the complaint,
- indicate specifically the work in question,
- identify the complainant,
- suggest how many others support the complaint,
- require the complainant to think through objections in order to make an intelligent statement on the text and complaint (1, 2, and 3),
- cause the complainant to evaluate the work for other groups than merely the one they first had in mind (4),
- establish the familiarity of the complainant with the work (5),
- give the complainant an opportunity to consider the criticism about the work and the teacher's purpose in using the work (6, 7, and 8), and
- give the complainant an opportunity to suggest alternative actions to be taken on the work (9 and 10).

The committee reviewing complaints should be available on short notice to consider the completed "Request for Reconsideration of a Work" and to call in the complainant and the teacher involved for a conference. Members of the committee should have reevaluated the work in advance of the meeting, and the group should be prepared to explain its findings. Membership of the committee should ordinarily include an administrator, the English department chair, and at least two classroom teachers of English. But the department might consider the advisability of including members from the community and the local or state NCTE affiliate. As a matter of course, recommendations from the committee would be forwarded to the superintendent, who would in turn submit them to the board of education, the legally constituted authority in the school.

Teachers and administrators should recognize that the responsibility for selecting texts for class study lies with classroom teachers and students, and that the responsibility for reevaluating any text begins with the review committee. Both teachers and administrators should refrain from discussing the objection with the complainant, the press, or community groups. Once the complaint has been filed, the authority for handling the situation must ultimately rest with the administration and school board.

Freedom of inquiry is essential to education in a democracy. To establish conditions essential for freedom, teachers and administrators need to follow procedures similar to those recommended here. Where schools resist unreasonable pressures, the cases are seldom publicized and students continue to read works as they wish. The community that entrusts students to the care of an English teacher should also trust that teacher to exercise professional judgment in selecting or recommending texts. The English teacher can be free to teach literacy, and students can be free to read whatever they wish only if informed and vigilant groups, within the profession and without, unite in resisting unfair pressures.

The Students' Right to Read

References

American Library Association (2013, March). *Banned & Challenged Classics*. http://www.ala
.org/advocacy/bbooks/frequentlychallengedbooks/classics (Accessed June 15, 2018).

American Library Association. (2018). *Top Ten Most Challenged Books Lists*. http://www.ala
.org/advocacy/bbooks/frequentlychallengedbooks/top10#Before%201990 (Accessed July
15, 2018)

American Library Association. (2018). *Top 10 Most Challenged Books of 2017: Resources &
Graphics*. http://www.ala.org/advocacy/bbooks/NLW-Top10 (Accessed July 15, 2018)

Stevens, W. (1957, April). Adagia Part One. *Poetry*, 41–44.

The Committee on the Right to Read of the National Council of Teachers of English:

- *Edward R. Gordon, Yale University, New Jersey, Chair*
- *Martin Steinmann, University of Minnesota, Associate Chair*
- *Harold B. Allen, University of Minnesota*
- *Frank A. Doggett, D. U. Fletcher High School, Jacksonville Beach, Florida*
- *Jack Fields, Great Neck South High School, New York*
- *Graham S. Frear, St. Olaf College, Minnesota*
- *Robert Gard, Camelback High School, Phoenix, Arizona*
- *Frank Ross, Detroit Public Schools, Michigan*
- *Warren Taylor, Oberlin College, Ohio*

Statement Authors

This document was revised by an NCTE working committee comprising the following:

- Benjamin "Benji" Chang, Education University of Hong Kong, Chair
- Anna Lavergne, Houston Independent School District, Texas
- Kim Pinkerton, Texas A&M University, Commerce
- Pernille Ripp, Oregon School District, Oregon, Wisconsin
- Gabe Silveri, Cypress Fairbanks Independent School District, Houston, Texas

Permission is granted to reproduce in whole or in part the material in this publication, with proper credit to the National Council of Teachers of English. Some schools may wish to modify the statements and arrange separately for printing or duplication. In such cases, of course, it should be made clear that revised statements appear under the authorization and sponsorship of the local school or association, not NCTE.

Article printed from NCTE: **http://www2.ncte.org**

URL to article: **http://www2.ncte.org/statement/righttoreadguideline/**

URLs in this post:

[1] Marjane Satrapi: **https://en.wikipedia.org/wiki/Marjane_Satrapi**

[2] http://www2.ncte.org/resources/ncte-intellectual-freedom-center/: **http://www2.ncte.org/
resources/ncte-intellectual-freedom-center/**

NCTE Beliefs about the Students' Right to Write

Approved by the NCTE Executive Committee, July 2014

During this era of high-stakes testing, technology-based instruction, and increased control over students' expression due to school violence, students' right to write must be protected. Censorship of writing not only stifles student voices but denies students important opportunities to grow as both writers and thinkers. Through the often messy process of writing, students develop strategies to help them come to understand lessons within the curriculum as well as how their language and ideas can be used to communicate, influence, reflect, explain, analyze, and create.

The National Council of Teachers of English believes

- The expression of ideas without fear of censorship is a fundamental right.

- Words are a powerful tool of expression, a means to clarify, explore, inquire, and learn as well as a way to record present moments for the benefit of future generations.

- Students need many opportunities to write for a variety of purposes and audiences in all classes. Teachers who regularly engage students in such writing should not be expected to read or grade all compositions.

- Teacher feedback should avoid indoctrination because of personal beliefs and should be respectful of both the writer and his/her ideas, even those with which the teacher disagrees.

- English language arts teachers are qualified to frame and assign student writing tasks, but students should, as much as possible, have choice and control over topics, forms, language, themes, and other aspects of their own writing while meeting course requirements.

- Teachers should avoid scripted writing that discourages individual creativity, voice, or expression of ideas.

- Teachers should engage students fully in a writing process that allows them the necessary freedom to formulate and evaluate ideas, develop voice, experiment with syntax and language, express creativity, elaborate on viewpoints, and refine arguments.

- Teachers should foster in students an understanding and appreciation of the responsibilities inherent in writing and publication by encouraging students to assume ownership of both the writing process and the final product.

- Teachers should explicitly teach the distinction between violent writing and violence in writing. Students should expect teachers to uphold the law in reporting all instances of violent writing.

- When writing for publication, students should be provided with high-quality writing instruction and be taught how to write material that is not obscene, libelous, or substantially disruptive of learning throughout the school.

NCTE Beliefs about the Students' Right to Write

- Administrators should work in collaboration with students who write for school publications such as school newspapers or literary magazines and, within the limits of state law or district/school policies, should avoid prior review.
- Districts should encourage the development and adoption of policies that support student writers as they learn to make choices in their writing that express their intent while still maintaining ethical and legal boundaries.

This position statement may be printed, copied, and disseminated without permission from NCTE.

Introduction: Where We Have Been, Where We Are, Where We Are Going

I begin this book by sharing a story with you of an incredible day of school, told to me by my father-in-law, Stan Hinden, an old-fashioned newspaper man. He started his career at age twelve and submitted his last published column in July 2016 at the age of eighty-nine. He wrote most of the years of his life for many publications, including *New York Newsday*, *The Washington Post*, and the AARP digital publication. He even published four editions of his own book. Because we were both writers, and as I was seeking common ground with him early in our relationship, I once asked him how he started as a journalist. He chuckled and told me that everything—all the years, the articles, the interviews and publications, all of it—traced back to one day in seventh grade in Far Rockaway, New York, approximately 1939.

It seems that day his class had a substitute teacher, who addressed the class that morning saying, "Today you will spend the day producing a newspaper. You can decide who the reporters are, what stories you need to write, who will get interviewed, and what will get published. We're publishing your newspaper at the end of the day." And then the teacher, so the story goes, left the students to themselves. Stan and three other friends took this opportunity to soar. They spent the entire school day interviewing the other students and writing stories. Their newspaper was published at the end of the day, and the four boys truly saw themselves as worthy reporters. After relating this story to me, Stan chuckled again and said, "You know, three of us went on to become reporters when we grew up. We caught the bug that day."

I never asked Stan the standard pedagogical questions like:

- "While you boys were writing, what were the other kids doing?"
- "How did the teacher actually publish and distribute the paper at the end of the day?"
- "How did the teacher help with editing and teach into revising?"
- "What happened the next day? Did your regular teacher let you continue your newspaper?"

What struck me was that seventy years after this experience, Stan still remembered that day and could recount how it changed the trajectory of his life. This was one teacher, opening up a classroom to become an authentic place of real writers, who wrote about what mattered most to them and their community and then published and shared their pieces with an authentic audience. Those boys knew their writing would impact their audience, because the audience of other seventh graders cared about that writing too.

I want to teach in that kind of classroom too. Don't you?

⤳

The flavor of Stan's 1939 seventh-grade day is deeply embedded in the content and intention of the NCTE position statement *NCTE Beliefs about the Students' Right to Write*, published in 2014. One point in this guiding statement is practically the lesson plan Stan's teacher followed that day:

> Teachers should foster in students an understanding and appreciation of their responsibilities inherent in writing and publication by encouraging students to assume ownership of both the writing process and the final product. (p. xxv; all page references to this position statement and to *The Students' Right to Read* map to the versions reprinted in the front matter of this book)

The rest of the position statement focuses on teaching the writers in our classrooms by honoring their voices and processes and helping them get their pieces out to real audiences who care about what they have to say. This position statement calls us to provide opportunities that encourage kids to write for formal and informal purposes, and when students are writing informally, they should be able to write without fear of our red pen judgment.

Likewise, a companion position statement, *The Students' Right to Read* (NCTE, 2018), guides us to build reading communities in our classrooms that honor kids as people who read, not just people who read for school. This statement asks us to examine our teaching practices so that books are freely shared and chosen and read in classrooms. We are encouraged through this document to make sure that the faces and stories on our classroom shelves reflect the faces and stories of the kids sitting in the desks in front of us. In fact, I like to call these two position statements NCTE's Golden Rules for Reading and Writing: Teach reading and writing as you would like to be taught; teach the readers and writers in your classroom as actual readers and writers.

⤳

Throughout my nearly three decades as a teacher, I've been striving to build classroom spaces and practices that align with these two important documents. Both position statements point to our shared professional knowledge that the apprenticeship student reader-writers receive in a workshop classroom should prepare them for life as literate people. Guiding the people I teach to build literate lives that extend beyond my classroom has always been my goal. I still have my very first copy of *In the Middle* by Nancie Atwell (1987). I bought it for an undergrad methods class in 1990. When I read about Atwell's dining room table classroom, what I now understand as a standard workshop setting, I absolutely imagined that my own classroom would be just like hers (pp. 19–20).

However, while I began my career with Atwell in hand, I also had traditional ideas about being an English teacher. I couldn't quite figure out how to have kids in reading and writing workshop every day, and I saw benefit in a community of readers reading a book together. I wanted to have a robust classroom library but had only enough money to cobble together a collection from garage sales, my mentor teacher's castoffs, thrift stores, and books I had carried with me since my own young adult days. I scheduled several book talks a week, and I asked kids to share with partners and the whole class the books they were reading. But I could plan only one day a week of independent reading workshop. I didn't know about conferencing yet, but I did know that I should be talking to kids naturally, one reader to another, about the books we read. I had a sense that as a community of readers, we should sometimes read books all together as a class, as Oprah was suggesting with her national book club initiatives. And I hoped that we would use our collective reading experiences to grow as people in the world, not just as an opportunity to study literature.

And while I believed I should be helping kids learn how to write literary essays about these books, I also had a notion that when we read books together as a class, kids might do amazing work if they were able to design and execute their own responses, which might be pieces of writing or pieces of visual art or music or even books they wrote themselves. I had a sense that kids might be more interested in what they were writing if they were able to pick their own topics. When possible, I tried to structure assignments so that kids could pick what they crafted. Every time I did that, they were more invested, and their work was a truer representation of their understanding and abilities. And I knew that real publication was ultimately the goal. I became good friends with our school district's printing office, and at least twice a year we published a book. As a new teacher, my early years were a good mix of a traditional ELA classroom with a generous amount of workshop time supporting all of the reading and writing we did together.

Over the years, I have learned so much about the myriad ways I can respect my students' rights to read and write as *real* readers and writers, not just as people who read and write for school. In recent years, however, as new mandates and resulting structured curricula and assessments came into my classroom, I recognized just how difficult combining a workshop setting with a mandated curriculum is—and often, I ended up forsaking "dining room table teaching" for fitting in lessons that met state and local mandates. For instance, every year I try to run the same kind of amazing writing groups that my teacher colleagues at the New York City Writing Project (NYCWP) create during our Summer Invitational Institute, but for many years, my classroom writing groups were a total flop. An NYCWP colleague, Alie Stumpf, and I were lamenting about our very weak student writing groups, and we realized the big difference between summer writing groups and school year writing groups wasn't the obvious one—that one group had teacher participants and one group had kid participants. The difference was much more significant. First, in the summer, the teachers *chose* what to write, which pieces meant something to them and which pieces were so important to share that they wanted to keep writing until they were nearing a feeling of "really good." And second, the teacher writers knew that they were going to share the pieces publicly with the rest of the summer group. Their writing was going beyond their notebooks to an audience that mattered to them.

How much this differed from our classrooms in the time of curricular mandates! Despite all we were learning in the summers, the kids in our classes were not choosing their own topics or writing for real audiences. Rather, they were often sharing their individual drafts of the same teacher-assigned prompted essay during writing groups. Not surprisingly, the conversations weren't rich and helpful, because everyone had almost the same essay, using almost the same evidence. The writing group feedback was thin and dull because, truthfully, there wasn't much to say. And their writing, with the exception of a quick "publishing party," during which students shared pieces of their work briefly, often planned as a gallery walk of drafts, wasn't really celebrated or experienced by interested readers. Publishing parties were most anticipated because of the snacks served. The kid writing groups didn't work because, even though the student writing was based on standards and grade-level expectations, it was not owned by the kids, so the kids didn't have much to be invested in when revising or sharing. Alie and I realized we didn't need to teach the kids better; we needed to create better writing invitations/tasks/assignments that met standards-based guidelines, but that also asked kids to write individual, original pieces that they cared about writing and sharing.

The notion that kids write better and are more interested, invested authors when they own the writing is a tenet at the core of *NCTE Beliefs about the Students' Right to Write*. Even though I had been teaching for many years, and this tenet was the main principle I had previously used to guide my practice, I'd forgotten about it as more strident expectations from outside agents directed my classroom work. This internal dissonance doesn't happen just to teachers like me, who've been teaching for more than twenty-five years, or to newer teachers like Alie, who learned to be a teacher in the early 2000s. I think this happens to all of us. And as new guidelines and expectations wall in our classrooms, it's quite easy to slowly transform our classrooms from places like Atwell's dining room table to Standards and Test-Prep Central.

In 2002, when the Elementary and Secondary Education Act became No Child Left Behind, and school funding was tied to standardized test scores, many of our ELA classrooms turned into tight spaces built around the conformity of test prep. The goal was high scores so that schools could measure their adequate yearly progress (AYP) and meet the levels the states laid out as successful and, therefore, funded. Even schools that used a workshop model included mini-lessons filled with reading skills designed specifically to help students pass tests. And writing workshops often became workshop in name only as the focus narrowed so that everyone was writing the same piece and working on the same author craft moves at the same time. Reading and writing workshops became standardized workshops. And in 2009, when Race to the Top funding and the Common Core State Standards took over curricula, ELA classrooms narrowed even further. Writing assignments were mostly argument based, and reading choices were nonfiction or literary texts that focused on "close reading" for meaning. Those of us who had been teaching in Atwellesque classrooms for years found ourselves in a pickle. How could we keep teaching in ways that we knew instinctively and experientially helped kids grow as readers and writers, when the curriculum mandates of our schools and districts, and eventually our country, had transformed so that the practices of authentic workshop classrooms were deemed unable to produce college and career readiness in our children?

~

NCTE was formed more than 100 years ago to address this issue—how to continue teaching what you know to be best for students when your school has decided otherwise. Leila Christenbury reminds us in her chapter "NCTE and the Shaping of American Literacy Education" in *Reading the Past, Writing the Future* (Lindemann, 2010) that in December of 1911, the sixty teachers who came together to imagine a professional home for English teachers agreed "to create an organization that could give voice and power to oppose the status quo" (p. 3). In fact, through NCTE's policy and belief statements, our organization has continued to support English teachers ever since. These organizational documents not only help NCTE at large to make decisions about how to develop new programming, join other like-minded organizations in political influence, create products, and plan meetings, but the policy documents are also the belief basis for the community of teachers who make NCTE their professional home.

In 1936, NCTE President Dora V. Smith pointed to a belief that underlies the two position statements guiding this book. Smith wrote that our goal as English teachers is to:

educate each pupil in terms of *his own uniqueness within the context of the group*. All this has special import for the curriculum. It cannot be done adequately if the aim is the reading of specific books by every member of the class, mastery of a set number of rules by all pupils, or attainment by everybody of specific standards in speech or writing. (qtd. in Christenbury, 2010, p. 2)

It's almost as though Smith was laying the groundwork for *NCTE Beliefs about the Students' Right to Write* and *The Students' Right to Read*.

At this point in education history, we know enough about how people learn and process new information and skills to recognize that for students to thrive, pedagogical differentiation is necessary. Kids need to be able to choose, at least sometimes, what they'd like to read. Students need to decide, at least sometimes, what and how they'd like to write. These two policy statements lay out for teachers exactly what we believe as an organization student readers and writers have the right to be able to do in their ELA classrooms. These statements give teachers the community backing of our organization to create opportunities for students to choose their own reading materials without regard for levels or curriculum mandates. Students have the right to see themselves in the books that are offered in classroom settings, both as independent reading choices and as larger group reading choices. Students have the right to be in conversation with other readers and place whatever they are reading in the context of their own experiences as well as the current world situation, and to use that literature to empower them to action. Students have the right to read for pleasure, without being graded. Likewise, kids have the right to write about what matters to them and about what they know of the world. They have the right to choose the form they'd like their pieces to take. They have the right to write in multiple languages, for real audiences, for purposes they deem important. And students have the right to write for fun, using their own voices.

No matter what a school district's ELA guidelines and programming consist of, the teachers in the school district are the means by which the guidelines and programming are delivered to students. Teachers build the classroom community that allows all students to thrive and grow. And middle school is a space where creating community is vitally necessary and very difficult. Middle school is a time in a kid's life during which the differences between self and other feel huge and unmanageable. Middle school friendships and allegiances can change drastically from morning homeroom to lunch. For middle school ELA teachers, reading and writing are great community builders. As a middle school kid, finding yourself in a book or saying who you are in the writing you share with others can help you manage the differences you feel between yourself and other kids in your school and in the world. Reading and writing for middle schoolers are inexorably intertwined as individuality-shaping and community-building tools. And middle school ELA teachers are the people who help kids learn to use those tools through the reading choices and writing variety their classrooms offer.

Teachers who are continuing to build classrooms around the practices laid out in *NCTE Beliefs about the Students' Right to Write* and *The Students' Right to Read* sometimes have to enact those practices in the spaces in between the curriculum they're currently expected to teach and the curriculum they know will truly help kids become lifelong readers and writers. And far too often, teachers are doing this work without the professional support of their schools. Because so many of the professional development offerings at district and school levels have narrowed to argument writing and close reading, teachers have increasingly been turning to the grassroots PD that is emerging on social media. Currently, thousands of teachers across the country utilize Twitter, Facebook, Instagram, and other social media platforms to connect with other teachers and literacy leaders and authors. A look at my Twitter feed for an hour confirms that everything NCTE lays out in the policy statements this book focuses on is also the focus of what teachers are talking about and trying to include in the work they do with students. And when they can't get support at school, they seek the support of other teachers they know virtually. There are dozens of weekly and monthly Twitter chats hosted by organizations such as NCTE and the National Writing Project (NWP) and the International Literacy Association (ILA), as well as offerings by online communities such as the Nerdy Book Club, the Educator Collaborative, and the #EduColor community that support and guide and highlight the work that teachers around the country are doing. When I engage with other teachers online about my practice and visit their classrooms through their posts, I feel like I'm part of a close community of people all over the country. These are teachers who dismantle the status quo of classrooms built around packaged curricula, stagnant assignments, unexamined canonical texts, and narrow ideas of children as readers and writers. This virtual community focuses on teaching kids to be thoughtful readers and writers, moving our country forward into a future that includes everyone's experiences and voices.

In this book, I hope to re-create that feeling of virtual support that I and so many others are finding in social media. I invite you, in Part I, to look at *NCTE Beliefs about the Students' Right to Write* and *The Students' Right to Read* as the Golden Rules of Reading and Writing. Think alongside me to consider these policies not as policies, but as the backbone elements of a common middle level classroom structure: the workshop setting. Notice how the elements of the policies support the conditions for learning in reading and writing workshops. And finally, you will be able to spend some time in two classrooms that employ the workshop setting to support the middle school readers and writers in those classrooms.

In Part II: Intervisitations, you'll have the chance to meet several teachers who are using their classrooms to promote students' rights to read and write in ways that help kids grow as lifelong readers and real writers with important ideas to share. The teachers open their classroom doors and invite you in to see various practices that fall within the guidelines of these two NCTE policy statements. At the end of each visit, I share what I noticed and ask you to think about what you might borrow for your own classroom.

In Part III: Shifting Our Shelves, you will have a chance to think about the need for inclusive and varied human experiences to be found on our classroom bookshelves. Then middle grade author and cofounder of the We Need Diverse Books Foundation (WNDB), Ellen Oh, shares the history of WNDB and who she was as a kid reader of color herself. Next, children's literature scholar Kristin McIlhagga answers frequently asked questions (FAQs) about how to examine our own classroom libraries and transform them into places that push boundaries and include kids who are too often invisible in more standard texts.

In Part IV: Reconsidering Composition, I invite you to think about the standard composing or writing process many teachers use to guide our writing practices in schools: what each phase of the process generally looks like in a middle grade classroom, as well as ideas that might help you reconsider those phases to include more writer-centered practices like those suggested in the policy statement.

Finally, Part V: Shoulders to Lean On and Arms to Link With, offers a look at the ways teachers are utilizing social media to create grassroots professional development that promotes students' rights to read and write freely and authentically. The different sections in this part will help guide you in creating your own virtual professional learning community and highlights specific online spaces you might be interested in including in your PD work. In particular, there are several active monthly Twitter chats that teachers turn to in order to engage with other teachers and literacy leaders on issues of labeling books and readers, how much choice should be included in reading workshop, ways to help kids write what they know, and the impact of choice and voice in and publishing of kid writing. Many professional groups host blogs or support leaders who regularly tweet and retweet smart thinking in the field of reading and writing with students, or about creating classroom spaces that promote authentic literacy. And thousands of teachers engage in conversations about reading and books on Facebook literacy pages based on popular and vital professional texts. Part V can help you begin to craft a professional learning network (PLN) based on virtual professional development that supports your belief in students' rights to read and write.

In addition to teaching full time in a middle school in New York City, I teach graduate students how to be ELA teachers. When I ask them why they want to be English teachers, they almost all say because they love to read and write, and they want to share that love with their students. The graduate students I teach imagine classrooms like my father-in-law Stan's seventh-grade classroom on the famous day of the substitute teacher: a place where writers, who happen to also be middle schoolers, are set free to write about what matters most to them, and to share that writing with their peers. The graduate students imagine classrooms like Nancie Atwell's dining room table, where they sit around chatting about books they're reading with other readers. I think that in teaching, all the business parts of school can easily take us away from that core love of being readers and writers and sharing that love with the kids in our classrooms. *NCTE Beliefs about Students' Right to Write* and *The Students' Right to Read* bring us back to that love. These policy statements frame for us how to create classrooms that encourage reading love and writing love authentically. My hope is that this book will help guide you in doing this literacy love work in your own classrooms.

Part I
The Golden Rules of Reading and Writing:
The Students' Right to Read and NCTE Beliefs about the Students' Right to Write

Some questions for you—before you read this chapter:

Where do you do your most comfortable reading?

How do you decide what to read next?

What happens when you don't really like a book? Do you abandon it, or keep going until the very end?

When you finish a book, how do you mark the occasion?

When do you read?

Do you have any series you're attached to? Any favorite authors or genres?

For me, my most comfortable reading takes place in my cozy living room, with blankets, or on my deck. Deciding what to read next for me is a challenge; my TBR (to be read) list is actually a whole wall of bookshelves. When we go on vacation to Cape Cod in the summer, I've been known to bring upwards of thirty books so I have choices, and please don't suggest a digital reading tablet; I'm a reader who likes to turn paper pages. I'm kind of bad at abandoning . . . it's more like I let the book languish. (Currently there's an Ann Patchett novel on my bedside table I've been "reading" for three years.) When I finish a book, I add it to my Goodreads page, but I also tell everyone I know if I love it. I might post on Facebook my adoration for the book, and if it's a kid's book, I immediately give a book talk to my classes. I have been known to still occasionally read a James Patterson or Patricia Cornwell mystery, but my dad and I share a love for Dan Brown novels, so we don't miss a chance to get anything new he writes. And when my grown-up book club gets together, we spend half our time trying to decide what we'll read next based on recommendations we've gotten from our greater reading circles. I look to my network of virtual teacher-scholar friends to give me reading suggestions that support my goal of antiracist and antibias being in the world and in my classroom. And of course, I have a huge stack of professional development books I can't wait to read and implement in my teaching.

As a reader, my reading life is rich with habits and choices and rituals. I bet yours is too. How do reading lives look in your classroom, though? What would your students say about their reading habits and choices and rituals?

And what about writing—how would you answer these writing questions?

Where do you do your most comfortable writing? Is it the same place you feel most concentrated and productive as a writer?

How do you decide what you'll write?

What is your composition process? How do you get started and how do you keep yourself going? Do you share with trusted readers along the way?

What about when you finish a piece? Is the piece just for you, or do you share it with a reading audience?

Do you have any genres you gravitate toward writing? Any genres that make you squirm and feel stuck?

And what do you do when you're writing and you feel stuck?

I have very specific processes that work for me to get words on the page. I wander around looking like I'm doing the dishes, driving, folding clothes, simply sitting, but actually, I'm composing whole paragraphs in my head before I'm ready to begin to write them on paper or into a document. In fact, I played around with three different ways to begin this chapter in the last two weeks before I settled on what you're now reading. All of that drafting work happened in my head as I was going about my days. I also like to draft and revise and edit by paragraph as I go. I've tried writing whole drafts of pieces and then going back to revise and edit, and it just doesn't work as well for me. And if I'm planning, as I did with this chapter and others in this book, I like to use webs; planning webs match my internal writing process the most closely. Please don't ever ask me to do an outline, because I just won't do it. When an issue arises in the world that feels important to me, I often take to social media and write bloggish kinds of posts asking big questions and offering my ideas. And if you ask me to just write, like "write for pleasure," I'm almost always going to craft a poem.

What about you? How do you live your writing life? How is your writing life different from the writing lives you help students shape in your classrooms?

In becoming familiar with the *The Students' Right to Read* and *NCTE Beliefs about the Students' Right to Write*, the two policy statements that guide the teaching and learning in this book, I have come to think of them as the Golden Rules of Reading and Writing. In other words, these two documents help teachers center their teaching of reading and writing in ways they might like to be taught or treated as readers and writers themselves. Both documents help teachers think about how to create classroom spaces, pedagogical structures, and teaching strategies that afford the students in their classes the most opportunities to read and write in the ways readers and writers behave in the real world.

Systems and structures in a literacy classroom that allow students to grow their literacy in the most natural ways can take many forms. In the middle grades, often we see these practices take the form of a workshop classroom. Although workshop literacy classrooms can look vastly different, and can even be structured around a purchased program, some common features tend to appear in most workshop-based classrooms. Following are the distinct phases most workshop classrooms move through on a particular day. If you've experienced workshop classrooms either as a teacher or a student, these "parts of a workshop" will sound familiar.

Mini-lessons. Most workshop days begin with a mini-lesson that offers direct instruction about some aspect of being a reader or a writer. During the mini-lesson, the teacher models a strategy or behavior or skill that will expand the students' repertoires as readers and writers. Often, students then practice or integrate into their own work whatever they've learned during that particular workshop session. Sometimes this takes the form of a quick-write and sharing out, and sometimes as one or more book talks by the teacher or other readers in the classroom. In this way, the student reader-writers have the chance to apprentice alongside others who are learning and with a seasoned reader-writer teacher.

The mini-lesson portion of a workshop varies greatly. In some classrooms, it's a skills-based time situated within a larger writing or reading unit of study. For instance, if the whole class is participating in literature circles based on historical fiction, the mini-lesson might focus on how to manage historical vocabulary that might be confusing to a reader's comprehension. In other workshop classrooms, the mini-lesson is authentically student driven. Perhaps the teacher realizes that many students are choosing to write narratives that include dialogue, and so the mini-lesson is direct instruction focusing on how to punctuate written dialogue. Either way, the job of the mini-lesson is to help grow students' literacy skills through the knowledge of a more skillful reader-writer, the teacher.

Time to work. The largest chunk of a workshop session is the student work portion. In some workshop classrooms, kids work with partners or in groups or on their own, putting into practice the ideas they gained from the mini-lesson. In this format of a workshop session, the teacher strategically moves through the class-room, listening in, observing, and conferencing with groups or individuals. This is the portion of the class during which students are doing the work, and the teacher is adjusting their teaching to the individuals in the class and to their understandings and abilities.

In other workshop classrooms, like those Nancie Atwell highlighted in her beloved workshop book, *In the Middle* (1987), and then broadened in *The Reading Zone* (2007) and subsequent editions of *In the Middle*, readers are all engrossed in reading different books, and writers are all engaged in various writing projects of their own choosing. In these classrooms, the working portion of the class is time for readers and writers to work on their reading and writing, and the teacher is meeting and conferencing with kids individually or in reading or writing partner-ships. For instance, if two kids choose to form a mini–book club around a favorite author's newest book, the teacher might meet with that partnership to check in on progress, comprehension, and engagement. If the workshop is a writing workshop, the teacher might be meeting with several individual writers and simply asking, "What are you working on? How can I help?," thereby differentiating teaching writer by writer. In his book *How's It Going?* (2000), Carl Anderson helped me think about how writing conferences can be structured to be the most helpful for individual writers. While a teacher is doing this, two or three students might be meeting in a writing group to share their work, ask for feedback, and suggest next steps to each other.

Time to share. In the final moments of most workshop classrooms, the whole class comes back together and readers and writers share their work in some way with the rest of the class. This sharing might take the form of a Say Something circle, which Kylene Beers explores in *When Kids Can't Read, What Teachers Can Do* (2002, p. 105). During a session of Say Something, everyone in the class is expected to share an idea about what they are reading with a small group of other kids. Gen-erally, the teacher doesn't respond but instead listens in as groups share, and then uses that listening in to plan further conferencing with individual readers. Alter-natively, the students may be on a more formal sharing schedule, especially during a writing workshop, with different kids knowing ahead of time that today is their day to share a piece they are working on, either as a completed piece or as a means to gather feedback for revision. In some classes, the teacher might give students an exit slip that asks them to account for what they accomplished that day, as well as their plans for next steps or homework. These reflections and plans might be shared out at tables or with writing groups. In other classrooms, reading partners and writing partners share out the interesting work of their peers for the rest of class to hear.

However the sharing occurs, this portion of the class is essential for two reasons. First, the sharing makes public the idea that readers and writers are always in a process of learning and growth and production. This is how reading and writing work outside of the classroom, making this portion of the class time mirror authentic practices of readers and writers. Second, the publishing of writing for an audience other than the teacher lends an urgency and seriousness to classroom writing tasks, which often feel artificial. Sharing, and ultimately publication, of student writing offers student writers the opportunity to experience the impact their written works have on authentic readers.

The phases of a workshop structure in a literacy classroom are well known and widely utilized in some way by many middle school literacy teachers. Delving a bit more deeply into the structure of a workshop classroom reveals several elements that remain present both in workshop teachers' minds and in classrooms. In fact, one of our most beloved writing teachers, Donald Graves, wrote in *A Fresh Look at Writing* (1994) (something Tom Newkirk and Penny Kittle later captured in their book, *Children Want to Write* [2013], about the work Graves did with young writers) that the "*conditions* for learning" are essential in a classroom space (pp. 58–66). The conditions for learning spelled out by Nancie Atwell in her workshop classroom are what allowed students to thrive as readers and writers while she was their teacher. Graves goes on to cite the essential conditions in a writing workshop classroom that help apprentice student writers grow. He names conditions we could all develop in our own classrooms.

Likewise, in *Reading in the Wild* (2014), Donalyn Miller with Susan Kelley wanted to ascertain the habits in the reading lives of "lifelong readers." They surveyed hundreds of adult readers and found that most lifelong readers share several characteristics, or conditions, in their reading lives that help them identify as people who are, in their hearts, readers. Both of these sets of practices (see Figure I.1)—the conditions Graves writes about for developing a writing workshop classroom and the self-identified characteristics of the lifelong readers that Miller and Kelley surveyed—honor the essence of *The Students' Right to Read* and *NCTE Beliefs about the Students' Right to Write*.

FIGURE I.1. Authentic literacy habits for reading and writing workshops. (Quotations in the left column are from Newkirk and Kittle's *Children Want to Write* [2013]; quotations in the right column are from Miller and Kelley's *Reading in the Wild* [2014].)

Donald Graves Suggests Conditions That Encourage Good Writing	Donalyn Miller and Susan Kelley Suggest Characteristics of Lifelong Readers
• Time: "They need daily writing time to be able to move their pieces along until they accomplish what they set out to do" (p. 59). • Choice: "Children need to learn how to choose their own topics when they write" (p. 60). • Response: "At the end of each class, time is set aside for sharing students' writing and their learning experiences during their writing" (p. 63). • Demonstration: "When you actually take your own text and put it on the chalkboard . . . and show your students how you read it, they will receive the clearest demonstration of what writing is all about" (p. 63). • Expectation: "To have high expectations is a sign of caring" (p. 64). • Room Structure: "The writing classroom requires a high degree of structure. . . . Teachers help the room to be predictable" (p. 65). • Evaluation: "I expect them to be prepared to tell me about their work and how it is going. This gives them practice in dealing with the structure of evaluation of work in progress" (p. 66).	• Dedicate time to read: "They spend substantial time reading in spite of their hectic lives" (p. xxiii). • Self-select reading material: "They are confident when selecting books to read and have the experience and skills to choose books successfully that meet their interests, needs, and reading abilities" (p. xxiii). • Share books and reading with other readers: "Reading communities provide a peer group of other readers who challenge and support us" (p. xxiv). • Have reading plans: "Wild readers plan to read beyond their current book" (p. xxiv). • Show preferences for genres, authors, and topics: "[W]ild readers often express strong preferences in the material they choose to read" (p. xxiv).

Below are elements of both reading and writing workshop structures and practices that you can use to honor *The Students' Right to Read* and *NCTE Beliefs about the Students' Right to Write*.

Elements of Reading Workshop You Could Accomplish to Honor Students' Right to Read

Maintain a Rich, Full Classroom Library

- Make sure you have full shelves or baskets of books that look new and interesting to middle school readers. Readers in the world love new and exciting looking covers and often don't want to read books that are ripped and torn.

- Make sure the books in your classroom library have varied levels. Include books and series that may even seem "too young" or "too easy" for middle

school kids. Readers in the world love revisiting favorite authors and series when new books are published. Reading over the years across a series or author is a perfectly normal behavior for readers in the world.

- Likewise, make sure your classroom library includes books that may have characters who are older, perhaps in high school, and are grappling with some of the difficult life experiences teenagers live through. Even though books that are written for older teens may seem challenging, often middle school kids are up to the complexity of young adult books and are hungry to read about how teenagers navigate the world as they get older. Readers in the world use stories to help them live through experiences they haven't yet had but may one day face.

- Make sure that your classroom library is filled with stories by and about traditionally marginalized people. The more books you have by authors who have experienced elements of the story themselves, the better . . . this is called #ownvoices (Duyvis, 2015). Readers in the world often seek out stories told by authors who have lived the stories themselves.

- Make sure the kids in your classes have access to books that represent the "real world," that show all aspects of lived human experience. Readers in the world use books to transport themselves to new experiences and places and also to be reminded of themselves. As well, readers in the world use books to build compassion and empathy for people who have different lives from their own.

Incorporate Real-World Reading Habits and Structures into Your Classroom Time

- Make sure, as much as your school environment allows, that you let kids choose to read whatever they want without strings attached or guidelines. All the while, ensure that you are continually introducing kids to exciting new book choices. Readers in the world use many sources of recommendations for what to read next, but they don't usually base those choices on reading levels or how much reading growth a book will help them achieve.

- Make sure you give authentic time for reading in your class. This time could begin with a mini-lesson that focuses on some aspect of authentically reading books and the behaviors readers in the world utilize in their reading lives. Then move into independent reading time. Kids should just read during this time. Anyone walking into your classroom when this is happening will see real readers reading. Consider reading for pleasure reasonable and valuable homework. Readers in the world often end their days with reading before they go to sleep.

- Make sure you help kids keep authentic records of what they have read and what they plan to read next. Readers in the world often do this by keeping notebooks of books finished or logging into websites like Goodreads.com to help them keep reading records. Also, understand that some readers don't choose to do this detailed record-keeping, but their reading lives are logged into memory and noted through great conversations with other readers.

- Make sure you "un-school" reading workshop as much as possible in a school setting. Obviously, reading workshop is a place where readers do the work of reading to grow as readers. And, obviously, because it's happening in school, teachers need to document growth for the kids in the class. But as you develop structures to gather data and monitor reading workshop, try to make those structures as close to ways that readers in the world manage their reading lives. Approach reading conferences with the interest of one reader talking to another reader about books. Don't grade amounts like numbers of pages or minutes or books. Instead, ask kids to record these amounts so they can see for themselves how much they've grown. When asking for reading responses in writing, ask the kinds of interesting questions that readers ask each other about books. Give kids lots of opportunities to talk about books with one another, in the way readers in the world share what they're reading with other readers.

- Make sure you are modeling, in all the teaching moves you make during reading workshop, being a reader in the world yourself. It is a legitimate teaching plan to move beyond conferencing and read while students are reading. Laugh out loud when your book is funny. Cry if a moving scene would naturally cause you to feel deeply. It's even teaching kids how readers in the world read if the timer goes off to end independent reading, and you say, "Five more minutes, please; I need to finish this chapter!"

When kids describe their reading life in your classroom, they should be filled with the book joy and excitement readers experience in the real world. When kids in your class describe their reading accomplishments, they should be talking about all the books they've loved or abandoned, discussing their favorite authors and series and books, and suggesting, one reader to another, great reads they think other people might also enjoy.

Elements of Writing Workshop You Could Accomplish to Honor Students' Right to Write

Provide Varied Writing Opportunities
- Make sure you support the philosophy that writers write for a variety of purposes and in a variety of genres. Writers in the world write for many reasons: sometimes to create new, imaginative pieces to share with the world; sometimes to add their voice to larger societal conversations; sometimes to engage in formal correspondence; sometimes to meet a formal

task like a test, application, or grant; sometimes to informally share ideas with friends and family; sometimes just for themselves. You can intentionally provide all of these writing experiences in your classroom as you move through days and the entire curricular year.

- Make sure you offer students many low-stakes writing opportunities. These opportunities help students build daily writing habits, increase their writing stamina, and offer them chances to try out ideas and genres that may be new to them. Students have the right to write without being assessed on all of their writing attempts. All school writing does not need to be graded, just as all professional writing is not written for publication. Writers in the real world often have a daily writing practice that is a time and space for them to keep their writing habits fresh and offers them a place to simply make note of the world and their observations. Sometimes more polished pieces are born of the daily writing and observations, but that is not the goal of daily informal writing. Likewise, having the opportunity to simply play with words and genres and forms helps writers discover what and how they want to give voice to ideas they may want to share more widely.

- Make sure you honor many different composing processes. Writing is an individual endeavor. When we expect every student to follow every step in a particular order in a composition process we have designed for the whole class, we don't honor writing brains that organize ideas and compose writing differently than the standardized process often expected of a whole class. Writers in the world generally follow some path of gathering ideas, writing drafts, sharing drafts with other writers, revising, and eventually publishing for many to read. But writers' processes often look very different from each other. In a series of mini-lessons, you could share multiple ways to collect ideas or begin drafting. You might share many organizing plans. But then let kids choose which process works best for them individually, thereby honoring who they are as writers.

- Make sure to give kids the chance to complete a writing task in various ways. If you are teaching argument, understand that poetry often argues a point, as do lyrics or graphic writing. If you are teaching narrative writing, understand that narratives might be memoirs or fictional stories. As well, when asking kids to write to a prompt, offer multiple entry points or variations as opportunities for writing to the prompt. In this way, the deep thinking of multiple writers is honored, while at the same time giving you the chance to closely analyze the thinking and writing they've done about the particular topic of study. When given a specific prompt or task, writers in the world make careful decisions about how they will approach that prompt or task so that they are able to maintain their own voice and style.

- Make sure, as often as you can, that you open up the writing spaces in your classroom for the middle school writers to pursue their own writing projects, projects they have imagined, conceived of, and designed on their own as writers. Writers in the real world pursue writing projects that interest and

excite them and that offer them opportunities to take risks in composing and sharing their voice.

Provide Varied Ways for Writers to Share Their Writing

- Make sure you offer low-stakes opportunities for students to share pieces that are in process. This might take the form of a trusted writing partner or writing group with which the writers share drafts to gain feedback from peers. You might also ask kids to pick one small portion of something they've just quickly written to share with the whole class so all the writing voices in the classroom are briefly heard. You might ask students who yearn for constant teacher feedback to pick one paragraph or stanza from a draft in progress to use in a conference with you. In this way, writers have the opportunity to receive encouragement and suggestions from you but aren't hindered by too much teacher feedback before a longer draft is ready for revision. Writers in the world often share pieces of drafts with writing groups or writer friends to showcase their writing projects and to get developing feedback from peers.

- Make sure you approach revision conferences as an interested, wondering reader. Instead of offering only suggestions for what could be changed, added, deleted, or edited, you might consider simply asking questions the piece makes you wonder as a reader. Teaching specific mini-lessons around how to include reader feedback in revision of a piece will help make the

revision sharing you ask kids to do throughout writing projects be purpose-
fully included as they continue to compose. Writers in the world share pieces
in progress with the intention of getting feedback that will help them make
their writing stronger and clearer for future readers.

- Make sure you honor and teach the idea that audience drives many specific
  writing moves and choices writers make when composing. Writers often
  compose pieces to be shared, and often have clear ideas about intended
  audiences for their pieces. In this way, writers alter their language, form,
  grammar, details, and tone based on whom they anticipate reading their
  pieces. When offering revision mini-lessons, specifically teach editing
  and revising for audience. Make clear that writers in the world are able
  to intentionally break standard language rules so that their pieces have an
  authentic tone readers will appreciate.

- Make sure you provide publishing opportunities that have audiences beyond
  yourself as the teacher. The reality for middle school writers is that the
  teacher is their expected audience; kids write for teachers for most writing
  tasks. Therefore, teachers are a fairly low-stakes audience for kids, even
  when the teacher's assessment affects a kid's grades. When the circle of
  readers widens beyond the teacher or a panel of teachers to other kids—in
  the writer's own class, other kids in the grade or in the school, or even
  wider, to readers beyond the school—students' urgency and interest in
  composing an engaging piece of writing heightens. Writers in the world
  spend lengthy amounts of writing time composing pieces they expect to
  publish for a wide audience to read. They try to achieve interesting, clear
  writing for the benefit of an audience of readers they care about. Providing
  spaces for publication will help student writers care about their writing in a
  more professional way.

The goal is for kids, when recounting their writing experiences in your class,
to remember being encouraged to own their pieces as real writers through the
composing choices they attempted and you respected. As they reflect on writing
with you, they should remember how you took their writing seriously as a reader,
not just as their teacher. You want them to leave your classroom understanding
that writing can be for both self-satisfaction and reflection, to meet strict academic
tasks, or to share their voice and ideas with a wide, interested audience. And teachers want students to remember fondly having had opportunities to compose for all
these purposes.

⤵

While neither *The Students' Right to Read* nor *NCTE Beliefs about the Students' Right
to Write* specifically mentions workshop-based classrooms, a careful reading of the
elements of each shows that the flavor of a workshop classroom is inherent in both.
Scholars in our field have guided us for decades through their writing and teaching

about workshop classrooms. We learn from scholars such as Donald Graves, Nancie Atwell, Donalyn Miller, and so many others as we plan, structure, and manage our own workshop classrooms. But we can also look to neighboring classrooms in schools all over the country to see how other teachers create workshop classrooms.

The following vignettes allow us to visit two middle school workshop classrooms, one in New York City and one in rural New Hampshire. Carole Mashamesh shows us the possible daily structure of a reading workshop classroom, and she allows us a glimpse at how she has built a huge classroom library. Linda Rief, whom many of you may know through her multiple books on workshop teaching, reflects on what to do when standard, tried-and-true workshop practices fall flat. If you are new to workshop teaching but like the two policy statements and think this teaching structure makes sense to you, these vignettes will give you ideas about where to begin. If you've been teaching in workshop classrooms for years, these vignettes offer some new ideas that will help you continue to build, as well as provide a model of how to reflect and revise your workshop practices.

A Visit to Room 354 at Tompkins Square Middle School

Carole Mashamesh is a longtime middle school teacher in New York City. Tompkins Square Middle School, located in Greenwich Village, employs the Teacher's College Reading and Writing Project Units of Study, a program that engages students in vigorous literacy workshop classrooms. Carole is especially known among her colleagues not only for having a vibrant classroom library of thousands of books, but also for sharing her deep book love and reading heart with the kids in her classes. Here, Carole shares with us some of the structures of her reading workshop classroom, as well as offering some tips for how to begin a reading workshop program yourself.

A Day in the Life of a Reading Workshop Classroom
Carole Mashamesh, Tompkins Square Middle School, New York, NY—Grade 8

Walking into our classroom, you'll see what teachers at school describe as a "comfy, lived-in space." You might think it chaotic—books line the shelves, the walls, the radiators. Every inch of our classroom is filled with books in bins labeled with all sorts of exciting tags, designed to make kids want to dive in. You'll see bins labeled "Girls in Tricky Situations" or "Boys Lost and Trying to Find Themselves." We have two meeting areas, one up front and one tucked away behind part of the library. Both spaces are always in use with either book clubs or small-group teaching. Book clubs meet in secluded areas so as not to distract the kids who are independently reading at tables. An especially passionate book club may need to bring cushions out into the hallway to continue their heated book discussion without disturbing anyone's reading. Some kids sit at teacher desks or in a quiet corner. We always keep a few spots open away from the main area for the kids who are easily distracted while reading. It helps to have a separate spot so they can stay lost in their books. This is what independent reading looks like in our classroom.

   One of the two teachers in our integrated co-teaching (ICT) classroom might be holding a reading conference with a student about their book choice (checking for comprehension) while the other teacher sits in with one of the book clubs, careful to only guide, not lead, the discussion, offering an occasional question to help the group think more deeply about what they've read. So our classroom is noisy and calm at the same time; there's space for everyone's needs. Students come up to us for book recommendations, but they also know to turn to their classmates for suggestions. It's great to have kids do one-minute "book talks" to pump up a book to classmates. There's always someone whispering about a great book they've read.

Through teacher guidance and library exploration at the beginning of the year, kids are able to find a book that's right for them, and they know where in the room to look for their favorites. We have many readers below grade level in our inclusive classroom (in ICT classes, 40 percent of the kids in each class are designated with a learning disability and have an individualized education program [IEP]), and we make sure to have bins of books with varied levels of complexity and picture support. Any kid having difficulty choosing a book to read, especially someone who doesn't feel confident in their independent reading abilities, knows to ask a teacher for help so that they don't have to wander the room every time they finish something. Kids who feel most comfortable reading books written for younger kids often finish books faster because the books they read are shorter. After reading several of the shorter, easier to manage books, kids often quickly become more interested in reading longer, more complex books. There is powerful satisfaction in moving up levels by reading through a bin of jointly chosen books. We design the room so that all kids feel they have ownership of the library and that they truly belong in the reading community we're creating.

I teach a humanities class, but reading is my number one priority for my students. I have always been a reader—as an only child I never felt alone as long as I had my book friends. I want to make sure that my students feel that same wonder in their books. I feel as though middle school is the last chance we have to help kids become integrated lifelong readers. In high school, they'll often be assigned books to read as a whole class, and in-school independent reading falls away, so it's important for them to develop this as a cherished habit while still in my care. And that means having a huge variety of books available to match all the diverse tastes, interests, and reading levels of my equally diverse students in our NYC classroom. I love when students are honest, because I want to know when I've got my work cut out for me. The greatest moments in teaching for me are when a student who tells me from day one that they don't like to read comes over to say they couldn't stop reading last night because they wanted to see what happened, or that their book made them cry. That's when they know what the joy of reading can be.

I have to say that, even though I am a reading specialist, my class peaks at about 85 percent passionate readers. As for the other 15 percent, getting them to finally finish books, when in the past they never had, is a huge accomplishment. And I'll tell you the key to achieving this: I read the books that my kids are reading and do the same work I ask of them in my own notebook. This practice will lead you too to have an incredibly awesome classroom library with books that fit all tastes and reading levels.

How Can You Help Kids Choose the Perfect Book?

The only way to make an honest recommendation about a book is to read it yourself and know which kids this book fits. If you use "'book ladders" in your classroom, you can think through "If they like *that*, then *this* would be a good fit." For more on book ladders, getting kids to read by thinking about what interests them, and choosing a lower-level book to progress in reading levels, try Teri Lesesne's *Reading Ladders* (2010).

Sometimes you get only one chance to make a book suggestion, and if it's the right one, kids will trust you enough to read anything. Nothing is worse than recommending a book that's a dud just because someone else online liked it. *You* have to like it and know which kids it will be a good fit for and which kids it won't. Know the books and know your kids.

Keeping up with all the hot books is not easy. I constantly scour magazines, library lists, and Amazon best books of the month to see what's new. Then I check the reviews to make sure actual readers agree, and then I add it to my list to read. I hang out in libraries and independent bookstores, which helps me gain insight into what books kids are reading this year from the people who see it happen. Many independent booksellers publish a quarterly newsletter listing noteworthy recent books for different ages and genres, including synopses of the books. I make time to read the newsletter from my local independent bookstore each week because it's part of my job, and if I incorporate it into my weekly schedule, I know I have to do it. I think of it as my reading homework. Summers are my time to dive into all the great books out there. I'm lucky enough to have time to myself and often spend a few days each week just reading. When I come back to school, I bring with me excitement about a new batch of books to recommend (and believe me, I really talk them up and model reading strategies with them so all the kids want to read them next). Plus, you can really get to know a student through a good book choice because they might open up about living through a problem similar to the character in the book.

How Can You Build an Awesome Classroom Library?

If education is truly meant to be "an effort to improve the quality of choices open to all students" (NCTE, 2018, p. xvi), that effort has to start with having many options of books in my classroom. That requires a lot of book hoarding, begging, stealing, and being creative with how you build your library. People are often left open-jawed when they see my classroom library, with more than 7,000 books, mostly organized into bins with titles that appeal to middle grade kids.

It's taken me years to build it, but anyone can have a library like mine if it's important to them. Kids taught me to stay on top of my library. My very first year of teaching I had some boys reading the Cirque du Freak series by Darren Shan (2000–2004), which quickly became one of my favorites for getting boys who "don't like books" to read, and they'd all started at book 8; the classroom library I'd inherited didn't have the earlier volumes. When I saw those students loving the characters and loving what was happening in spite of not being familiar with the background, I immediately went out to get all the books in the series and then encouraged students to start reading from the beginning. And they did! That's when I realized that I have to stay on top of my library, because kids are desperate to read if the right books are available. I spent a ton of money those first years and also took out library books constantly to make sure I kept finding books that spoke to my students' issues, backgrounds, fantasies, and preferences. Those boys taught me that I need to always be on a quest to supplement my library.

How do I do it? First off, I look to DonorsChoose.org as a source for new and hot books because there are always people out there who feel good about donating books to an underfunded classroom. I always write and share a project grant on the site before the holidays. I ask family and friends who want to get me a gift to donate to my library and get a tax deduction for the end of the year. That also goes for gift cards (from Barnes and Noble, Amazon, or a favorite local bookstore). If giving teachers holiday gifts is a practice for the families at your school, let them know you're always looking for new books or book-based gift cards. Also, send out a letter to parents when you have a project posted on DonorsChoose so that they can participate too. Every spring, DonorsChoose has a special day when all the projects seem to get funded. I make sure to have a project ready for when that happens—free books!

I am constantly on the lookout for any program that gives books to classrooms. For instance, I bring a group of students to the National Book Awards Teen Press Conference every fall. While there, kids receive a copy of the award-winning books, and I always try to "borrow" a few copies; it's a great way to have some of the best new YA literature in my room. In New York City, teachers at Title I schools are invited to get new and slightly used books through a program called Project Cicero. This is a one-day book giveaway during which teachers can take as many books as they can grab and carry during their designated hour in the project's book room. Most teachers bring a huge suitcase to the event! Check to see if you have any local book giveaways like this that could help you supplement your classroom library. First Book is another organization for teachers working in Title 1 schools across the country. This nonprofit maintains many book programs, including a marketplace website on which teachers can purchase new books for a fraction of the retail cost. Teachers need only sign up for an account using their school's free and reduced lunch percentage to begin purchasing. In addition, First Book has book giveaways and specials for teachers throughout the school year. Generally, teachers need only pay for shipping in order to be sent boxes of free books during the giveaway specials. Publishers also have advanced reader copies (ARCs) to give away. Publishers are interested in getting new books into readers' hands, and often developing friendly relationships with publishers will help you build your library with great new titles. Asking kids to "try out" the new books and offer the publishers real kid reader feedback is a good way to build these relationships.

My favorite option is when libraries have book sales or fundraisers. On summer vacation, during my travels I look up all the libraries that hold fundraisers—when I tell them that I'm a teacher all the way from New York who's going to ship the books back to my classroom, they usually charge me twenty-five cents per kid book! Librarians often have a soft spot for a slightly obsessed but dedicated teacher looking to build a classroom library. I don't worry about shipping so much because the post office offers a cheap media mail rate for shipping books. You can send a medium-size box (around twenty-two to twenty-five books) for around seven to eight dollars, which is about thirty-five cents per book. I'm always on the hunt at yard sales and church sales; sometimes they'll just give you the books when they find out you're a teacher.

Once I get books into my classroom, I try to make sure they are returned after kids borrow them. At the end of the year, I hold a raffle—for each book a kid brings back, they get a raffle ticket. I buy cheap AMC movie passes from Costco, and kids can win one from each class. If kids want to increase their odds, they can bring in their own books from home and get three raffle tickets per book they donate to our library. Usually parents are happy to clean out their shelves. If you get books out of your age range, trade them with another teacher a few grades above or below you.

One last option that requires a lot of initiative but will get your kids excited about reading is asking an author to do a book fair at a local Barnes and Noble or independent bookstore. In the past, I have hounded authors (through email, showing up at their tables at book fairs, going to their readings/public appearances), even offered to treat them to dinner, in an attempt to get them to visit my school. However, I understand that visiting schools is actually part of an author's job and is, in fact, an element of earning their livelihood. Authors rightly expect to be paid for visits, but fundraising or securing other funding to pay an author has a huge reading payoff for kids. If your school doesn't have a way to fund an author visit, one option is to sponsor a reading at a bookstore. At a bookstore reading, the author sells copies of their signed books, and kids are at the bookstore, spending time among the shelves as they wait. It's important to have as many kids as possible read the author's books ahead of time so the kids are excited about the visit and knowledgeable about the author. When they get to finally meet the author, it'll be like meeting a rock star. Often bookstores will offer schools incentives to partner in these kinds of events. For instance, Barnes and Noble encourages teachers to make wish lists of books that parents can donate to classrooms. The store also gives a percentage of the money made on the school book fairs and author events back to the school in the form of gift cards—which you can spend on more books!

How Can You Manage All Those Books?

Honestly, sometimes I feel as though managing my library is a full-time job I somehow eke out in an already busy day. The best thing you can do is to train student assistants. Every year I ask students to write me a letter about why they want to be a librarian. Usually these are kids who love being in the library and are always reading. They become my classroom librarians. It's good to have kids who don't mind giving up their lunch periods and have great organizational skills. We put book pockets in every book with lined library cards that kids sign when they check out a book (you can get these from Demco in their library supplies department). When new books come in, the librarians fill out index cards for the books and stick them in the book pockets. And here's a tip: these book pockets are also a great place for kids to keep their reading logs while reading the book. We keep a box for each class to hold their library cards for the book they've checked out. When kids are done with their book, they find their card in the box, replace it in the back of the book, and leave the book in the return bin for the librarians. It's better to have the librarians re-file the books because they'll know exactly where the books belong. Teaching them to understand the library on that organizational level takes time.

Arranging the books is important too. You want to make sure the bins are placed into sections that both make sense to you and are easy for kids to get to. Labeling the bins with exciting sticky notes with titles and pictures will draw in students (it's always good to have at least one librarian who's artistic).

Now That You Have the Library, Get Kids to Read!

None of what I do with my library matters if kids aren't reading the books. To help them become voracious readers, I join book clubs with them. In a higher-level book club, this might look like me throwing some questions to a group, pointing out important text they may have missed, or asking a question that challenges their thinking. Again, my goal is to steer but not lead the conversations. Another technique that works with the higher-level book clubs centers on my display of a poster of banned books that names a number of classics I would love kids to read. Students always ask, "Why was *Of Mice and Men* banned? Why was *To Kill a Mockingbird* banned?" Then they ask if they can read those books. I tell them I need to get their parents' permission because the book is *banned* and perhaps dangerous—well, the best way to get any middle school kid interested in a book is to tell them that they can't read it!

The more difficult book clubs to manage are those with kids who describe themselves as not liking to read or kids who struggle because reading is just plain

hard for them. Middle school kids in this group often don't want to be seen reading books that third graders are reading; they want to read what other eighth graders are reading. I find the best way to help kids in this situation move into more complex books (we use the Teachers College Reading and Writing Project leveling system, from the work of Irene Fountas and Gay Su Pinnell) is to actually model what reading—and thinking about reading—looks and sounds like. While the rest of the class is independently reading, I'll sit with a favorite book that's at their level (or maybe a touch higher) such as *The One and Only Ivan* by Katherine Applegate (2012) or *The Miraculous Journey of Edward Tulane* by Kate DiCamillo (2006), books that are simple in terms of reading level but that have deeper meaning when closely read. Then we read the book together in a small group. These groups are either five to six kids in a class during reading time or a small group of eight dedicated kids who'll come gather at lunch once a week. We go slowly and do close reading, similar to Chris Lehman and Kate Roberts's approach in *Falling in Love with Close Reading* (2013), paying attention to the most important text in each short chapter. We talk about what the excerpt could mean and how it changes or builds on ideas they already have. I also pause to have kids visualize what's happening in the text, a skill I find that kids who get stuck reading usually don't exercise while reading. Kids feel safe in such a book club and often aren't afraid to take chances with their thinking and wondering. As a teacher, watching them build complex ideas about a book is a remarkable experience. A student named Jada, after reading *The One and Only Ivan*, said to me, "Why aren't all books as good as this one?" I explained to her that many books are "that good" as long as you do the work of thinking and visualizing as you read. After this kind of experience, students are more likely to accept my book suggestions and maybe even choose to read together again as a book club and share their thinking.

Having a strong reading workshop classroom, stocked with tons of great books, and a teacher who loves to read too is a change maker for many kids. Developing this kind of classroom reading program can help change a few reluctant readers into book lovers and gives kids who love to read a space to thrive as readers. Isn't this one reason we teach English language arts?

Questions to start a reading conference or to assign as homework:

- The very basic **What's going on in your book?** This is good for checking comprehension: Are kids giving you a full retell, because they can't decide what's important, or a summary, which shows they can synthesize what they're reading? Are kids using the characters' names, showing that they're holding on to the information?

- **Which of the characters would you be best friends with and why?** Here I'm asking for simple ideas, and it gets them talking. The "why" shows me how they support their ideas. If they don't have a favorite character, I ask them who would be their enemy and why.

- A higher comprehension question to start a discussion is **What decisions is your character making that you don't like, and why do you think they're doing that?** I'm really looking to see if they understand what motivates the character's behavior. Next I ask, **What advice would you give them?** This makes a great homework prompt.

- **Which character can you relate to and why?** Once kids see characters as someone they can identify with, it helps them become attached to the book and perhaps help them figure out a problem in their own life.

- I also ask kids to describe how they **visualize a scene in their book**. Here I'm looking to see if they just repeat what the story says or whether they add little details that tell me they're actually visualizing what they read. Good readers live in the world of their books, and kids who struggle need modeling of and constant practice in how to visualize.

Ways to encourage kids to keep reading:

1. The best way to keep kids reading their book is to pair them up with a friend or friends. Kids hold each other accountable. They don't want to be left out of the partnership or group and will read so as not to be left out. Having them talk about the book makes the reading more exciting and helps with comprehension. Students who might not be comfortable asking a teacher what's happening may be more likely to ask a friend.

2. I may read the book with students. Knowing we'll have a check-in about the book makes them keep up and feel special. Middle schoolers (as much as they complain about it) want that special attention.

3. I ask when they anticipate finishing the book. When I explain that I have kids dying to read this book next (and I'll mention a few kids' names), they begin to see that they're part of a club that loves to read, especially that hot book they're reading now.

4. I also drop hints that something exciting is going to happen soon, like "Just wait to see what [the character] is going to do; it's crazy!"

5. Oftentimes if a kid struggles with reading and they want to read a book that feels too difficult to navigate, I suggest they use that book as a reading goal they can achieve by reading lower-leveled books first and reading their way up. I keep reassuring them that if they can only get through a few more books, they can read the one they want, and they'll really be able to enjoy it. I try to make a reading plan with them so they're aware of exactly how many books they need to read on the path to their goal.

A Visit to Room 201 at Oyster River Middle School

Linda Rief has been guiding middle school teachers in our country toward workshop teaching for years. Her several books are on teacher shelves, at the ready, when a question arises about launching writing-reading notebooks in a classroom or for ideas about how to implement daily quick-writes. When people think of Linda Rief's classroom, I'm sure most imagine a seamless writing and reading workshop, a hum of kids working along in authentic writer or reader roles. But just like everyone else, sometimes Linda's class doesn't hum so smoothly; sometimes there is awkward silence as shy middle schoolers wait for someone else to read a piece of writing first, wait for someone else to "put themselves out there." In this piece, Linda shares with us ways to think about a writing workshop that did not go as expected, guiding us once again to be reflective practitioners when what we planned and what has always worked goes awry in our classroom.

Choices and Challenges in the Writing Workshop
Linda Rief, Oyster River Middle School, Durham, NH—Grade 8

We are halfway through the eighth-grade year in a writing workshop. Today I push all the tables against the wall and arrange the chairs in a big circle. I place a package of sticky notes on each chair and wait with great anticipation for the kids to come in. I am excited for them to hear all the wonderful writing their classmates are doing. This is always the best day. A celebration of the hard work they have put in as writers. A chance to hear each voice.

As the students arrive there are only questions: *What's going on? Why are all the tables against the wall? Why are the chairs in a circle? We're what? No, . . . no, . . . no way. I am not sharing my writing.*

I am not deterred. I sit down in a chair, my writing in my lap, a pack of sticky notes and a pen in my hand. I have explained for days that we will be sharing our writing, the piece we like the most so far this year, with the rest of the class. Today I explain that these are best drafts, and we will each write down what we hear or notice that works well as the writer reads. After reading aloud, the writer will hand their piece around for each of us to tack on our note.

I model how this works by reading my writing—the text of a picture book I have been working on all year. I send the written piece around and students attach their notes. I thank them and say, "Who would like to go next?"

Silence. No eyes look at me. I wait. And wait. I keep looking up at the clock. The minute hand appears to be stuck. Have only three minutes passed? "I won't make anyone read," I say, "but you have all done some wonderful writing. Doesn't anyone want to read? . . . It feels good to get compliments from each other. Anyone?" And we wait. Ten minutes. Nineteen minutes. Twenty-seven agonizing, painful, never-ending minutes.

Twenty-three silent fourteen-year-olds. *Silent.* As if a cough or sigh will bring attention to them. We are sitting in a circle. We are facing each other. No one utters a single word. Thirty-two minutes. Forty-one minutes. Are they even breathing, I wonder?

Another teacher passes by in the hall with a glance into the room. He steps back, pokes his head in, walks over to me, bends down and whispers, "What the hell is going on?"

I am wondering the same thing—what *is* going on? The silence continues in all classes—all . . . day . . . long.

But I am a glutton for punishment and stick with my plan to try it a second day. Slight improvement. One or two students read, despite painful pauses of complete silence in the forty-five minutes.

Did I not tell the students they would be sharing their writing, reading their writing to the whole class? I did. Yes, I did. Did they not believe me?

I told the students earlier in the week that we would be sharing our writing. They were reluctant, downright hostile in some cases, but I was sure it would not be a problem. I would take them through the same process I have used for years: The writer reads and then listeners write down on a sticky note what they heard or noticed, what stayed with them, what made the writing especially engaging and compelling. The writer would hand their writing around for other students to attach their notes. When everyone had read, I would hand them their writing with all the wonderful comments their classmates wrote. They would feel good about engaging an audience of their peers. They would say what other kids have said in the past: "These notes feel like hugs, even from kids I don't know really well."

I would start with my piece if no one volunteered and then watch as one student after another read his or her best piece, anxious to hear what their peers had noticed.

Not this time. Or during any of the other three classes. Four classes of students sitting silent, portfolios balanced on their legs, staring at the floor, for more than forty painfully agonizing silent minutes. For two days!

What is going on?

Bear with me as I try to figure this out.

Eighth-grade language arts is essentially a writing-reading workshop. Through the work of Peter Elbow, Janet Emig, John Dewey, Louise Rosenblatt, Donald Graves, Nancie Atwell, Donald Murray, Tom Newkirk, and Mary Ellen Giacobbe (just to name a few), I learned the conditions that need to exist to create a workshop approach to reading and writing. In its simplest form it looks like this:

Our students need:

- Reading that engages, interests, challenges
- Real writing for real reasons for real audiences

Our students deserve teachers who:

- Read and have the courage to write
- Are reflective practitioners
- Have high expectations
- Teach with their head and their heart
- Recognize, encourage, and build on the diverse strengths and promises of their students

Students can do their best work when given:

- TIME
- CHOICE
- RESPONSE (toward revision, while drafting)
    - this is what you did well
    - questions you need to consider
    - suggestions
- MODELS and MODELING of fine reading and writing (both fiction and nonfiction)
- STRATEGIES for entering into, strengthening, and extending that writing and reading
- A WRITING-READING NOTEBOOK—a place to consistently initiate and collect their thinking
- ENCOURAGEMENT to use visual tools to show their thinking as writers and their understandings as readers

From my eighth graders I expect good reading and writing in which one process enriches the other, in which students' ideas and wonderings and questions invite risks, taking them to the outer edges of what they know and what they can do. I expect good reading and writing, in which process and product are woven tightly into literate tapestries of wonder and awe.

On a weekly basis, what does the workshop look like? Monday, Tuesday, and Wednesday we do a quick-write (in the writing-reading notebook that each student keeps) at the beginning of the class, and I often point out through a brief mini-lesson a craft move the kids might notice in the mentor text we just used for the quick-write. The students then turn to their own writing, and I move from student to student with "How can I help you?" The focus is on the writing.

On Thursday and Friday, students read for fifteen minutes at the beginning of the period. I move around quickly in a touch-base conference ("What are you reading now? What page are you on? How's it going?"). On these days, we might read a few mentor texts focused on the kind of writing they are working on in order to look more closely at what a writer is doing. Or we might be looking at reading strategies.

Writing and reading, process and product, woven tightly into tapestries of wonder and awe. Sounds good. I try. But as you can see from the opening vignette, it does not always happen as smoothly and as seamlessly as we are expected to believe.

The reading of their writing aloud is meant to be a celebration of all we have done and learned in the workshop approach. Something has gone wrong this year.

I told the kids we would read aloud. I put the chairs in a big circle. Read my own piece first, after talking about positive response on sticky notes. Then we sat in silence—for TWO DAYS! Finally, three kids in one class read. After two days, I put the tables and chairs back. Kids came in the third day—"What? Why aren't we reading aloud?" After two days of near silence, they want to know why we aren't trying for a third day. Really?

I asked them to write in their notebooks why they hadn't read for the first two days. "Too embarrassing . . . Don't like my writing . . . Too personal . . . Too long . . . Too short . . . Not good enough . . . I was worried about what kids might say."

One student said, "I haven't done any writing worth reading." I think I plagiarized Ben Franklin when I said, "Then do something worth writing about!" Yikes, did I say that? I think I did. It had been a frustrating two days.

What does this experience tell me?

I have not created the kind of writing community where kids feel safe with one another, where they trust themselves and their peers to offer the kinds of feedback that keep the writer moving forward with their thinking. I have not created enough time for them to read their writing to each other in small groups. This is essential in a workshop classroom—teaching kids how to talk to each other in constructive ways about their writing and giving them the time to do it.

But something else has changed, and I am wondering if this, too, has had an effect on the ability to create a trusting community of writers. Computers.

In previous years, students had to bring in a hard copy of their writing because we had no computers. They worked face to face with each other, often saying, "Listen to this. Tell me what you think." Writing conversations were natural, spontaneous—happening as kids wrote by hand in their notebooks, or on computers the few times we were able to get them. Feedback was always (well, almost always!) positive and nurturing. That's what I love about workshop. The kids at tables facing each other but looking up and talking as the need arises. It becomes natural. They internalize what they hear me saying as I go table to table: "How can I help you? Read it to me. . . . I heard you say . . . This stuck with me . . . I noticed . . . Here's a question that popped into my head: . . . What if you . . ." There is a comfort that comes from this kind of talk. It builds a community of writers who trust one another.

We have gone to one-to-one personal laptops. Students carry them from class to class. Instead of sitting face to face with each other, they are staring at computers. I love the fact that we don't have to schedule the few computers we used to have in the building around 500 other students, but it has changed the dynamics in the classroom. This *may* be contributing to why students are not comfortable reading their writing to each other.

At a recent language arts meeting, my colleagues actually cheered when I said I thought I liked Google Classroom and was using it to have students send their writing to me. But there's the rub. It is convenient. It is easier. But sometimes I misread students' intent. Sometimes they misread my feedback. I am not face to face with the writer as I need to be, as I want to be. Something changes when reading writing on the computer in contrast to having the student sitting next to me where I can hear the intent in their voice. I can sense their degree of comfort or discomfort with the piece. I can focus on the content, not the mechanics as they read. And as they read, they notice for themselves when their writing doesn't say what they meant it to say, and they correct it accordingly.

Additionally, in one-on-one conferences, other students hear the writing, often adding their own comments once I leave the table. They begin to trust me and trust each other, trust that the comments will be constructive and positive. They are meant to move the writer forward in their quest to strengthen their voice.

What will I do now, realizing what might be getting in the way of a trusting classroom community?

Our administration wants to go paperless. I had to seek special dispensation (in the form of a little begging over a few weeks) for our students to be allowed to print from their computers. I had to explain again and again why it was important for writers to have hard copies in front of them as we talked about their writing and had the opportunity to listen to each other. I understand there are computer programs that allow kids to share their writing and talk to each other, but it's not the same. Perhaps I am stuck in the old world, but I think there is a need in schools, especially in workshop classrooms, for students to see, hear, and talk to one another, face to face, over the products they are making.

Writing is nurtured when there is a purpose and an audience, one that gives us positive, constructive feedback. It has to happen on a daily basis if we want to help kids trust each other as they build a writing community. Isn't that what we want in our classrooms, ways to help students become articulate, compassionate, nurturing citizens of the world, who trust each other, know each other, and talk to each other?

I do think, and several teachers in workshops I have led have mentioned to me, that there are ways to still maintain a workshop approach when everyone is working directly from and on computers. These teachers have their students read their writing to them directly from their personal computers while the teacher writes comments, questions, and suggestions on their computer and then sends the comments digitally to the writer. If that works to keep the students growing as writers, then they should keep at it that way.

For me, the computers pose more of a distraction, perhaps because I am not as efficient on them, or perhaps because I really want to make direct eye contact with the writer in my attempts to understand all the complexities involved with writing—*and* the writer.

Now that I've figured out that the presence of digital composing seems to have changed the human interaction I have with the writers in my room, as well as the interactions they have with each other, my next step is to figure out how the live human voice that so moves writers can still be a viable part of our workshop classroom. Computers are so helpful in the composing process. But stepping out from behind them might be more helpful as students get feedback.

Perhaps it's as simple as asking kids to bring in or print out a hard copy of their draft when they are ready to receive feedback. Through modeling conferences and my written feedback, and then having students share in partners or small groups with a hard copy the writer reads aloud, these face-to-face interactions will continue to help students strengthen their writing and to trust each other enough to be willing to share their best pieces with the entire class.

Hearing each other, not silence, is what keeps our kids moving forward and growing as writers.

A Final Thought from Jen

My early desire to have a "dining room table" classroom like Nancie Atwell's mirrors the spaces that both Carole and Linda show us as we look inside their classroom doors. The comfy spaces for reading, the chatting about books, the time to read . . . I've always wanted the readers in my classroom to have access to those conditions as they spend the year with me. Likewise, sitting with writers, asking about their pieces, sharing ideas for revision, hearing the writing voices shared in a circle of trust and support are some of the aspects of writing with kids I've tried to incorporate into my classroom. For me, these two teachers have structured their classrooms around the Golden Rules of Reading and Writing. They are providing reading and writing time and space and experience in classrooms I would love to learn in as a reader and writer myself. I appreciate how Carole and Linda offered a peek into their processes and reflective practices as they share their time with the readers and writers they teach.

In the next section, you'll have a chance to visit five more classrooms from very different areas of our country: suburban Oklahoma and Missouri, New York City, and rural Mississippi. Each teacher invites you into their classroom to see other ways they are actively bringing the principles of *The Students' Right to Read* and *NCTE Beliefs about the Students' Right to Write* into their classroom work with the middle school kids they teach.

Part II
Intervisitations

At least one cycle of our professional development work at my school every year is dedicated to intervisitations. We are paired with another ELA teacher in our department who has a schedule that meshes with our own, and we then visit each other's classrooms. Sometimes this visit is prompted; we may both be considering independent reading structures or listening in on conferencing with kids, so we observe and learn from each other. Sometimes the visit is feedback focused; the teacher being visited wants feedback on a new structure or strategy, or is hoping to revise an existing structure or strategy, making the new eyes and ears of a partner in the room quite helpful. Sometimes the visit is open-ended; we come in, sit and watch and listen and consider and learn, and then chat together afterward. I look forward to this portion of our school-wide PD plan because I learn so much every time. Even when we plan together, as a school, department, grade team, or teaching partners, there is something different about sitting in the back of someone else's classroom and watching that person teach kids that engages the observer's own depth of understanding and pedagogical portfolio.

In my years of participating in back-of-the-room observations of my colleagues, I have learned from the seventh-grade teachers different ways to more authentically teach vocabulary, a skill I greatly lacked and often ignored in my own classroom. From the sixth-grade teachers in my school, I learned how to run excellent simultaneous small groups in a co-teaching classroom. My teaching partner and I now use this strategy multiple times in a unit, based on our colleagues' guidance. And I always "steal" charts and whiteboard notes when I sit in the other eighth-grade teacher's classroom. Another visit that has changed my way of thinking comes from watching the bilingual literacy teacher at my school teach. The way she authentically includes the grammar of English while engaging kids in the writing and reading of real writers and readers is so thoughtful and rigorous, and it is exactly what any of us would want for our own children's classroom experiences.

In this section, I hope you enjoy "sitting" in the back of the classrooms of five middle school teachers. We will watch how they very intentionally incorporate aspects of *The Students' Right to Read* and *NCTE Beliefs about the Students' Right to*

Write into their pedagogical practices, despite curricular mandates that ask them to teach within structures that are not traditional workshop settings. I hope that visiting these teachers will encourage you to develop ways and open up spaces in your own curriculum that incorporate the ideals of these two policy statements even when you are teaching to mandates that seem to go against these ideals.

In their respective settings, April Fulstone and Heather Anderson show us how to use ideas within the policy statements to encourage authentic reading and writing practices when you are teaching a whole-class novel. Shelly Unsicker-Durham shows us how you might rethink "writing to the test" to include practices that honor middle school people as writers. Finally, Alex Corbitt and Chad Everett respectively let us watch how they encourage the middle school writers and readers they teach to drive the work they do in their classrooms. In all, I hope you'll enjoy your time in each classroom, and I'll stop by at the end of each visit to share what I'm borrowing from each teacher for my own classroom. I invite you to think about your own teaching and the ways you can further honor students' rights to read and write as the already seasoned readers and writers they are in middle school.

A Visit to Room 219 at Wydown Middle School

The Giver *by Lois Lowry is one of the most commonly taught whole-class texts in middle school, and one of the core texts in the seventh-grade curriculum in April Fulstone's school. April wanted to challenge her students to examine the notion of dystopia, not just as a literary genre but as a definition of the world we are currently living in as Americans. Using the essential questions "What is value? Who determines it?," students analyzed what makes a dystopian society and how a person can challenge the status quo. On completion of a standard literary analysis of the novel, April used the students' thinking as a bridge for students to consider the dystopia of the United States during the Civil Rights era and today's remaining dystopian system of institutional and systemic racism. Students chose one out of ten historical fiction or nonfiction titles that address a Civil Rights era theme. In book clubs, students practiced critical thinking about the rules of a society and who benefits most from those rules, as well as who loses. Ultimately, they made connections to the legacy of the Civil Rights era and human rights violations in today's society. Then they shared what they learned with the wider audience of their school community.*

The Giver and the Real World: "The Perilous but Wondrous Times We Live In"
April Fulstone, Wydown Middle School, Clayton, MO—Grade 7

As one of the few teachers of color my students will have in their Clayton Schools experience, I look for opportunities to incorporate my own questionings about the world, my stories of seeking who I am, and literature and media that counter the status quo narratives of the mainstream literacy curriculum. I strongly believe that teachers need to be vulnerable in front of students and to share ourselves openly as learners and thinkers, as humans, not just as content deliverers.

Some background to the project I describe in these pages: I spent a decade among sixth graders teaching an integrated social studies and literacy curriculum; using literature and primary sources to build empathy for diverse perspectives was my main objective. Then, in the fall of 2014, I joined the seventh-grade literacy team. I felt my way through the year of a new curriculum a bit blindly, thankfully with supportive colleagues to help guide me. I had a few anchors: the three core texts (*The Outsiders*, *Maus I*, and *The Giver*); the essential questions, "What is value? Who determines it?"; and our common practices of writers workshop, literature circles, and independent reading. Still, the first year felt a bit hollow. I realized I needed to make the curriculum my own, and as the year progressed I rearranged a few things to make it feel more like home. I reflected on my first year of teaching seventh grade and looked for ways to "redecorate."

The questions I considered as I made these changes:

- If units feel disconnected, what are the unifying threads and how can essential questions be used to connect them?
- If student work feels inauthentic, what connections can be made to the real world?
- If students have to read a required book, how can I guide supplementary reading to give them choice and also an opportunity to think about diverse perspectives that connect in both literature and the real world?

As the next year and my second time teaching this grade began, I implemented some changes based on these questions: my literacy colleague, Lisa, and I opened the year with a double-sided mask project, asking students to symbolize on the front how others perceive them and on the back how they perceive themselves. I incorporated some new readings into the curriculum, adding "Fish Cheeks" by Amy Tan (1987) into the memoir unit and excerpts from Richard Wright's "The Ethics of Living Jim Crow" (1937) into a Great Migration unit that I created (and have since expanded) because the era produced so much amazing creative expression in the name of resistance. I reorganized a short story unit to teach it thematically throughout the year rather than as a genre of writing. These moves helped me to be the teacher that I needed to be for my students.

Of course, the core texts were nonnegotiable. I have always been somewhat conflicted about core texts. I know that whole-class shared reading is extremely valuable for close reading, author study, and practicing the use of textual evidence in analysis, among other reasons. I know that it's unrealistic to expect our students to have choice in their reading all the time, especially in the upper grades when high school is essentially college prep, which is really about learning the accepted canon. Luckily, the texts required in our seventh-grade year are fairly universally engaging.

However, I still felt as though something was missing. When I joined the seventh-grade team, I inherited a core text unit for Lowry's *The Giver* (1993). This unit began with a utopia project, during which students looked at the founding documents of the United States and then worked in groups to decide on the qualities of their own utopian society. At the conclusion of the unit, groups took turns presenting their imagined utopias to the class. Throughout the unit, students met in book clubs, and I was supposed to point out close reading quotes for the whole class to analyze. Students wrote a literary analysis about a theme of their choosing, using textual evidence to support this idea.

The utopia group project, for my first round of seventh graders, ended up revealing surface-level thinking and felt disconnected from the real world. Some groups were saying things like "Once people turn sixty-five, they have to go to a center for the elderly" without much reasoning behind the statement, or focusing so much on the technological accoutrements of their imagined world that the idea of government went out the window. I concluded that seventh graders have their own forms of wisdom but haven't lived long enough to engage with the nuances of building a perfect community. Yes, they had fun, but what did they really get out of this experience? I wanted them to dig deeper and see how relevant *The Giver*'s themes are to our own lives, past and present. I wanted students to think more critically about the yearlong essential questions, "What is value? Who determines it?," in response to Jonas's story.

After reflecting on my dissatisfaction with the kind of engagement my students displayed in that first year, I realized why I felt that way: I did not *create*, but was simply *executing*, the units I was teaching. And this is a telling point. Good teachers put their heart into what they teach, or it doesn't feel real to them or to their students, and creating assignments is a crucial part of that heart. I am fortunate to work in a district where teachers are trusted to develop much of the curriculum, and I'm quite sure that my team members who were part of the creation process of these assignments were doing a better job than I was. After all, they had written the units; they owned the teaching of this work in a way I couldn't quite manage yet. This realization led me to new reflective questions:

- In most educational settings, how much are teachers expected to execute rather than create, and thus engage, in content?

- What kinds of curriculum might emerge if teachers were the primary creators, able to use their own (and their students') questions, their own (and their students') life experiences, and their own (and their students') expertise to drive teaching and learning?

So in round two of teaching this course, I turned to creating. I decided to scrap the utopia project and instead help students make connections to current and historical events from a variety of news media, and to think about dystopias and attempted utopias in the real world. As stated in the *The Students' Right to Read*: "English teachers must be free to employ books, classic or contemporary, which do not hide, or lie to the young about, the perilous but wondrous times we live in" (NCTE, 2018, p. xvii). I wanted students to think about Jonas's perilous but wondrous world as he discovers the disturbing amount of control his government has over his community. I wanted them to see that we also live in a perilous but wondrous world, or as Ta-Nehisi Coates puts it, the Beautiful Struggle (Coates, 2008).

The Giver unit was the perfect opportunity to raise issues about this perilous world and to return to my three driving questions:

- If units feel disconnected, what are the unifying threads and how can essential questions be used to connect them?
- If student work feels inauthentic, what connections can be made to the real world?
- If students have to read a required book, how can I guide supplementary reading to give them choice and an opportunity to think about diverse perspectives that connect in both literature and the real world?

To connect *The Giver* unit to the preceding and following units, I focused more on the idea of dystopia and how lives are valued differently in the real world. A previous core text we had studied as a class was *Maus I* by Art Spiegelman (1980). During that unit, we discussed how people in power place value on the lives of people within their society. In my revised *The Giver* unit, students looked at the meanings of utopia and dystopia using a video from Study.com. With our definitions in common, we discussed how Hitler created a real-life dystopia during the Holocaust. We then made connections to the unit just before *The Giver*, which was a research-based argument about the value of technology versus human interaction in our lives today. In the previous unit, students had read "The Veldt" by Ray Bradbury (1951) and then chosen their topics, with many opportunities to share with each other about their emerging claims and evidence. Many kids focused on the topic of cyberbullying during this research and recognized the dehumanizing tendencies of social media. When we began considering notions of value and dystopia in response to *The Giver*, it made sense to revisit their previous topics of research.

To make deeper connections to the real world as we moved into *The Giver* unit, students read several current events articles about places like Bhutan; North Korea; Kowloon; and Ferguson, Missouri, with the option of extending their knowledge through independent research about one of these places. We had been working on annotation with nonfiction articles since the beginning of the year, so students knew they were not just reading for information, but questioning, connecting, and reacting to the information. Many students, especially the African American students, connected with the dystopia of the militarization of police in Ferguson, a community fifteen minutes away from our school by highway (and one in which some of our voluntary transfer students lived). Students talked in their groups about the essential questions in *The Giver*, but also made connections to how values cause unity or conflict in real life. As a whole class, we looked at multiple sources discussing North Korea—its history, Kim Il Sung's utopian hopes, its appearance on the surface and the dystopia beneath the surface. Students made connections to what they had already learned about America's foundation of racism and terrorism during a sixth-grade unit about slavery and in our fall semester about Jim Crow.

The original common assessment for *The Giver* unit had been a literary analysis of themes within the book. I extended this to ask students to make connections between *The Giver* and the nonfiction sources they had analyzed during the unit. They could also make connections to an independent reading of a dystopian novel. Some kids completed this further novel reading in book clubs in half the time it took the rest of the class. I differentiated ways that students could extend their analysis. Some students chose to focus on a theme in the book, which was enough of a challenge. Others incorporated evidence from another article or novel. A few used information from independent research to contemplate whether utopia is possible, still anchoring their argument in evidence from *The Giver* as well.

Real-life topics that students can connect to dystopia in literature:

- Militarization of police at peaceful protests
- Mass incarceration
- School shootings

Usually at the end of the unit, we watch the film version and talk about the adaptation and how it affected the meaning for students. In *The Giver* film, there is a scene toward the end in which the Giver touches Jonas to give him strength for his escape, the touch provoking flashes of famous protests throughout global history. This scene is a great visual connection to start talking about how one person can stand up to generations of conformity by questioning unjust norms. It really helped more concrete thinkers make the connection between Jonas's resistance and resistance to oppression in the real world. I could reference this scene as we began our study of the modern Civil Rights Movement. During our Civil Rights book club conversations, students found evidence of characters experiencing dystopia during that specific time of American history.

To give students the opportunity to learn more about and express their own social activism, the next unit was our Human Rights Project. For this project, students chose both their subject and how they would tell the story to raise awareness about injustice in their lives. Using literature to evoke connections between human experience and resistance set the stage for students to investigate what needs to change in their own worlds and how they can share their convictions. Many students either connected back to topics from earlier in the year,

Civil Rights YA titles that I use:

- *X: A Novel* by Ilyasah Shabazz and Kekla Magoon (2015)
- *Betty before X* by Ilyasah Shabazz with Renee Watson (2018)
- *Claudette Colvin: Twice toward Justice* by Phillip Hoose (2009)
- *The Greatest: Muhammad Ali* by Walter Dean Myers (2001)
- *The Lions of Little Rock* by Kristin Levine (2012)

A few human rights activists whom students might want to research:

- Cesar Chavez
- Yuri Kochiyama
- Grace Lee Boggs
- The Black Panthers
- Huey Newton
- Angela Davis

whether it was segregated educational systems (still remaining all around us) or police brutality, or chose a current issue close to their hearts, such as the Syrian refugee crisis, undocumented immigration, or #BlackLivesMatter, to name a few. The students practiced using reliable web sources, paraphrasing notes, and organizing their thoughts to form a claim about actions that should be taken to support or raise awareness about their human rights issues. Some students worked in the art studio with one of our art teachers to communicate their message via collage, painting, sculpture, or installation and artist statements. In the end, we invited our school community to an exhibition of student work (see Figure II.1).

As I get closer to this year's Human Rights Project, I already have some revisions in mind. I want to narrow the scope of our topics to the local St. Louis region and make the product action oriented. Some of my students witness injustice as part of their daily lives, while others have never known what it feels like to have any part of their humanity questioned. The project is a vehicle for students to learn from one another about how our environment and identity shape the lives we lead and the opportunities we can easily access.

I know that many teachers are hesitant about bringing up race and other seemingly controversial topics in the classroom, especially teachers who have never had to talk about these topics themselves, or who feel they don't have the life experience or authority to properly address the issues. But our students desperately need safe spaces and sufficient time to process the very real issues surrounding them; they are bombarded by images, misinformation, and stereotypes at a rate that is preposterous. Without guidance, how will they make sense of this media and their roles in society? Rather than ignoring the hard topics, we need to face them bravely for the sake of all kids. Teachers don't need to be experts; we just need to facilitate a safe space.

The Students' Right to Read says, "One of the most important responsibilities of the English teacher is developing rapport and respect among students" (NCTE, 2018, p. xvii). This cannot happen without the teacher modeling and giving that rapport and respect. So when we spend a whole class period learning and talking about systemic racism, I start with my own stories—when I became aware of race, when I began to question prejudicial treatment toward myself and others. In professional development that I lead for colleagues, I often hear white teachers say that they don't have the experience to teach about topics of race and identity. However, I believe students need to hear white teachers being vulnerable about their own

Fictional diary entry by Saida Robles-Razzaq:

March 12, 2016

Dear Diary,

Today we left Syria. The civil war has killed some of our friends and we just couldn't stay in our town because of all the violence around us. Our house had been bombed by Isis, and there were many Isis fighters around. A lot of our family had already left Syria to go to Turkey, and we wanted to join them. But my parents were worried that we wouldn't be allowed into Turkey because they had closed their borders. The trip to Turkey was terrifying, because I felt like we could be caught any second. We could only fit what we could put in our car. We paid a smuggler to take us out. We made it to Turkey safely, but we didn't have much money left because we had to pay the smuggler a lot.

Sincerely,
Laila Ahmed

Sculpture about minimum wage by Daphne Kraushaar:

Collage about Angela Davis by Katherine Rice:

FIGURE II.1. Student samples.

identity, what whiteness means, and how everyone, especially white Americans, have weight to carry in conversations about race, even if it's only to listen intently. I say again and again to my students that they didn't create this world (like *The Giver's* Jonas), but they are responsible for being aware of injustice and acting on it when necessary (like Jonas). This may be as simple as spreading truthful knowledge or becoming an activist in the greater community.

Jen's Observation Notes

- I love the questions that April used to help her "redecorate" (what great phrasing!) her curriculum. They helped her think about how to make a curriculum that others had developed feel more matched to who she is as a teacher. These questions are a great starting point for any teacher or group of teachers beginning to revise a curriculum. In reality, when we are handed a curriculum developed by someone else, we do need to sit with the work and find ways to incorporate what we know and who we are as teachers into the plans. I'm flagging these questions to take to my grade team.

- I wrote this quote from April, "Yes, they had fun, but what did they really get out of this experience?," on a sticky note and stuck it in the front of my lesson plan book. What a smart way to assess a project. I always want to be able to answer this question when reflecting on how the work I've asked students to do corresponds to how they've grown as thinkers, knowers, readers, writers, people. I appreciate being pushed to question my own practice so that I'm continually refining my work with kids.

- Being in April's classroom reminds me of two important aspects of my teaching life: first, being in a place of constant analysis and revision of my units so that the work the students are doing continues to be relevant and asks them to grow as literate people; and second, that there are ways to weave important social justice work into the fabric of my already packed curriculum, and that not doing that work with kids could be detrimental to our democracy.

And finally, teaching within the NCTE policy statement on reading:

April's teaching of *The Giver* reminds me of the following excerpt from *The Students' Right to Read*:

Literature keeps "students in touch with the reality of the world outside the classroom" and asks questions like "'What is the nature of humanity?' 'Why do people praise individuality and practice conformity?' 'What do people need for a good life?' and 'What is the nature of a good person?'" (p. xvii)

In connecting this classic piece of young adult literature to the notion of dystopia, not just in literature but also in real-life dystopian situations, both in other countries and right in their own neighboring communities, students were able to examine these important questions from the policy brief as means to think about how they could effect change in the world themselves. In April's upcoming versions of this unit, her plans to include an action-oriented piece to the final writing will push kids beyond the literature and into a world that desperately needs their empathy and work.

What are your observations as you "sit" in the back of April's classroom?

- What new ideas does her work suggest for you?

- What changes might you make in your own teaching?

- What new wonderings do you have?

A Visit to Room 151 at Stillwater Junior High School

Heather Anderson wanted to create a way for her eighth graders to see current connections to a classic text that just celebrated its fiftieth anniversary. In her Oklahoma middle school, she uses The Outsiders *as a starting point for her students to examine issues of stereotypes and what those stereotypes do to a community. Through a series of activities, students identified the stereotypes in not only* The Outsiders, *but also in their school building, in Oklahoma, in the United States, and around the globe. Following these activities, students were invited to think critically about the group(s) they belong to individually and to break down which stereotypes might affect them due to the labels they wear, both literally and figuratively. Heather then asked kids to compose an essay, song, or poem that reflected how stereotypes affected them and their future. Finally, encouraging students to use their newly formed ideas to act in the world, Heather asked students to brainstorm ways to apply what they'd learned about stereotypes to enlighten and aid the community in a hunger banquet as part of a spring community service project.*

Nike Socks and Ceiling Tiles: Conversations That Push and Clarify
Heather Anderson, Stillwater Junior High School, Stillwater, OK—Grade 8

"So there's this kid named Ponyboy. He's a Greaser. Greasers aren't well off. They live in the crappy part of town, and they have a rep for stealing stuff and carryin' big switchblades and bein' 'bad boys.' They wear a bunch of grease in their long hair and tight white shirts that show off their muscles and, ya know, grungy, and crap, kinda like the guys from *Grease*, you know . . . that musical . . . but tougher! Just 'cause they look real greasy, everybody thinks they're stupid and dangerous. Ponyboy doesn't know if he wants to be a Greaser, but he's proud of it at the same time. He's got this inner struggle goin' on. Then there's the Socs. They're the Greasers' enemy. They think they're all that and rich and stuff. They wear these, like, plaid shirts, real fancy. They like to beat up Greasers just cuz they can. But not all of them are bad."

Although rudimentary, this summary, a conversation heard in the hallway between two eighth graders, hits at the heart of S. E. Hinton's *The Outsiders* and touches on the imperative lessons of acceptance and systemic social injustice featured in the novel.

On our end-of-the-year class surveys, students consistently name reading Hinton's *The Outsiders* (1967) as the most impactful experience. However, it also continues to be the most challenged book in my curriculum. Many parents criticize the novel's lack of gender diversity, violent content, and inclusion of suicide. Last year alone, a dozen parents emailed me with concerns about the violent nature of the characters in the novel, worried our reading would inspire violent acts in their children. Two parents asked for an alternate reading assignment. Despite these criticisms, I continue to share Ponyboy's story with my students because of its unique ability to help them identify stereotypes, as well as to open up safe channels of discussion about death, suicide, bullying, and classism.

Hinton's characterization of thirteen-year-old Ponyboy Curtis strikes a nerve with the eighth-grade Oklahoman students I teach each year. He is a character who experiences the joy, heartache, and hormones each teenager in my classroom experiences. It is Hinton's raw, authentic teenage voice that resonated with the public fifty years ago, and that continues to resonate with my students each year. Most important, I continue to read this text with my eighth graders because it allows me to personally connect with them and create a classroom community where people feel safe to share their ideas, world perspectives, writing, and voices.

The Beginning: Examining Privilege and Status Symbols

We started our unit on *The Outsiders* by linking some specific vocabulary words students would encounter in the novel to our own lives. Students researched the words using Vocabulary.com and considered the meanings provided through the lens of their own life experiences. To help students make these word-to-text-to-real-life connections, we began with a vocabulary quick-write. I asked the students to choose a vocabulary word and write about that word in the world of Stillwater Jr. High.

This day, I asked the kids in my Pre-AP course, "How can you tell if someone is *elite* at Stillwater Jr. High?" Even though Vocabulary.com offered us several definitions of the word, most kids in this class gravitated toward the first one: appearance.

One pungent eighth grader, fresh from PE, wrote that at our school, Nike socks are a status symbol. He told us that these seemingly inconsequential items of clothing can elevate a kid into the "popular" crowd, and gave us distinct rules for ownership:

> If you can convince your parents to buy you these socks, $20 pair of socks, you need to keep them pristine. Don't let any dirt embed itself into the immaculate white ridges of your Nike socks. If you do, people will laugh and then shun you. Do not wear them while playing outdoor sports. The swoosh should remain black. Do not allow it to fade from washing or sunlight to a muddy grey. If this happens, take a black Sharpie and color it in. But then, hand wash the socks in the sink with a toothbrush so the Sharpie does not bleed onto the white.

After this student shared his writing, other students began sharing their own experiences with the word, becoming comfortable using it in conversation and writing. Students shared stories of feeling elite and just the opposite. They examined their privilege and identified the criteria for what makes one "elite" in modern society.

This is how we began our time with Ponyboy, the Greasers, and their nemeses, the Socs.

While Reading: Putting the Pieces Together

In the blissful, silent morning before all my students arrive, I tape a sign to my ceiling: "YES! I totally, most utterly agree." To the floor, I tape: "NOPE. NO. NO. NO. UH-UH." To the seat of a chair in a desk sitting prominently at the front of the room, I tape a visible: "Meh. Sorta."

As students pour into my classroom, I gingerly stand on the surface of the desk at the front of the room and place my right index finger on the ceiling. Curious eyes dart from mine to the ceiling, to a friend, and to the signs posted around the room. Eyebrows arch in confusion. I use the remote in my left hand to beckon the almighty Whiteboard awake. Students' eyes frantically read the statement projected in front of them:

"You can tell a great deal about a person from what they wear."

Silence. Fingers stroke chins and twist braids in thought. "Well, are you going to move?" I ask. "Stand on a desk, lie on the floor, sit in a chair! Choose now! Just please don't lift my ceiling tiles from their places. You don't want to let loose what's living up there." Now it's all coming together for them; today English class will be a little different!

Slowly students rise from their straight rows. Some crouch to lie on the floor, some help each other onto their desks, giggling at the thought of the principal walking in at such a moment. Some stay seated, unsure of themselves or their opinion on the matter. Once everyone finds an initial spot, I set the expectations for the activity.

"Today we are going to talk about issues and topics that affect each and every one of us, and some of us on a very personal level.

"First, I want you to know this is a safe space. When you share your ideas, your voice in this room, you are respected, heard, and valued.

"Next, you may agree or disagree with what anyone says in this room, including with what I have to say. But we will disagree in a way that says, 'Hey, I see where you're coming from, and I respect that. Here's my perspective. Let's find some common ground.'

"Finally, this safe space needs to stay safe, even when things get heated. We will not point fingers. We will not name drop or discuss specific events in your personal life that will incriminate or blame others. Instead, this will be a time to discuss real-life stereotypes and how they affect people globally, statewide, and even here at SJHS.

"So what exactly are we doing today, besides standing on desks or lying on the floor? We're going to start by conducting what's called a 'Values Continuum,' which will gauge your stance on a few of the major issues you've seen so far in *The Outsiders*. You've already taken a stance on the first statement. This is all about appearances. Turn and talk to two nearby partners about your stances. Hearing someone else's ideas might just make you change your position, literally! When you're finished sharing, we'll come back together and hear from two people on the floor, two sitting in their seats, and two people with their hands on the ceiling. Go!"

As students share their thoughts on the statement before them, many rise and fall, swayed by the moving speeches of their peers. After six students have spoken their piece, I project on the Smartboard an image of a forlorn-looking student with long, greasy black hair wearing an ill-fitting black shirt and faded baggy black pants. He's holding a skateboard and has Sharpie marker tattoos down each arm.

"Please look at this image. I have three questions for you. First, what kinds of grades do you think this student receives?"

Most students reply, a D or a C average.

"What do you think this student will do for a living?"

Many students infer that he will be a high school dropout, require a drug rehabilitation program, or work in fast food.

"Finally, if you saw this person walk through these doors right now, how many of you would view him as a potential friend?"

Only two hands raised out of thirty.

I project another image on the board. A clean-cut boy in a Nike shirt and shorts set holds a book to one side, with a foot resting on a soccer ball. He has a smile on his face, and his blonde hair is neatly parted to one side.

"Now look at this image. I have the same three questions for you. What kinds of grades do you think this student receives?"

Most infer an A to B average.

"What do you think this student will do for a living?"

Answers range from a CEO to an entrepreneur to a doctor.

"If he walked into this room, would you view him as a potential friend?"

Roughly three-fourths of the class raise their hands.

At this point, I feel students need a little nudge to understand how their assumptions are connected to stereotypes and their conversations about our vocabulary.

"So, let me get this straight. Based on absolutely no information about these two gentlemen other than what they are wearing and how they do their hair, you have been able to decipher their grades, their future occupation, and whether or not you would be friends with them at a glance? Isn't this stereotyping? Unfortunately, this is what we do on a daily basis. We make snap judgments about people, just like in *The Outsiders*. What do you think about this? How has this affected you?"

Eventually the conversation comes back around to the Nike socks, prompting one student to shout, "It shouldn't matter about the freaking Nike socks! They go on the smelliest part of your body! Half the time people can't even see the Nike symbol! It's really just about if your parents have money. That's what it comes down to, isn't it? And it's not just at the junior high. This is worldwide. The Nike socks are just a symbol. It's like we're being programmed at an early age to believe that money is everything and if you don't have it, then you're not worthy of being valued as a person! I'm definitely getting that vibe from Ponyboy when he gets beat up for just walking down the freaking street. He can't afford the fancy car to drive him home from the movies. For all we know, the grungy looking guy in the picture could be a super genius!"

A breakthrough! Students are beginning to take on multiple perspectives and understand how stereotypes and assumptions based on appearance can be damaging to those affected.

I then project many more statements onto the Smartboard, including:

- "Wealthy students don't get punished as often in school as nonwealthy students."
- "Kids who get bad grades have bad behavior too."
- "Teenagers are too inexperienced to write a novel."

Not only are students delighted with the opportunity to stand on top of their desks, but also these statements turn into excellent conversations about issues that seem taboo in other classes and even among their peers: classism, race relations in the United States, the school-to-prison pipeline, and even the school dress code!

Examining Stereotypes in Modern Society and the Social Hierarchy of a Junior High School

Following the values continuum exercise, I numbered students off into small groups of four to five and provided each group with a short list: Americans, women, people who own trucks, Canadians, Asians, police officers, Mexicans, blondes, African Americans, Oklahomans, teachers, students. This list was compiled based on the stereotypes that students most frequently encounter in our reading of *The*

Outsiders and in the media. It is worthwhile noting, however, that I didn't ask students to think of stereotypes of the dominant culture in my classes. Groups such as white people, men, and college graduates were unintentionally left off the list. Following this activity, this omission was pointed out to me, and I was chagrined at my oversight. Perhaps I was protecting the dominant culture in my classes from self-criticism? Given the opportunity to repeat this activity, I would provide students with a more comprehensive list.

Once again, I felt that setting expectations for our class discussion was vital to aid students in a respectful, productive analysis of not only the text but also modern society.

"As a group, I want you to come up with three to four stereotypes for each of the groups on your list. Now, I want to make one thing clear. Just because you name a stereotype doesn't mean we all think you believe this stereotype is true. For example, if I say, 'a stereotype for blondes is they are dumb,' it doesn't mean that I personally believe this stereotype is true. We are being open and honest about the falsehoods that are out there about groups of people, how these falsehoods affect real people, and what we can do to combat these stereotypes, so please don't feel bad about writing something down. Just be delicate—and school appropriate—about your wording."

And off they went. According to my eighth graders, some stereotypes for Oklahomans are that we all ride horses to school or work, speak with atrociously thick, twangy accents, are all extremely closed-minded, and are all Bible-thumping Christians. Together, we analyzed how these stereotypes came about, how they don't represent every Oklahoman, how they might be damaging for our state, and what we can do to end these stereotypes. Unfortunately, some stereotypes are far more damaging than "they all ride horses to school." For example, students noted that Muslim Americans are being dehumanized and treated with hostility and hatred on a daily basis due to the stereotype that Muslims are anti-American terrorists. When students name a stereotype like this, I know it's important for them to have more information to combat the stereotype. When kids noted the stereotype about people who are Muslim, we watched Tara Miele's YouTube video "Meet a Muslim" (2016), which illustrates that people who worship the Muslim faith are also people just like the families at our school, with joys, desires, sorrows, and, likely, Nike socks.

Following this activity, students delved into the stereotypes of groups at Stillwater Jr. High. Standing with marker poised in hand, I asked students as a whole group, "What groups exist at the junior high? Remember, this is a safe space. Be delicate with the naming, but be honest."

Group names jumped into the air. Jocks! Nerds! Gamers! Choir kids! Band geeks! Artsy kids! Techies! Grungy kids! Preps! ISP (in-school suspension) kids!

Smokers! Theater kids! LGBTQ kids! Cheerleaders!

"Okay. Now I want you to draw a pyramid on your piece of paper. I want you to place these groups in a hierarchy. A hierarchy is essentially a ranking system where people with more authority or more status go at the top of the pyramid, and people with the lowest status go at the bottom. This is going to be tough, but if you choose, no one will see your paper but you. You can base this hierarchy on your personal perception, or you can base it on which groups you believe the entire school perceives to be at the top, bottom, and so forth. Go!"

In almost all of my classes, the "jock," "prep," and "cheerleader" groups were at the top of the pyramid, and the "grungy," "smoker," and "ISP" groups were at the bottom.

One student noticed a pattern in the pyramids we constructed.

"Hey, Mrs. A, I noticed that most of the groups we chose were based on action, you know, like, hobbies, or stuff we like to do. But when we put them in a hierarchy, it ends up looking like we ranked them based on money. Like the jocks and preps who usually have more money are at the top, and the kids that usually come from poverty are at the bottom."

A wonderful revelation. In small groups, students discussed the reasoning behind these perceptions and how these ideas connected to the themes and characters in *The Outsiders*. One group noted how Ponyboy and his gang of Greasers were stereotyped as filthy troublemakers due to their greasy, unkempt hair and disheveled clothing, much as students in the class had judged the "grungy" boy depicted in the photo I projected. However, students reflected that the main character, Ponyboy, breaks this stereotype through his introspective, gentle, and studious nature. One group commented that the Socs would be on the top of our social hierarchy pyramid due to their clean-cut appearance and lavish lifestyles. It was clear, despite the controversial content of the novel, that students understood the consequences of these stereotypes through the in-depth analysis of their own life experiences. This understanding validates reading this banned book in my classroom, where students are exercising their right to read, as outlined in *The Students' Right to Read*:

> One of the foundations of a democratic society is the individual's right to read. This right is based on an assumption that the educated possess judgment and understanding and can be trusted with the determination of their own actions. . . . The reader is not limited by birth, geographic location, or time, since reading allows meeting people, debating philosophies, and experiencing events far beyond the narrow confines of an individual's own existence. (NCTE, 2018, p. xvi)

As this position statement declares, the right to read transcends one's own life experiences, allowing students to understand the consequences of choices through the examination of characters' actions. By reflecting on the motivations and actions of the Greasers and Socs in *The Outsiders*, my students can better understand how their own choices and assumptions impact those around them.

After Reading: Critical Writing

After days of critical discussion, students' minds were now ready for critical writing. First, students revisited their quick-write from the beginning of the unit and expanded on or addressed any changes in their thoughts or beliefs. Students were then invited to compose an essay, song, or poem that reflected on how stereotypes affect them and their future. To help students develop their individual voices and provide choice in my classroom, I gave no strict requirements for this assignment. Students were instructed to simply (or not so simply) illustrate in written form their understanding of stereotyping and how it has affected their lives. No length requirements. No directions such as "you must include at least two metaphors, one hyperbole, and one simile." Just the power of words.

Kids wrote beautiful pieces, like the one by a student who wrote about her identity as a dancer and all the stereotypes that come with that identity. In her poem, she was able to clearly analyze and illustrate how stereotypes have affected her life, delving deeply into the ramifications of making assumptions about someone based on their appearance and other criteria. Despite being an eighth grader, this student wrote a poem that was quite analytical, incorporating the social and human ideas she had encountered in *The Outsiders* while crafting an artful argument about her own stances on the topic. Most students wrote pieces that illustrated each writer's depth of understanding, not just about the novel, but also about how our middle school community supported yet also stereotyped everyone.

When kids performed their pieces for the class, they were able to connect with one another in ways they hadn't before. They understood each other's passions and drives as they worked toward goals like becoming a dancer. They also understood through each other's pieces that committing to a singular identity like "dancer" causes burnout from intense practice and a sense of isolation if your friends don't share your passion. Through their personal reflections, students were able to relate to the characters in *The Outsiders* and understand how to prevent the negative consequences of stereotyping in the real world.

Though this writing assignment was not a structured reading response that required a thesis statement, textual evidence, or a counterclaim, as my state writing test requires, it allowed students to explore their unique voices and solidified their right to write. *NCTE Beliefs about the Students' Right to Write* states:

> During this era of high-stakes testing, technology-based instruction, and increased control over students' expression due to school violence, students' right to write must be protected. . . . Through the often messy process of writing, students develop

strategies to help them come to understand lessons within the curriculum as well as how their language and ideas can be used to communicate, influence, reflect, explain, analyze, and create. (2014, p. xxv)

By giving my students the opportunity to freely express themselves by writing in any format, students were better able to see the connections not only between *The Outsiders* and their own lives, but also the connections they have with each other and with others around the school, state, nation, and world. Sometimes teachers must break away from clinical state mandates to help children develop humanity.

So What?

However, making these real-world connections on paper is not enough. I didn't want to allow the critical writing assignment to be the end of the unit. I desired to call my students to action, to use what they learned to drive change. In my classroom, I have a sign by my whiteboard that simply states, "So what?!" If a student points to this sign, I must be able to provide an answer for why the activity I have assigned is relevant to their lives and how it will ultimately be beneficial for their future. Following the critical writing assignment, I asked myself, "So what?" What do I want my students to do based on what they have learned? How will this impact them in their future careers? Tomorrow in the hallways? How can I help them amplify their voices? This inner struggle led me to the Call to Action unit assignment. I asked students to design and implement a project that would raise awareness for the issues presented in *The Outsiders*. I grouped students into teams of four and gave them a week to create a project proposal. They then "pitched" their project to the class, and the class voted on which project to implement.

The winning project was a hunger banquet designed to raise awareness about poverty and hunger in Payne County, Oklahoma. This project also aimed to illustrate privilege and shed light on common stereotypes about those experiencing the cycle of poverty. Using as a model the hunger banquet activity developed by an Oklahoma City nonprofit, World Neighbors, the students decided to invite members of the Stillwater community to the high school for a meal. This activity is meant to simulate the overwhelming food shortages people face in our own country and in developing countries around the world, and then create discussion among participants about how to help solve world hunger issues. When the students' guests arrived, they would be given a role to play. The vast majority of guests would be seated at the "Developing" tables, representing so-called "Third World" nations, while only a select few would be seated at the smaller "Developed—First World" tables. According to their seating assignment and role, guests might be asked to walk a fair distance to obtain very little food and water, or they might be fortunate enough to dine on a five-course meal. During the meal, activities would allow participants to converse about their roles and misconceptions about those in each area, as well as to reflect on the feelings the banquet evokes.

To prepare for this event, students divided themselves into specific committees: decorations, fundraising, activities, marketing, and an executive committee. Each committee made a list of the overall goals and perceived jobs they should perform leading up to and during the event. Students then shared their lists with one another, focusing on the big picture and minding any gaps that would need to be filled in by specific committees. During this stage of the planning, I encouraged the idea that control of the classroom shift to my students. Rather than provide them with step-by-step tasks, I allowed the planning process to occur to students naturally, guiding them back to their big picture and stated goals when I felt a committee's plans were steering off course. I did a great deal of walking around the classroom, answering questions and helping students find resources.

In these daily walks, I noted key conversations: "It kinda feels like I'm doing a job. This is what actual adults do if they're into jobs like event planning or marketing. I can so see myself doing this."

"We should have the First World people sit right where the line for food forms for the developing countries. That way they'll feel guilty. How many dirty looks do you think they'll get? Wait! This could be a good conversation starter about privilege and stereotyping!"

"I don't think my family'll come to this event. My mom isn't too happy we're reading *The Outsiders*. She thinks it encourages Greaser behavior. I'm pretty sure if I didn't rob stores and carry a switchblade before I read the book, I'm not going to after. I don't think she gets that it's a 'what not to do' kind of book."

Upon overhearing this last student's conversation, I couldn't help but be moved. This is exactly why I believe in my students' right to read and write. This is why I will continue to teach *The Outsiders*, despite the pushback from those who would censor it.

Final Thoughts

Although students didn't get the chance to implement the event due to scheduling conflicts, I truly feel that students' lives were changed for the better through this unit. Not only did students critically think about the world around them and their actions in society, but they also made connections from their reading to their daily lives, applying their knowledge to call an authentic audience to action. Above all, students learned that words are "a powerful tool of expression, a means to clarify, explore, inquire, and learn as well as a way to record present moments for the benefit of future generations" (NCTE, 2014, p. xxv). This unit solidified my belief that middle school students are fully capable of mature discourse, able to address controversial topics given a safe environment in which to do so. These topics should not be victims of a null curriculum, unspoken out of fear. Students are already exposed to and grappling with these topics in their daily lives. Why not allow them to navigate these rough waters in a space where they know their ideas are valued, where they know they have the right to know, read, write, think, believe? Despite challenges that may arise, I will continually fight for these rights so that my students can become empowered, thriving, communicative members of modern society.

Jen's Observation Notes

- Throughout my career, vocabulary instruction has been one of the weakest elements of my classroom practices. I've read countless research studies and pedagogical works to help me think about authentically including vocabulary instruction in my daily or weekly lessons. And always, it falls by the wayside. I think we probably all have some aspect of ELA teaching that we let fall by the wayside because our curriculum is often overflowing. I haven't stopped challenging myself to find ways to "fit in" vocabulary, and I love the idea of vocabulary quick-writes. Being in Heather's classroom offered me the idea of connecting vocabulary to who the students are as people. We already engage in quick-writes every other day in my classroom as part of building writing stamina, interest, and voice. Including vocabulary quick-writes into the rotation is a thoughtful way to begin working with vocabulary during a classroom structure my students and I already utilize and value.

- "Hearing someone else's ideas might just make you change your position, literally!" I love the on-top-of-the-table, lying-on-the-floor silliness that Heather used to launch middle schoolers into serious conversations. Heather's movement-based values continuum honors the weirdness and energy of middle school kids while asking them to take each other's ideas seriously. Next time an anticipation guide is in our plans, my co-teacher and I are going to use this genius structure.

- I love Heather's reminder that a literary response can be a creative response inspired by the ideas in the piece of literature. I sometimes forget to incorporate other forms of creating and composing in my classroom beyond writing. While I do often include creative narrative responses as writing options, asking kids to compose a piece in whatever genre or medium helps them best represent their understandings and arguments honors all the modes of creativity students choose.

- I've already made my "So what?" sign to post in the front of my classroom! Being able to name the "why" of all I'm doing in my classroom is not only important for me to be able to do for myself in terms of examining my own practices; the question "So what?" is also important for me to be able to answer for my students. Many middle schoolers' focus of urgency lies far outside the classrooms they spend all day in, and being able to say to them, "What we're doing is important for you because . . ." can help them build urgency for their time inside their classrooms as well.

- Beyond the simple coolness of a hunger banquet, I really appreciate asking students in an ELA classroom to engage in real-world projects that can impact their immediate community. Helping students have a voice and the means to feel deeply about issues they can be activists for in their world is a practice squarely in the middle of an ELA classroom. Even though Heather and her students didn't get to actually hold the hunger banquet, the seriousness of their planning conversations was invaluable to their growth as people. I am reminded that when I share my classroom with other teachers, it's just as valuable to share what didn't go exactly as planned as it is to show my most stellar moments.

And finally, teaching within the NCTE policy statement on reading:

Heather's teaching of *The Outsiders* reminds me of the following excerpts from *The Students' Right to Read*:

> Some groups and individuals have also raised objections to literature written specifically for young people. . . . But many contemporary novels for adolescents focus on the real world of young people. (p. xiv)

and

> In selecting texts to read by young people, English teachers consider the contribution each work may make to the education of the reader, its aesthetic value, its honesty, its readability for a particular group of students, and its appeal to young children and adolescents. (p. xvi)

In continuing to read this classic, oft-challenged novel with her classes, Heather is able to bring to the reading "the real work of young people." In addition, she continually connects the themes and details of the novel to the real lives of the kids in her classes, helping them gain guidance from Ponyboy and his friends in ways that books written for a more adult audience might not be able to do so clearly. In her classroom, Heather makes the case for teaching books that benefit kids even if some adults don't see the value of books written for kids with gritty plots and themes.

What are your observations as you "sit" in the back of Heather's classroom?

- What new ideas does her work suggest for you?

- What changes might you make in your own teaching?

- What new wonderings do you have?

A Visit to Room 905 at Central Junior High School

With the Common Core State Standards (CCSS) driving the curriculum in Shelly Unsicker-Durham's suburban Oklahoma school district, she was encouraged and assisted by her school's literacy coach to begin the school year with argument writing, one of the highlights of the CCSS framework. Shelly had previously structured her classroom to be "as close to Nancie Atwell's classroom as possible!" Beginning the year with a structured argument unit felt constricting, but the new curriculum required that she try. Students lacked the excitement and drive to write and revise as real authors do when writing a piece they care about. Even Atwell-like conferencing with young writers didn't help. The following year, Shelly combined the curriculum mandates with teaching that she knew promoted authentic writing. She reimagined the argument unit by including three modes of writing: narrative, informative, and argument. She asked kids to interrogate a topic close to them, a state law that was being considered about the wearing of hoodies in Oklahoma schools. By offering kids various points of entry into a topic they cared about, every student was able to write a piece that they felt successfully shared their thinking about a law that would affect them.

Grappling with Passage-Based Writing
Shelly K. Unsicker-Durham, Central Junior High School, Moore, OK—Grade 8

"Ms. Durham, you know how this makes me feel?" Maria's big brown eyes looked directly into mine, and I thought I could hear enthusiasm in her voice.

I smiled at Maria and asked, "How does this make you feel?"

"Stupid. Trying to learn this kind of writing makes me feel STUPID."

This is an essay about students like Maria and about how teaching writing has turned into a balancing act between what we know—from years of experience and research—about teaching writing, and what we are increasingly required to do in the age of testing. It's an essay about how we find balance, learn new ways of teaching, and support student writing even in challenging times and circumstances. It's about my growth as a teacher, my continued commitment to our students' right to write, and the compromises I have come to embrace. It's about when teaching writing made *me* feel stupid, and how I came back to find myself as the teacher I'd always been.

Let me start by setting the stage for Maria's response. We'd been working in my class on preparing for our state's second year of an eighth-grade passage-based writing assessment, an on-demand writing task based in the three modes of writing sanctioned by the Common Core State Standards (informative, argument, and narrative.) The test the year before had used an informative prompt, so we were anticipating an on-demand writing task for an argument. In this lesson, presented by our literacy coach, Maria and her classmates had completed a V-chart, a graphic organizer to help us understand claims and counterclaims. During the culminating activity, a class debate, Maria stole the spotlight. She stood with confidence as she shared her claim, cited textual evidence, and acknowledged a counterclaim. Then she explained why her stance was the strongest. Overjoyed that she and a few other students were catching on, I tried to keep an open mind about making room for the new demands on my curriculum, even if that meant letting go of *my way* of teaching writing.

For the ten years prior to this event, my way of teaching writing began with writer's notebooks, heart maps, and giving students choices in topics and genres. My way began with student writers exploring the topics from their own lives—in a way that allowed them to name their world. "When you write, you are the master of your universe" was a mantra repeated in my classroom. My way focused on writing as a process and learning one writing trait at a time, beginning with idea development—helping students discover their own ideas about the world. My way focused on the other traits—organization, word choice, sentence style—long before tackling academic writing. My way immersed students in a diverse mix of mentor texts, allowing them to choose what they found interesting to try out in their own writing—rather than follow a particular structure or formula they had not discovered for themselves. My way honored NCTE's suggestion in *NCTE Beliefs about the Students' Right to Write* as they engaged "fully in a writing process" allowing "them the necessary freedom to formulate and evaluate ideas, develop voice, experiment[,] . . . and . . . express creativity . . ." (2014, p. xxv). My way felt purposeful to me and, I think, to my students as well.

However, my district's confidence in embracing CCSS and the evolution of the state writing assessment moved me away from my way, what had become for me a comfortable and sound pedagogy. My district's curricular shifts required a steep learning curve for me. Learning takes time. And the time I spent grappling with new expectations left little time for the writing practices that had once been routine in my classroom. Our literacy coach led the effort to embrace passage-based writing. Her enthusiasm was contagious as I watched her engage my students in collaborative reading and writing activities. After her lesson, it was my job to transfer the gist of what we learned together into writing individual essays, fully developed and organized, incorporating textual evidence from specific passages for support—passage-based writing.

Maria and I sat side by side at her round table that day, mulling over ideas for expanding her initial paragraph into an essay. Although she had already told me that she liked it the way it was, I was determined that she write more since, after all, we were practicing for essay writing on the test. After a few more moments of what I thought of as engaged one-on-one coaching, Maria brushed her wavy black hair away from her face and over her shoulder and let me know how "stupid" all of this made her feel.

I sat there, stunned, feeling the weight of Maria's frustration, along with my own. Was Maria simply refusing to write more because she didn't want to? Or was she frustrated because she lacked the experience and confidence in extending her thinking into writing a fully developed idea? Either way, I realized I had spent so much time prepping her and her classmates for the new assessments—assessments I did not fully understand myself—that I had failed to help Maria see herself as a writer.

◞

Maria's experience remained with me the following year. It would be the third year since our state abandoned what had been a simple and consistent writing rubric based on writing traits, a rubric I'd used in class like an anchor chart. The new rubric attempted to follow the old, but with the focus on CCSS modes of writing— narrative, informative, and argument—the rubric became convoluted, breaking into different pathways and expectations depending on the mode. It's not that I was opposed to learning new kinds of writing and teaching. Once I let go of my frustrations with the changes to the rubric, I found value in passage-based writing as a way to use skills we already practiced (e.g., close reading, annotating, making connections) to scaffold students into authentic research. As Calkins, Ehrenworth, and Lehman (2012) suggested, I moved from responding to CCSS as a "curmudgeon" to a treasure hunter, digging for gold (p. 3). While this was not my most comfortable teaching structure, I realized I could make space for passage-based writing within my pedagogy.

With Maria's words ever on my mind, I knew I needed to integrate the best of the writing practices I had used for years with new skills that would allow students to not only engage with nonfiction texts but also produce a formidable piece of writing demonstrating comprehension and synthesis. The biggest challenge lay in preparing students for a significantly more complex writing and reading assessment while restructuring my classroom curriculum. The time once spent on engaging writing activities packed with student choice had to be replaced with preparations for district benchmark assessments, usually with texts that seemed far removed from my students lives, interests, and vocabularies. I struggled to make time for both.

◞

By January 2015, my state made its way into national news when one of our law-
makers wrote a bill that the Huffington Post dubbed "The Hoodie Law" (Bobic,
2015). The article was about more than hoodies, and a hyperlink in the article
took readers to another article that gave background information about the Black
Lives Matter movement. As I read these two texts, both informational, I considered how they might possibly work in the classroom as we prepared for the state
writing assessment. Then, not two weeks later, a pastor made the local news when
he christened the following Sunday "Hoodie Sunday," asking willing members of
his congregation to wear their hoodies to church (Martin, 2015). The first article
had initially grabbed my attention because I knew that a bill outlawing the wearing
of hoodies would engage student interest. If we closely examined all three articles
as a class, students could choose at least two to practice integrating them into their
writing.

Time presented yet another challenge, however. Close reading and annotating of three passages, then planning for, drafting, and revising an essay, could
easily take a week or more. In most classes, my students ranged from third-grade
to post–high school reading levels. I worried that many readers would end up losing their stamina after the first practice assessment, which focused on argument.
I needed to get everyone prepared for the possibility of three different modes of
writing without students losing their willingness to think deeply or feel engaged.
As I grappled with how to manage both time and stamina, I wondered, *What if I use
the same three articles for the three different writing tasks?* Once students were familiar
with the three texts, adjusting their writing could be as simple as changing their
stance as writers—a way of teaching that harkened back to my deep beliefs about
teaching writing.

Taking a stance. That thought made room for more brainstorming. I'd had
many conversations with colleagues in which we compared being a writer to the
work of a movie director. Writers use word choice, sentence style, and other
descriptive strategies to create snapshots and scenes for readers to visualize (Lane,
1999). This is especially true in narrative writing. So, when we practiced the narrative mode, students would be *writing like a movie director*. What about the other
modes? Argument writing with claims, evidence, and counterclaims, closely aligned
with defending a case in court, and so became *writing like a lawyer*. Informative
writing, presenting credible information from an unbiased perspective, allowing
readers to draw their own conclusions, could be *writing like a reporter*. All three
stances—telling a story, arguing, and telling it like it is—seemed to fit well with
middle school personalities. Additionally, I hoped students would find taking on a
professional point of view engaging.

Wanting to provide a familiar anchor for my students to return to, I adapted a graphic organizer I used to teach organization and planning. In my mind, it resembles a bridge—the metaphor being that writing is like a bridge connecting the reader to the writer in a way that allows deep understanding of the ideas being conveyed. In actuality, it mostly resembles a lot of rectangles boxed together. Adapted for the argument writing, it looked something like Figure II.2.

FIGURE II.2. The argument writing organizer.

Introduction: Argument Writing
Hook:
Thesis/Claim:

Counterclaim:

Main Idea/Subclaim #1	Main Idea/Subclaim #2	Main Idea/Subclaim #3

For each main idea/subclaim, provide support with details, reasons, examples, and evidence.		
•	•	•
•	•	•
•	•	•
•	•	•
•	•	•
•	•	•
•	•	•

Conclusion:

I know. This organizer closely resembles the five-paragraph essay. But the three middle columns are meant to represent the columns of a bridge. I began by having students examine images of several actual bridges and discuss how the bridges serve different purposes, modes of crossing, and those crossing over the bridge. So too with writing. While some bridges have ten or more columns supporting the weight of traffic, others have only two. Writers plan a structure for their main points (or subclaims) in a way that supports the claim in the introduction. While I teach using this organizer explicitly, once they've practiced with it, students are invited to plan their writing in whatever way makes the most sense to them. If students were more comfortable with a method like webbing, Four Square, an umbrella-shaped organizer, or some other method previously learned, I encouraged them to use whatever worked best. Using their own method of planning, students were able to refer to the writing elements mapped out on my "bridge" graphic.

The only difference between the informative and argument organizers is the additional section for the counterclaim. The adaptation for the narrative organizer was a little more complex. Wanting to incorporate narrative elements learned from Barry Lane (1999), I revised the layout from portrait to landscape and included a back side to create space for collecting "domain-appropriate" and other descriptive words, along with a place to think about sentence style. The front of the organizer looked like Figure II.3.

With the graphic organizers set and the three articles chosen, my teaching partner and I sat down together to craft writing prompts that might resemble what students would find on a state writing assessment. Here they are in the order presented to students (Figures II.4, II.5, and II.6). At that time, our state department was in flux about terminology, so we tried to cover our bases.

I chose to begin with the argument mode because students love to argue. In fact, past eighth graders loved arguing so much that they struggled to let go of their personal biases when writing informative essays. To scaffold students into writing an argument, I began by focusing first on the prompt. The prompt should give students instructions about the mode. Then, depending on the mode, students would decide the stance to assume as writers. If they were being asked to write an argument, their stance would be to write like a lawyer. If students were going to write like a lawyer, then learning to read like a lawyer would involve scouring the text to both deepen their understanding and search for evidence. As students read closely the three texts, they highlighted parts they found compelling or with which they strongly agreed or disagreed. In the margins, students noted their thinking. After reading the texts, students used an organizer to jot down a plan for structuring an argument. Finally, students wrote rough draft essays that they filed in their writing folders.

FIGURE II.3. The narrative writing organizer.

Introduction: Narrative Writing			CHARACTER & CONTEXT
Hook/Lead:			Every story begins with a
Theme (lesson learned by narrator or main character):			CHARACTER who wants something:
Part One	Part Two	Part Three	
	SNAPSHOT + THOUGHTSHOT + DIALOGUE = SCENE		
			SETTING: Know the when and where in order to create snapshots and scenes for your readers.
Conclusion:			

Students followed a similar pattern for the informative prompt. After studying the prompt, we discussed the stance of writing like a news reporter, then reread the three articles for information that could be conveyed without bias, treating both sides fairly. Students highlighted in a second color and continued marking the text. Using the informative organizer and writing from this stance seemed to present a greater challenge for students. At one point, a student in second hour, Blane, tall and lanky, burst out with "Hey, this is hard!" Shaking his head, then stretching into a lopsided grin, he admitted, "But it really does make me feel like a journalist!"

In the final round of practice, students analyzed the narrative prompt, then went back to the text, circling words and phrases to add to a word bank on the back of the narrative organizer. This time I asked students to write like a movie director. This comparison extended previous lessons in *visualization* as readers, as well as *showing versus telling* as writers. Next, students brainstormed possible characters—focusing on those with whom students could relate, imagine, and write about. I modeled this process by using student ideas to complete a class graphic organizer and write a rough introduction. Students then planned their own characters, conflict, and scenes. Once students had rough drafts of the three possible modes of writing, they chose one to revise and edit.

FIGURE II.4. Our persuasive/argument writing prompt.

Writing Prompt: Persuasive/Argument

Every year, legislators propose and vote on new laws, which may represent the interests of a few while impacting the lives of many. After reading the hoodie articles, *take a stance and write an argument about whether the proposed Oklahoma hoodie law is fair and just to all. State and develop a clear claim, but also address a counterclaim*. Support your discussion with evidence from all three articles:
1. "Wearing a Hoodie in Oklahoma Could Soon Cost You a $500 Fine,"
2. "50 Years after the March on Washington: Creatively Pursuing the Paths of Glory," and
3. "OKC Pastor to Wear Hoodie during Sunday Service."

FIGURE II.5. Our expository/informative writing prompt.

Writing Prompt: Expository/Informative

Every year, legislators propose and vote on new laws, which may represent the interests of a few while impacting the lives of many. After reading the hoodie articles, *write an expository essay that examines the issues surrounding the proposed Oklahoma hoodie law. Inform your readers of the concerns on both sides*. Support your discussion with evidence from all three articles:
1. "Wearing a Hoodie in Oklahoma Could Soon Cost You a $500 Fine,"
2. "50 Years after the March on Washington: Creatively Pursuing the Paths of Glory," and
3. "OKC Pastor to Wear Hoodie during Sunday Service."

FIGURE II.6. Our narrative writing prompt.

Writing Prompt: Narrative

Imagine the Oklahoma hoodie law passed. Write a narrative that describes the experience of someone wearing a hoodie who is approached by law enforcement. Your writing should include setting and character description as you develop a plot. What challenges will your character face, and what actions will he or she take in response? As you plan and write your narrative, include details from all three articles:
1. "Wearing a Hoodie in Oklahoma Could Soon Cost You a $500 Fine,"
2. "50 Years after the March on Washington: Creatively Pursuing the Paths of Glory," and
3. "OKC Pastor to Wear Hoodie during Sunday Service."

I wish I could tell you this worked so well that student writing scores soared that year. But that was one of the years our state dismissed writing scores due to issues with the testing company. I did, though, keep a couple of student exemplars from that experiment. One belongs to Blane, tall and lanky with a lopsided grin. He's the student who discovered both the challenge and the joy of writing like a reporter. In the conclusion of his informative essay, Blane wrote:

> Many are still concerned about the proposal and Oklahoma has a big decision to
> make. Is state Senator Don Barrington trying to keep us safe, or violate our rights?
> Are Pastor Jesse Jackson's concerns reasonable? One thing is for sure, people every-
> where are stepping up like Daniel Maree and the Million Hoodies Foundation.

Blane's a-ha moment, writing like a reporter, affirmed my decision to move from argument writing first to informative writing second. With room to make his own decisions as a writer and his "freedom to formulate and evaluate ideas" (NCTE, 2014, p. xxv), Blane chose to go beyond two sides to include a third perspective.

Narrative was Anna's favorite of the three modes she practiced with the three hoodie articles. Always thoughtful and deliberate in her writing, Anna, with bright eyes and a wide, beautiful smile, wrote a story titled "Because of Barrington," il-lustrating her skill with details and dialogue. She wrote:

> "This new hoodie law is stupid! Even Pastor Jesse thinks so. I remember when he told
> us all to where [sic] hoodies to church one Sunday as he wore one while preaching.
> Who would follow the law anyway?" asked Chuck.
> "People who can't afford to pay $500 dollars," I replied shivering.

Michael, her narrator and main character, might be "shivering" because of Bar-rington's law—he is not wearing a hoodie. Her story is set in the winter of an imagined time, as if the bill had become law. Anna invested time with all three modes, but with the freedom to choose which one she would move forward toward a final draft and, ultimately, her final portfolio, her right to write for her own pur-poses encouraged a space for experimenting and expressing her creativity.

As I reread both of these students' full essays, I'm struck by the things they both did well in idea development, organization, and word choice. I'm struck by the things they might have done differently, mostly in editing, but also in under-standing more deeply the wording of the bill and its implications for institutional racism and discrimination. Which leads me to reflect on my classroom practice.

I learned that short, nonfiction texts are a highly effective way to scaffold students into research and academic writing. Before this, when I was teaching writ-ing *my way*, I postponed our research project until the end of the school year. Most of the time, research overwhelmed me and my students. This kind of practice did not. Additionally, working with articles about current events also taught me the importance of curating the kinds of texts that will engage my students. Incorporat-ing more of this kind of writing earlier in the year might open up time for students to choose their own topics to research and find their own articles.

Passage-based writing or any other curriculum mandate does not have to be a burden leaving me powerless or my students feeling *stupid*. The willingness to grapple with things that are hard can push us—both teachers and our students—into deeper understanding and more fulfilling literacy habits. Most important, I learned that my way of teaching has the capacity to grow without trampling on my students' right to write.

Jen's Observation Notes

- First, I really appreciate Shelly walking us through her struggle with trying to "teach to a test." In many states, the reality for teachers is they are given mandates to follow and assessment designed by people far outside their classrooms. When teachers are asked to teach within strict structures, encountering policies like *The Students' Right to Read* and *NCTE Beliefs about the Students' Right to Write* often causes teachers to groan and think, "I'd love to do all this, but I just can't!" Shelly's journey shows us ways that we can incorporate the ideals of the two policies even when we are teaching to state- and district-mandated curricula.

- "Writing like a movie director," "Writing like a lawyer," and "Writing like a reporter"—what a genius way for students to really begin to understand purpose and audience and how their writer voices need to shift based on intent. Middle school kids often live in the future, saying things like "When I grow up, I want to be in the NBA, be a lawyer, and be a neurosurgeon." Their goals are passionate and grand, but their notions of how adult work works are obviously limited by their age and experiences. Asking them to take on the writing personas of adult writing stances works so well with their "when I grow up" goals.

- When preparing kids for passage-based writing, the reading, annotating, discussing, and analyzing of texts takes classroom time that always runs short. I appreciate that in Shelly's class, we're reminded that we can use the same deeply read texts for multiple purposes. Reusing texts for more than one evidence-based piece provides stronger writing because the students' familiarity with the texts helps them hone in on just the right piece of evidence to utilize for each different writing need.

And finally, teaching within the NCTE policy statement on writing:

Shelly's teaching of passage-based writing reminds me of the following excerpts from *Beliefs about Students' Right to Write*:

> Students need many opportunities to write for a variety of purposes and audiences.
> (p. xxv)

and

> English language arts teachers are qualified to frame and assign student writing tasks, but students should, as much as possible, have choice and control over topics, forms, language, themes, and other aspects of their own writing while meeting course requirements. (p. xxv)

In developing three different persona stances to write from, and offering kids multiple texts to use as evidence within the forms they chose, Shelly managed to incorporate various aspects of this policy while still satisfying the mandates of the curricular shifts within her state and district. This is really smart teaching during really trying times.

What are your observations as you "sit" in the back of Shelly's classroom?

- What new ideas does her work suggest for you?

- What changes might you make in your own teaching?

- What new wonderings do you have?

A Visit to Room 422 at The Bronx School of Young Leaders

Like many progressive schools, Alex Corbitt's school in the Bronx tries to carefully balance the federal accountability mandates of standardized test scores with authentic teaching and learning. Within the confines of state mandates, Alex's school has encouraged him to create a Teen Activism course. In this class, the kids decided that they wanted to write, produce, and distribute an anonymous zine that discussed issues of tolerance and inclusion throughout their school community. The argument writing that was the basis of the zine was natural and rigorous as these middle schoolers wrote pieces to encourage their fellow students to help them create a school environment where everyone counted. Alex believes that good literacy teaching can be a means to important activism.

Teen Activists: Designing Curricula Today, Shaping the World Tomorrow
Alex Corbitt, The Bronx School of Young Leaders, Bronx, NY—Grade 7

Jen Ochoa, our workshop leader, wasn't laughing. Her sharp wit and contagious laughter were replaced with a stern tone. Her eyes traced across the room. It was late July, and our 2016 New York City Writing Project Summer Institute was coming to an end.

"Next month we will return to our classrooms," she stated. "The presidential election is underway and hate speech is part of our nation's discourse. We must grant students opportunities to process the condition of our country. Our silence allows oppressive narratives to dominate." All summer long, Jen had guided our thinking about writing and reading in our classrooms, but today, she reminded us that teaching is a political act. What follows is my attempt to answer her call to action.

I started developing my Teen Activism course in the latter weeks of August, after I'd had a few weeks to mull over the summer institute and Jen's words. The class was initially offered as an English elective for seventh and eighth graders about documentary films. Fifteen students had expressed interest in the class that past June. With their permission, however, I hoped to revise our focus to emphasize social justice work, and not just in film. I wanted our Teen Activism course to be legitimately student centered; thus, my preliminary unit planning was intentionally vague. I did not want to center the class on my experiences, perspectives, or biases. Instead, my goal was to create a radically inquiry-based syllabus. The students, I hoped, would dictate the trajectory of their learning; my role was to listen and facilitate.

Summer ended, and the first day of school was upon us. "Welcome back," I said, looking around a circle of thirteen-year-olds. My smile masked an amalgam of anxieties. How would I pitch a Teen Activism course to this group of students expecting a Documentary Film course? How would we rally around social justice issues? I didn't have answers, but I had an approach: allow students voice and choice every step of the way. I believed I would have their buy-in if their reading, writing, and questioning sincerely stemmed from their interests and decision making.

We began that day with an icebreaker and stories about our summers. A few students had us rolling with laughter. This low-stakes icebreaker was intentional. If we were to explore heavy content together, we had to create a warm, supportive space—one that emphasized culture before content.

During a lull in our summer debriefing, I took a moment to frame why we were gathered together. I expressed my hope that we use the class to explore social justice issues affecting the school community. Trying to model vulnerability, I expressed my frustrations with the hate speech that had dominated our country. As my students chimed in, I stepped back to listen. I challenged myself to quietly release the trajectory of the conversation to the students. As a teacher, even one who generally centers student voice in the class, turning over the class completely to kids felt scary. I was nervous. During the discussion they would intermittently ask me who should speak next, or whether their statements were "correct." I explained that I intended to help them learn about topics they cared about without being "in charge" of the class. Realizing that it would take practice for the kids to own the classroom space, I suggested we create classroom norms that centered the kids' agency. Here are the norms they generated:

1. We lead our discussions.
2. We ask our own questions.
3. We don't need to raise our hands.
4. We can include everyone.
5. We can confidently say what is on our minds.
6. We can respectfully disagree with Mr. Corbitt.
7. We can help decide what we learn and how class is run.

Over the next week, my students scoured newspapers for social issues they cared about. We engaged in open discussions that married current events with the students' lived experiences. They raised a variety of concerns that centered on safety and belonging: Would undocumented families be deported? Why is there a large police presence in the community? How do we protect women's rights? Based on these discussions, one student stood up at the whiteboard to document potential unit topics. A list formed: bullying, drug abuse, police brutality, LGBTQ+ identities, animal rights, mental health, sexism, environmentalism. I suggested we take a vote on the issue that we wanted to investigate first. Students decided to explore "Racism in Society" for unit 1. After reassuring students that I would find documentaries related to their inquiry (after all, they had signed on to a documentary film class), I asked if they would be interested in reading articles and book passages too. They all responded in the affirmative.

We launched our Racism in Society unit with a screening of *Precious Knowledge* (Palos, 2011). *Precious Knowledge* is a documentary that chronicles the development of the Ethnic Studies Program in the Tucson (Arizona) Unified School District. The program sought to empower underserved Latinx communities with culturally relevant pedagogy. This initiative was subsequently dismantled by politicians deeming the endeavor "anti-American." The film centers on a group of teachers and students who valiantly resist political oppression in a tragic fight for inclusive curricula. My students and I were inspired by the unbounded tenacity with which the teenagers pursued inquiry and self-knowledge.

The injustices highlighted in *Precious Knowledge* were sobering. "Mr. Corbitt, this class is very important, but it's also very stressful," said one student during a post-film reflection. Launching our first unit uncovered many shared fears and anxieties. The threats of policing, deportation, incarceration, and marginalization weren't hypothetical; they were real and frightening. We had to acknowledge the potentially traumatizing nature of our inquiries. Another student suggested we create a "safety protocol" for moments when our conversations got too intense for comfort. The safety protocol we created followed three simple steps:

1. Pause an upsetting conversation.
2. Play a lighthearted, team-building game.
3. Resume the discussion when ready.

Anyone could initiate the protocol as needed, no questions asked. It soon became apparent that emotional safety and community were fundamental to studying social justice issues. The students and I decided to wear blue wristbands as a visible sign of our solidarity and support of one another. We would clink wristbands together during hallway transitions throughout the day. This was our secret way of communicating "I've got your back" to one another.

Further into our Racism in Society unit, my role as text curator became clearer: I did research, gathered relevant texts, and laid them out into menus. These menus featured a wealth of unit-related texts, organized by genre, laid out across double-sided paper. Students selected documents that built onto our evolving inquiries and discussions. Students were free to determine how many texts we analyzed; I avoided imposing any rigid calendars or limits. The texts we covered included periodicals, excerpts from Michelle Alexander's *The New Jim Crow* (2010), presidential debate footage, and two additional documentaries: *2 Fists Up* (Lee, 2016) and *13th* (DuVernay, 2016). Some of our readings even came from newspapers I purchased at the local bodega. I wanted students to understand that analysis-worthy texts that spoke to our inquiries were everywhere.

My students pushed beyond their comfort zones when analyzing texts "above their reading level" such as *The New Jim Crow* and *13th*. We typically explored challenging texts in a whole-group format. To normalize productive struggle, we practiced pausing and clarifying whenever a reading or documentary became confusing. Any member of the class could request to pause a text without fear of judgment. For example, we paused *13th* for an impromptu math lesson to understand how Black and Latinx people are disproportionately incarcerated compared to their white counterparts. My students' determination taught me to never restrict a child's access to rigorous texts that are supposedly "above" his or her reading level. When a text answers a need within authentic inquiry, it is worthy of the hard work it might take to navigate the difficulty in comprehension.

Authentic projects, designed by the students, captured our learning throughout the year. My students gave presentations to peers, filmed public service announcements, started an activism Twitter account, and posted self-help posters around the school. Perhaps the most innovative student-led project was an anonymous underground newspaper titled *Whisper*, a double-sided sheet of paper littered with poetry, prose, quotes, artwork, and magazine cutouts. The project took inspiration from old punk zines of the 1970s. The theme of the paper was inclusion, and the project's philosophy was to replace hateful discourses with words of love and affirmation.

To create *Whisper*, students collaborated in Google Docs. They drafted submissions and commented on one another's work with feedback. Once their submissions were adequately workshopped, they signed them with cryptic monikers (to preserve anonymity) and printed them out. A few artistically inclined students compiled the writings and artwork into a master copy and ran off enough photocopies for the entire student body. After dismissal, we ran down the hallways stuffing *Whisper* into every locker throughout the building. The following morning, homeroom was particularly quiet; kids were reading the mysterious paper and discussing who could have created it. My Teen Activism students even included an email address at the bottom of the paper for other kids to contribute writings for subsequent publications.

The length of each Teen Activism unit was up to the discretion of my students. I would ask, "Are we done?" and they would let me know. Whereas our Racism in Society and Prison Industrial Complex units encompassed nearly half the year, our Nutrition unit barely lasted a week. The less I imposed parameters, the more my students owned their learning. I once suggested we all become vegetarians for a week . . . you can imagine the ensuing revolt. By the end of the year, we had studied racism, the prison industrial complex, mental health, animal rights, nutrition, bullying, sexism, and substance abuse.

This year I am unable to facilitate my Teen Activism course due to scheduling changes. But perhaps this isn't a total loss; the lessons I learned about inquiry and student-led instruction should live in *every* class I facilitate. Here are takeaways that continue to inform my pedagogy:

1. Invite students to develop relevant, high-interest unit topics.
2. Curate text menus that allow for student choice.
3. Allow students access to texts of varying rigor, regardless of students' "reading levels."
4. Establish emotional safety protocols before exploring thorny content.
5. Create authentic projects that target audiences beyond the classroom.
6. Empower students to be leaders in the classroom and own their learning.

My next step is to work on an initiative I call "The Mirrors Project." The project aims to create a teacher-student book club that focuses on culturally relevant YA literature. The books are selected by students and, upon club consensus, eventually integrated into our school's curriculum. The student club members become TAs in the classroom, helping their teachers facilitate conversations about the new literature. Thus, our school becomes a "mirror" that reflects the interests, identities, and direction of our students (Bishop, 1990). I don't know how this project will be received among my teaching colleagues who still feel more comfortable holding the reins in their classrooms. But my Teen Activism course taught me that students owning their learning and being leaders in the classroom is very well received amongst middle school kids.

Students' rights to read and write are a matter of agency. The voice and choice we allow kids in the classroom lay the foundation for an engaged citizenry—a cohort: not rendered passive to cope with injustice, but empowered to shape society for an equitable world.

Jen's Observation Notes

- "My role was to listen and facilitate." The very notion that the kids in the class would create the class curriculum and the teacher would provide the support they needed is a radical one. Watching Alex accomplish this feat in his classroom is an example of a truly revolutionary pedagogy that exhibits many of the tenets of our two policy statements. I am in awe.

- I appreciate that Alex shows us that having this kind of student-centered, student-run classroom requires practice and negotiation from both the teacher and the students. Developing the norms together was a way to model how to create a productive space in which everyone could share and thrive and learn. I know many teachers who create class norms with kids, but when I've attempted to do the student-centered work Alex describes, I have not always remembered this very essential step.

- As well, developing a safety protocol when engaging in classroom discussions or texts that may be triggering is an important reminder for teachers who would like to open their classrooms for the important work of students "empowered to shape society for an equitable world."

- Alex's list of takeaways from teaching this course is going straight into the front of my lesson plan book. Any work I do with kids in my classroom will benefit from one or many of Alex's takeaways.

And finally, teaching within the NCTE policy statements:

Alex's Teen Activism course reminds me of the following excerpts from *NCTE Beliefs about the Students' Right to Write* and *The Students' Right to Read:*

[W]e respect the right of individuals to be selective in their own reading. (2018, p. xvi)

and

Words are a powerful tool of expression, a means to clarify, explore, inquire, and learn. (2014, p. xxv)

and

Teachers should foster in students an understanding and appreciation of the responsibilities inherent in writing and publication by encouraging students to assume ownership of both the writing process and the final product. (2014, p. xxv)

Alex's Teen Activism course really lives the essence of both of these policies, especially *NCTE Beliefs about the Students' Right to Write*. Alex shows us what believing in middle school kids as thoughtful agents of their own educational experiences based on their own assessed needs looks like in a classroom. In this classroom, nothing was irrelevant because the students chose what they needed to learn and what they felt was important to know, and then they decided how to create a format that would help them share what they learned with their peers.

What are your observations as you "sit" in the back of Alex's classroom?

- What new ideas does his work suggest for you?

- What changes might you make in your own teaching?

- What new wonderings do you have?

A Visit to Room 223 at Horn Lake Middle School

When the We Need Diverse Books campaign hit social media in 2014, kidlit writers of color banded together to challenge the publishing industry, librarians, and teachers to include books with kids of color or kids from diverse backgrounds in the books they shared with children. The #WNDB hashtag is now synonymous among educators with expanding curricula to consciously include stories of children who don't typically make the shelves of classroom libraries. Teachers who are consciously diversifying their classroom libraries are consciously diversifying the reading lives of the kids in their classrooms. Chad Everett shares with us how independent reading can be harnessed as an opportunity to help students foster positive self-identities and develop empathy and understanding for others. He tells us how the books he shares help all kids in the classroom find themselves in a story and learn about those who are different from themselves. He also shares how independent reading can be used to move beyond simply providing access to diverse texts to critically examining how to incorporate diverse texts within instruction, which diversifies the entire curriculum.

Access and Care: Supporting a Student's Right to Read

Chad Everett, Horn Lake Middle School, Horn Lake, Mississippi—Grade 8

Evan

He walked into the building as a sixth grader already the embodiment of all that is middle school cool—the eighth graders followed him. Now, here he is, sitting in Room 223 with me. I know that these first few moments will set the tone for the remainder of the year. I'm wondering how our classroom space will evolve, as much as I guess he's wondering who he will be in this space. Evan takes his seat. He is watching me, and all of the other students are watching him.

Knowing My Students: Creating Identity Webs

Evan, as well as the rest of my students, did not enter my room as an empty notebook with wordless pages. They, like me, entered this room with a story—their story. My first priority is learning the stories on the pages that come before the chapter I arrived in.

> But first, I begin my walk through the important preliminary matters:
> "Lunch is at 12:40."
> "You can go to the bathroom whenever you need to."

"I do not give packets, but I do expect you to read for twenty minutes every night—yes, every night."

After the collective eye roll has finished, we begin our work together.

Even though many of the young bodies sitting before me see themselves as fully developed, I know that they will become different people in our time together; after all, that's what happens in middle school. I know they wonder: Will I be valued? Will I be considered a full member of this new community we are forming? As we start our journey, I want my students to press deeper than physical attributes as they seek to define themselves and one another. Ultimately, I hope they move beyond trying to define one another, but instead get to know one another in authentic ways as we construct a community.

I gaze around, the first-day quiet still in full effect. Well, there's not time to waste.

"Who are you?"

Blank stares. I rephrase my question.

"What types of things define us individually and together? What types of things do we use to define ourselves and others?"

The answers begin to come slowly:

"If you're boy or girl."

"The way you look."

"Family."

"Race."

I base this portion of my work on *Upstanders: How to Engage Middle School Hearts and Minds with Inquiry* by Sara Ahmed and Harvey Daniels (2015) and facinghistory.org. As students continue to think and share, I continue to write down each response on a separate index card. These categories will provide a starting place for this beginning assignment that sits in the center of our community building: our identity web construction (pp. 35–37). I often turn to *Upstanders* and Facing History and Ourselves because both provide concrete ways we can support students as they press deeper than surface-level aspects of identity. After the kids have exhausted their initial identity brainstorming, I tape each of the index cards with the student responses to my board to create a web with an empty space in the middle. At this point, the only things listed are generic categories (e.g., socioeconomic status, education, etc.). Later, when students create their own webs, they will list their personal characteristics (e.g., middle class, formally educated, etc.). For example, our co-constructed web will have race and physical appearance as aspects of identity, but a student's personal web will have "African American" or "6'0 and athletic," depending on their unique identity. Next, I write my name at the center of the web and draw lines connecting each of the categories to my name. After this, I show students an example of an identity web I have created for myself (see Figure II.7). After this collaborative introduction, I invite my students to construct identity webs for themselves, with the collaborative web on the board and its category labels serving as a support for students who need it. We revisit these webs across the year as students continue to evolve.

This is only the first step toward where we are headed on our journey of exploring identity; however, I have found this step is crucial as my students begin to evaluate how they define themselves. As students are constructing their identity webs, they peer over one another's shoulders and start to make connections between their webs and those of their peers.

I can hear some of the boys who play football tease each other about who should be able to list "athlete" as a component of their identity. I chuckle for a moment and think about something: as we create labels for ourselves and place ourselves into categories, we are working to meet our basic need to feel as though we belong somewhere, in some community. However, this categorization also poses the danger of seeing different people as *other*. The way we define those falling within the "other" category has a significant impact on our ability to empathize with them.

Once they have completed their identity webs, I invite students to share theirs with a classmate with whom they feel as though they do not share many

FIGURE II.7. My web.

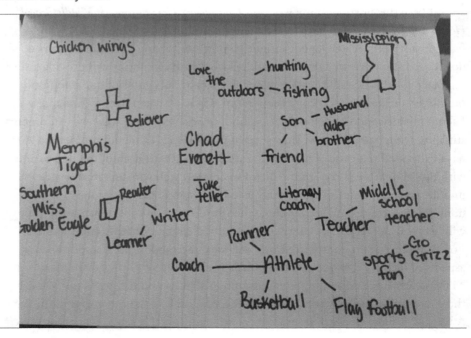

common aspects of identity. This process allows them to intentionally connect with people unlike themselves. Perhaps not surprisingly, they usually also find more commonalities than they expected. Sharing in this way nudges them to push beyond initial assumptions and visible aspects of identity. As they share together, I move around the room conferring with individual students and pairs who are sharing.

As my students finish the initial construction of their identity webs, I make a lap around the room to see if Evan is finished—he is. I ease toward the table that sits in the back corner of my room to get ready for the first of many one-on-one conferences—the beginning of my yearlong investigation into my students' lives and needs. I open the notebook where I will keep my conference notes over the course of the year, a repository for observations about who my students are as individuals, and get ready to talk to them about their identity webs. This notebook helps me keep track of my students' needs, especially ensuring my students have access to texts that both accurately reflect their lives and introduce them to the lives of those different from them. I begin calling their names and they approach me for conferences.

"Evan, will you bring your identity web and join me back here?"

He slides into the seat across from me—hairline extra crisp and every detail of his outfit perfectly coordinated, down to the creaseless Space Jam 11s. The look on his face lets me know he is still unsure about this whole identity work thing.

"What's up, man."

"Nothing."

"All right, take me on a tour of your identity web."

I pay close attention to the place Evan begins this tour. Each of us makes strategic decisions about the parts of our identity we accentuate to others. I learn as much about Evan from HOW he introduces me to his map as I do from WHAT he puts on his map. Once he is finished, I continue.

"So, can you tell me about a time when someone *othered* your narrative— about a time when someone focused on one part of your identity and tried to make it the totality of who you are? Or about a time when someone made assumptions about you based on one part of your identity?"

This question resonates deeply with him, I can tell by the look on his face. It's a question that resonates deeply with me too, and usually with my students. Evan points to the part of his identity web where he wrote about his family.

"People assume that because people in my family have been to jail for drugs and stuff that I'm the same way. That I do the same stuff."

He knows all too well the feeling of having his narrative othered, an impor-tant lesson I want all my students to think about carefully. Yet I don't want this examination of their webs to end here. I don't want my students to feel as though they have to accept the boxes that others try to prescribe for them. I want them, first, to recognize the value of *all* narratives. And second, I want them to continue reflecting on the impact they may have had on people's lives as they have othered—as we all do—the narratives of those we know well and those we don't. In other words, I want them to recognize that we all come from story, are part of a larger story, and, along our journey to the completion of our individual stories, we should endeavor to find beauty in the stories of others.

Putting into practice what I learn from these one-on-one conferences about students' first drafts of their identity webs, I shift focus to consider how their stories are included in my classroom. I want students to find themselves authentically reflected in our curriculum and on our classroom library shelves. I want them to have the opportunity to encounter stories of people not like them.

To illustrate how I try to do this: Last year, my students and I engaged in the Reading Without Walls Challenge developed by Gene Luen Yang, then National Ambassador for Young People's Literature, to help achieve the goal of reading about lives different from their own. Students set individual reading goals that are not just standards driven, but driven by our desire to know and understand others. For example, one of my students set a goal to read more sports biographies about female athletes so that he could better understand how their experiences are different from those of male athletes. Another one of my students wanted to better understand the experiences of those who have experienced police brutality and decided to read *All American Boys* by Jason Reynolds and Brendan Kiely (2015) in addition to nonfiction pieces on police-community interactions. Each of my students track in their reader's notebook how their chosen books are shaping the way they view the world. To help monitor our progress toward achieving these goals, we do a biweekly quick-write answering the question: *How is your current reading changing or challenging you?* It is important to note that many of these goals cannot be achieved through the reading of just one text. For example, the student who read *All American Boys* didn't have a comprehensive understanding of those who have experienced brutality when he finished reading. However, he did walk away with the understanding that not everyone has the same types of experiences when interacting with law enforcement. He walked away understanding that his narrative is not the only narrative.

The Right to Read: Reflecting the Full Range of Students' Humanity

One of my goals as a teacher is to connect my students with books as soon as possible and to keep connecting them with books throughout the year. As Evan continued to trust me with his life experiences, I immediately thought of Rashad in *All American Boys*. Evan's experiences with law enforcement were quite similar to

Rashad's. He had been profiled and accused of things that he had not done. I suggested the book to Evan in our next reading conference. He hesitantly took it and agreed to give it at least fifty pages.

I floated around his table the next few days during independent reading looking for any sign that he was enjoying it. All signs pointed to the fact that he wasn't. On day three, he confirmed my suspicions. He returned the book and told me that it wasn't a good fit for him.

I was puzzled. This book had to be a perfect fit for him, right? I had taken the time to get to know him and make sure that his lived reality was reflected in the pages. I took the time to search for a book that pushed back against stereotypes and tropes. However, Evan's hesitation about this book confirmed one of the realities of teaching: you can follow all the steps suggested by "experts" and still not reap the desired outcome. This is why teaching is both art and science: It's not simply about following a prescribed process. It's also about creating meaningful relationships that help you know students more deeply than all of their outer layers.

As I spent time reflecting on which book I would next recommend to Evan, something occurred to me—I had othered his narrative. I had focused on just one element of his identity—his race in connection to law enforcement—placing less focus on other parts of his identity.

A student's right to read includes the right to read across their full humanity, the right to read books that reflect the full depth of their identities. One of the dangers of the current push for diverse literature is that we, as teachers, lose sight of those aspects of students' identities that are often overlooked. We forget that they are beings living within complex intersectionalities. Finding books, like *All American Boys*, that accurately portray the experiences of my students' interactions with police is important as I curate my classroom library, but I also need to remember that students are more than any singular aspect of their identity, even if that aspect connects them with a marginalized group.

Evan taught me a lot of things across the year we spent together, but that first reading conference together shaped my perspective and approach to supporting a student's right to read.

Evan had lived *All American Boys*. He didn't want to be reminded of the realities of growing up as a young Black male in America or have his experiences validated. He needed me to recognize all the other things that made Evan who he is, so that's what I set out to do. I focused on trying to identify the biases and lenses that may be distorting the perspective I had of him, and that's when I saw Evan for Evan. So I took a step back and asked myself these questions: *What did I think of Evan initially? Why did I think that?*, and *Is my perspective deficit based or asset based?* In reflecting, I realized that the view I had of Evan was shaped by my interactions with other males from inner cities, not my interactions with Evan specifically. I had made the mistake of generalizing Evan and his story, rather than pressing to get to know the intricacies of *his* story. I was, perhaps, moving too quickly.

Evan and his friends had been passing books from Jeff Smith's Bone graphic novel series between one another. Evan just wanted to laugh. He wanted to be a middle school boy and be seen as one. Most of life dictated that he be more mature than his age. Independent reading provided him with the opportunity to just be himself.

Reading Conferences: Supporting a Reader's Journey

I have always valued the time I get to spend one on one with students recommending books, but now when I sit down with a student, I am more cognizant of the need to see where they are on their journey as a reader. Evan taught me that. One way I do this is by inviting students at the beginning of the year to create reading timelines where they map out the significant people, places, and texts on their journeys as readers. I now place these timelines side by side with students' identity webs when making book recommendations. The integration of these two artifacts has helped me to see the books that students have read not as individual anomalies but as important markers on their journeys as readers and individuals.

Taking this approach has helped me to support students as they encounter people different from themselves along their journeys, people who exist both inside and outside of books. Students must take the knowledge they develop through their reading and in their classrooms and engage with the world. Therefore, we cannot assume that because we have read about the refugee experience, for example, we have empathy for refugees. Instead, after I have read a text about a character with whom I do not share many common aspects of identity, I must ask what I need to do to make what I am learning and feeling actionable. How is this information going to change the way I live my life each day? And this is where I focus my reading conferences. To do so, I draw on questions developed by my friend and fellow educator Katharine Hale to help with this work.

1. In what parts of the text do you *see* yourself? Why?
2. In what parts of the text do you *see* someone else? Who?
3. How did this book help you see this person and their experience more clearly?
4. What are you curious about now? What do you want to look into more?

If we create our classroom so that we walk alongside students as they endeavor on this journey, modeling our own journey along the way, encounters with stories different from students' lives will not only exist on our shelves—those encounters will exist in our personal lives and the lives of our students. Likewise, empathy won't just be a feeling, it will be an action. We will want to encounter those different from ourselves not only in texts but in our personal lives as well.

Throughout the year, Evan and I found ourselves around that table often as I worked to find texts that he would enjoy. He enjoyed George O'Connor's Olympians graphic novels, but for the most part, we found ourselves back at texts filled with humor: the Bone series, Kinney's Diary of a Wimpy Kid series, and the I Funny series by James Patterson. Each of those texts represented stops along his journey as a reader, a journey that is as unique as each reader. It is not our role as teachers to dictate this journey to our students; rather, we might see ourselves more like tour guides—knowledgeable about all the possibilities and finding our reward in seeing our travelers enjoy themselves no matter what stops they decide to make.

I don't want to give the impression that Evan loved all of my recommendations or that we always got along beautifully. Embracing and respecting a student's fully humanity means continuing to embrace and respect them when they act as though they don't want to be embraced. Around October of that year, Evan and I struggled. For two weeks, he refused to read and appeared to not care about anything I had to say, and with each day I felt my frustration increase. Helping students connect with texts must be grounded in our love for students themselves. So, during that two weeks, I continued to remember the love that I had for Evan.

When he refused to read, I continued to love him. When he refused to listen to anything I said, I continued to love him. We eventually worked through that rough patch, and I got to see Evan flourish, academically and personally—not because I made the perfect reading recommendation but because I continued to love him. I tried to remember that sometimes respecting a student's right to read includes respecting the spaces in our lives when our brains and our hearts don't really feel like reading. It happens to me. It happens to my reader friends. And it happens to students like Evan.

Access to Texts

There is no doubt that a teacher cannot truly believe in a student's right to read if they do not intentionally curate a library of texts that allow students to read across their full humanity. This means that when students approach my classroom library, they can both find themselves represented within the pages and on the covers of books and also find the lives of people different from themselves accurately represented there. Literature paints a picture for readers of what has been, what is, and what could be. In her essay "Mirrors, Windows, and Sliding Glass Doors," Rudine Sims Bishop states, "[W]hen children cannot find themselves reflected in the books they read, or when the images they see are distorted, negative, or laughable, they learn a powerful lesson about how they are devalued in the society of which they are a part" (Bishop, 2009, p. 1). One cannot be in the business of caring for children and ignore that some students' stories have been pushed out of our schools. In allowing students to read texts that affirm and develop identity as well as empathy, we guarantee that "the reader is not limited by birth, geographic location, or time" (Lesesne & Chance, 2002, p. 61). Students experience a world and people beyond their individual existence. The right to read includes students' right to read books that reflect their individual and collective identities. In exercising their right to read, students are doing part of the work of creating the world that we dream of for our children's children.

Jen's Observation Notes

- Being in Chad's classroom encouraged me to get out my copy of *Upstanders*, Sara Ahmed's first book, written with Harvey Daniels, to consider how I might include that smart identity work in my classroom this year. In addition to creating our own identity webs, we've started creating identity webs for the characters we meet in our independent reading books and our whole-class shared reading.

- "One of the dangers of the current push for diverse literature is that we, as teachers, lose sight of those aspects of students' identities that are often overlooked." This sentence is so important to remember as we work to help the readers in our classrooms find books that really meet who they are, not just singular aspects of who they are. Since being in Chad's classroom, my reading conferences with kids have been framed around this notion. Such an important reminder!

- Chad also reminds me to stay in patient, loving acceptance of wherever a particular kid is on their journey of building a reading life. When he and Evan had their time of struggle, I immediately thought of all the kids with whom I have times of struggle during a school year. I am often patient with them as they struggle in terms of our interactions, but I find myself impatient when they are in the "not reading" periods of their lives. Chad reminds me that I have those times in my own reading life and need to honor and help kids live through those times in their own lives. He makes me consider what I could help kids plan to do during the times they just aren't feeling like reading while we're having reading workshop in our classroom.

- The set of questions Chad offers us from his colleague Katharine Hale are a really smart way to help students build empathy through the characters and stories they encounter in the books they read. I am going to include these in the reading focus choices I invite kids to answer about what they're reading.

And finally, teaching within the NCTE policy brief on reading:

Chad's model of his journey in coming to know his readers more thoroughly reminds me of the following excerpts from *The Students' Right to Read*:

> One of the foundations of a democratic society is the individual's right to read, and also the individual's right to freely choose what they would like to read. (p. xvi)

and

> The reader is not limited by birth, geographic location, or time since reading allows meeting people, debating philosophies, and experiencing events far beyond the narrow confines of an individual's own existence. (p. xvi)

and

> One of the most important responsibilities of the English teacher is developing rapport and respect among students. (p. xvii)

Chad's careful consideration of each reader's full humanity through the beginning-of-the-year identity work helps him conference with readers in a more complete way. This enables him to find books for each specific kid instead of for constructed genres of kids. His use of Bishop's "mirrors, windows, and sliding glass doors" as a thread weaving throughout the reading work in his classroom allows him to move kids beyond reading within their own experiences, out into the greater world portrayed in the books on the classroom shelves. Both of these ideals are central to readers' rights.

What are your observations as you "sit" in the back of Chad's classroom?

- What new ideas does his work suggest for you?

- What changes might you make in your own teaching?

- What new wonderings do you have?

A Final Thought from Jen

Although I have incorporated the ideals of *The Students' Right to Read* and *NCTE Beliefs about the Students' Right to Write* in my classroom for most of my career, writing this book was the first time I had considered the actual policy statements deeply. Reading through the policies, and juxtaposing them with what I knew was happening in many middle schools of colleagues around the country, I was worried. I thought I might not be able to find many teachers using the ideals of the policies in their classrooms beyond having a workshop classroom. I was especially worried considering recent curricular changes stemming from the Common Core State Standards, which forced many colleagues into helping kids learn how to write only argumentatively and to read only nonfiction articles. In some cases, creative teachers who had spent years cultivating progressive, student-centered classrooms had been instructed to begin using a standardized boxed curriculum. I wondered whether I'd be able to find teachers I could introduce you to here who would help you reconsider your own teaching.

I was happily surprised to meet many teachers in early inquiries across my networks who were incorporating the policy ideals despite teaching in schools that had revised ELA curricula to match the CCSS. Teachers like April and Heather and Shelly were incorporating aspects of students' rights to read and write within and around curriculum they had inherited or had revised to meet new standards. I was excited to meet teachers who were using their classrooms as spaces to help middle school students think deeply about the world they live in, and then consider how they might impact that world so that everyone had more equitable lives and opportunities. I was happy to meet teachers who, like Alex, were encouraging students to create their own learning spaces built around what middle school people felt were important topics and skills to learn more about. And then using what they learned, kids in classrooms like Alex's were doing real work in their school and larger communities. And finally, I loved talking with teachers like Chad who were reflecting on their practice so deeply that they were moving beyond what they assumed they knew about kids to actually listen to kids, and then change their teaching accordingly.

I encourage you to sit in the back of *your* colleagues' classrooms and learn from them as we learned from the teachers in this section. If you begin paying close attention to the work of the teachers in your own networks, I bet you will find, as I did, that teachers are trying hard to find ways to honor their middle school students as the readers and writers they are in the world, not just in their classrooms.

As you look forward to the next two sections, Shifting Our Shelves and Reconsidering Composition, expect to find other ways you might think about expanding the voices and human experiences you share with your students through literature. You'll be able to consider how you approach the composition process in your own classroom, and how you might expand that process to be the most inclusive of all writers. In this section, you've visited several middle school classrooms to watch how teachers use the ideals *The Students' Right to Read* and *NCTE Beliefs about the Students' Right to Write* to plan, reflect, and teach the readers and writers in their classes. Now I'd like to invite you to my own middle school classroom, Room A205 at MS 324, The Patria Mirabel School in New York City. I'd like to share with you some ways I've used the policy statements in my own teaching, and I'd like you to meet a few other people who have helped guide my thinking.

Part III
Shifting Our Shelves: Intentional Book Sharing and the We Need Diverse Books Movement

I was in junior high from 1982 to 1984. Our school had an independent reading program called Sustained Reading. For twenty-five minutes after lunch every day, the whole school stopped and everyone read; no matter where you were or who you were, the teachers and principals and secretaries would be reading during this time too. If you were in math or gym or band, you read during this time. You could read, literally, whatever you wanted, and I honestly don't recall a day, in all three years, of anyone playing around and disrupting this reading time. As a middle school teacher now, recalling this experience, it seems miraculous that it worked so well, without question or pushback. This school in suburban Detroit had a huge, well-stocked library, and as a voracious reader, I checked books out many times a week. For most of seventh and eighth grade, I read dozens of books in a romance series called Sweet Dreams. Each book was nearly identical: a mousy girl with a very popular best friend would somehow get to be the romantic partner of the cute, popular, sometimes troubled boy of her dreams. I had a very romantic heart and I gulped those books down whole. The only problem was, in every book, in order to imagine myself as the main character, I had to translate. You see, I was that mousy girl with a very popular best friend, but I didn't like boys; I secretly liked girls. In the mid-1980s, I had no images in the books I read (or in popular culture either) that showed me images of who I was or how my life might look. Even though the classic YA book *Annie on My Mind* by Nancy Garden was published in 1982, I never found it on the shelves of that beautiful junior high library. Instead I was left to transpose the images of a strapping male love interest with the artsy girls I had crushes on.

I didn't read *Annie on My Mind* until I was a ninth-grade teacher in the mid-1990s. When I finished that book, I wept. I cried for the teenager I had been who so needed this beautiful story about two girls deeply connecting and loving each other. I cried because I had finally found a teen romance I didn't need to translate. I went on in the next few years to complete my master's thesis based on LGBTQ+ young adult literature. I think I was still in search of books my junior high self would have loved reading instead of the Sweet Dreams romances.

Rudine Sims Bishop reminds us in her groundbreaking piece on diversity in children's literature, "Mirrors, Windows, and Sliding Glass Doors" (1990), that seeing images and experiences of ourselves in literature affirms our existence; it helps us imagine our own humanity within the greater picture of humanity. These images help us understand we exist as we are, outside of the standard boundary lines. Books providing stories of the vast varieties of human experience are necessary for all kids to consume, but especially for those of us who have to work hard to find ourselves on the shelves in our school classrooms and libraries. However, as teachers with limited budgets and physical spaces, as well as deep attachments to favorite titles, figuring out how to shift our shelves to make space for stories of experiences currently absent or limited in our classrooms can seem daunting.

I clearly remember sitting in a district curriculum meeting in the mid-1990s. This particular meeting was part of a series during which selected teachers came together to revise the district's curriculum vertically, K–12. As expected, the conversation had turned to books, as in, Which books would we "teach" in each grade? (Don't ask English teachers to talk about which books they want to teach to their whole class; that conversation is a never-ending debate!) On this day, the department chair of one of the high schools said, "Well, if we have to have a woman and we have to have a minority [people of color, or POC, wasn't a term we used at that time], then how about we just use *Their Eyes Were Watching God* by Zora Neale Hurston, and then we kill two birds with one stone." I'm sure you are appalled. I was. Despite the incredible merit of that novel, how in the world could it be reduced to "killing two birds with one stone"? And yet, I fear, as we look at the books we use in our classrooms, in whole-class reading, small-group instruction, and independent reading or read-alouds, we might be silently searching for books that cover multiple bases of personhood. And I think if we examine current curricula across the country, we'd probably find an abundance of assigned books containing problematic representations of all different kinds of people living outside the standard framework of white, able-bodied, cisgendered, Christian, middle-class, straight kids.

When I think of some of my own favorite books to read with kids, it pains me to think about the problematic language or representation I know exists within the pages. Does that mean I can't read those books with my classes anymore? Or does it mean I need to find ways to help kids read with lenses that watch for places in texts that might make readers feel othered or invisible? In this section, I suggest ways that we can begin examining the books we share with kids, and how we might begin shifting our shelves to include wider, more inclusive stories of humanity, written by a variety of authors from varied backgrounds. First, I share a few ways that I've begun to examine which books I share with the kids in my classes. Then we'll hear from #WNDB (We Need Diverse Books) founder and middle grade author Ellen Oh about the founding of this organization and the work it's doing to impact children's book publishing. And finally, children's literature scholar Kristin McIlhagga shares some frequently asked questions you may have as you begin to examine your shelves for problematic books and think about how to choose books that help kids read about the most varied human experiences, as well as to see themselves in books.

From a Classroom

Room 205 at MS 324, The Patria Mirabel School
Jennifer Ochoa

Shifting Whole-Class Reads

"Did you see this, Ms. Ochoa? *Stargirl* won! Ugh! Does that mean you're really going to keep it for next year?"

Three eighth-grade girls called me out into the hallway as they stood, scanning the bulletin board I'd just put up. On it were the results of the eighth grade's Literary Merit Essay and Vote. The results were clear: the novel *Stargirl* by Jerry Spinelli (2000) received the highest number of votes from the eighth-grade class as having the most literary merit, thereby ensuring, so we'd told the kids, it would be kept in the eighth-grade curriculum next year. But these girls were worried. As we had read the book together in class, they had continually pointed out that even though the whole book was about a girl, it was told from a boy's point of view.

They had wondered, in their verbal reactions and written responses, if there were no good books we could have read that offered a girl giving her own point of view about her experiences. As a teacher interacting with other literacy teachers on social media, we were all in a time of expanding our thinking around diversity in children's literature. My students' laments underscored the discomfort I had with continuing to use this book—in the limited time of 185 school days—as one of our two whole-class books. But, I kept thinking, lots of kids really engage with this novel.

Another kid waiting to get into my classroom said, "I LOVED *Stargirl*! It's one of the best books we've read in middle school. It teaches us about the regret we might feel when we're older after we've been mean."

A girl from the original group chimed in, "Well, I'm just glad enough people voted for 'Am I Blue?' It's really important for LGBTQ kids to get to read about themselves in school too, and that story really showed how you might know many gay people who just haven't come out to you yet. There's no way you can get rid of that story next year. It's too important." It was true; many kids had written about "Am I Blue?," a short story by Bruce Coville (1995).

"Yeah," another girl said, "and 'Am I Blue?' is good to show that you might be questioning your identity and that's OK too. Ms. Ochoa," she continued, "is there any way you do something next year so kids didn't ONLY read *Stargirl*? I mean obvi, people like it from the vote, but what about mirrors and windows?" I loved that this student recalled the lessons on literary merit in which we used portions of Bishop's (1990) theory that literature should be "mirrors, windows, and sliding glass doors." We used Bishop to help us navigate meeting characters with whom some of us shared many experiences and feelings, and also meeting characters who had different experiences, life circumstances, and reactions from our own.

During our literary study of several short stories and this novel, we asked kids to think about the concept of literary merit. Students deeply considered each story we read and determined which elements caused each story to have a great impact on a reader. We used the work of Bishop to think about how the stories connected to our hearts, and we used the more traditional English class concepts of writer's craft and literature elements to analyze how we experienced the stories as literary scholars. The kids developed a two-part list called "Elements of Literary Merit: Cool Craft Moves Authors Use" and "Cool Ways Authors Teach Us to Be in the World." We used this kid-created literary critique guide in the discussions and writing that followed.

After we finished reading several short stories and *Stargirl* together, the kids each decided which story they believed exhibited the most literary merit based on the elements they had developed. They wrote letters to us, their teachers, arguing for the story they'd each chosen to stay in the curriculum. We told them we actually do take their letters into consideration when drafting the curriculum for the following year. For instance, no one argued we should keep "All Summer in a Day" by Ray Bradbury (1954) two years in a row. In the second year of reading this Bradbury tale, a student argued passionately that we needed to replace it because the bullying was too harsh. As promised, we jettisoned the story. A year after that, one student wrote in her literary merit essay that we should definitely keep "Eleven" by Sandra Cisneros (1991) because, had we noticed, most of the stories were "written by boys, and half of the kids in the grade were girls, so we needed to hear female voices too." This kid's essay prompted us to review the stories, and even though there were several favorites written by male authors that most eighth graders historically loved, we moved those aside to include "Fish Cheeks" by Amy Tan (1987) and the picture book *Each Kindness* by Jacqueline Woodson (2012).

Listening to the girls' disappointment in *Stargirl*'s winning results, I remembered one heated class discussion about the book's merit near the end of our reading. A girl in one of my classes passionately argued, as only a middle school kid can (she even stood up and gave a speech), that this book was not fair. She argued that *Stargirl* was not a good book for girls or boys to read because the main character, Leo, tells the whole story of his girlfriend, Stargirl. She argued that boys always get to tell girls' stories, and girls should get their own voices. She said the story was distorted because we never really heard what Stargirl thought about herself. She swayed almost all the girls in the class that day. And when I later admitted to the kids I had been wanting to change our curriculum to include something other than *Stargirl* for a couple of years, those girls were happy to vote for a story that they felt had a more authentic voice, like "Am I Blue."

Their disappointment in the results of the vote was real. Their sureness that this vote was the ultimate way that their teachers determined the texts we read together showed that they were readers looking for representation, hoping their advocacy could change curriculum. In truth, I agreed with those girls. Originally, I hoped we'd replace Spinelli's classic with a book that may well become a new classic, *Piecing Me Together* by Renee Watson (2017). The literary merit vote complicated that curricular decision. I took the passionate anti-*Stargirl* readers aside and told them that even though the majority of the grade voted for a book they so passionately disliked, I really agreed with much of what they had written in their essays. Then I book-talked *Piecing Me Together* to the whole class. I explained what literature circles are and asked if people thought maybe, for next year's eighth-grade kids, we should switch to literature circles, which could include both of those books, and perhaps others that dealt with conformity. Immediately kids were buzzing, suggesting titles and talking about how cool it would be to have choices of books to read and discuss with the class. Their voices were passionate and thoughtful, and mentioned how having more mirror and window choices would help other kids understand more peoples' experiences. And many kids thought it would be amazing to read about kids like themselves in school.

Shifting the Read-Aloud

I love picture books. It's not just a little crush; I am fully, deeply in love with picture books. For years I've snuck them into my daily curriculum here and there. For years I have been buying beautiful, funny, informative, quirky picture books to include in my classroom library. I have probably ten milk crates stuffed with all kinds of picture books along one wall of my classroom. The sign above the milk crates says, "Break Books," because in our room, whenever you need a break, picture books are there for you. I carefully choose the books I include in those bins. I make sure there are lots of different kinds of experiences represented, and many kinds of faces in the pictures and on the covers. And this year I'm sharing the books in those stuffed bins more strategically and more often than I have before. This year we read a picture book several times a week to start our class time together.

I've long been inspired by the tremendous Classroom Book a Day program Jillian Heise created in her middle school classroom. She blogs about her experiences reading a picture book every day of the school year to her seventh and eighth graders, and how that practice raised the literacy levels, empathy levels, and community levels in her classroom (http://heisewrites.blogspot.com/2014/09/180-bookaday-read-alouds.html). This year my teaching partner and I began a picture book read-aloud time called the Community Read. We supplement picture books with poems, intriguing headlines, interesting definitions, and other short texts, but mostly we read picture books. The kids favor funny picture books. They love books that are clever or wry. They love interesting illustrations and they love stories that they can read with their hearts. And while I have loads of books about historical diversity and biographies about incredible people who aren't often celebrated, when I choose a read-aloud, I often gravitate toward books I know will make the kids laugh or gasp or feel deeply. I sometimes choose based on whatever theme or topic we're studying. And I try to always share current picture books that are most often discussed in the children's literature circles.

While the bins are stuffed with nonfiction and informational picture books, I don't often choose those books as read-alouds. I'm not really sure why. I think I always assumed students would pick informational, historical, or biographical picture books on their own, while I shared more story-based books with our whole class. But Fernando changed that practice for me.

On Halloween, I told the kids that we were going to read many picture books to celebrate the creepy, the ghostly, and the unknown. They were excited by the book stack on the front table when they walked in, as we usually only read one picture book a day. That morning I had pulled several books out of the crates for our mega read-aloud day. Among titles such as *The Dark* by Lemony Snickett (2013), *The Monsters' Monster* by Patrick McDonnell (2012), and *Leo: A Ghost Story* by Mac Barnett (2015), I included *Día de los Muertos* by Roseanne Greenfield Thong (2015) in the stack. That day we managed to read three picture books before we moved on to working on our own creepy story writing. The next day we read a couple more, as we were all still in a Halloween mood. Finally, on November 2, as I was ushering people into the classroom, encouraging them to get out their three essentials— independent reading book, notebook, and something to write with—Fernando came up to me holding *Día de los Muertos*. "We're going to read this one today, right, Miss?" he asked.

I hadn't read that book from the stack yet because it didn't contain a story like the others. It's a beautifully illustrated book that explains the Mexican cultural practice of celebrating Día de los Muertos in a rhyming verse that extends throughout the book. Being Mexican American myself, I bought it for my classroom to honor my own family history, but I'd never actually used it during a read-aloud. It just didn't seem like that kind of book. For some reason, this book didn't seem to fit into my own inner-teacher criteria of what kinds of picture books make good read-alouds. Fernando's request caught me off guard, not because someone was asking me to read a book to the class—that happens several days a week. I was surprised because *Fernando* was asking me. He was a really quiet kid. He smiled big and nodded often but said little. Even during reading and writing conferences, he didn't say much; he simply nodded and took notes. He wasn't shy; I'd often seen him talking to friends and laughing and joking around. But he was very respectful of adults, and that respect manifested in a quiet classroom personality.

"Would you like me to read this today, Fernando?" I countered.

"Yes! I saw it on Halloween, and I've been waiting for us to read it. It's just like my family!" he said. "I've been waiting for us to read this since I saw it in the stack!" I knew from parent-teacher conferences that Fernando came from a large family that had immigrated to New York City from Mexico when Fernando was a baby. Looking at his excited face, holding out a book to me that represented one of his family's most loving holidays, reminded me that every move I make in my classroom is carefully observed and matters.

"Of course we're reading this one today! That's why I left it out!" I said. "I know we were supposed to read it yesterday, but we ran out of time. After we're done, if you'd like to, you can share how your family celebrated this year."

Of course we read the book. Of course Fernando beamed the whole time. And of course he shared that on the previous night at his house the *ofrendas* were for his grandparents who had lived in Puebla and had died since his family's immigration, how his mom made *pan de muerto*, and his uncles came over to sing and celebrate. He encouraged Rosa to share because he knew her family celebrated too. She did. Everyone in our class seemed excited to learn about this holiday. Most of the kids at my school come from Dominican American households, so they asked lots of questions about a holiday that was familiar yet new for them. Smiles abounded.

Often teachers get cultural sharing wrong. They fill their classrooms with special treats from people's family cultures, and there might even be dancing or cultural costumes that no one from that culture actually wears. I've done that as a teacher. I thought we were being diverse and I thought I was including everyone. But I think those diversity celebrations I hosted were tokenism. We didn't go deeply into the cultural origins of the celebrations or how celebrations change as people migrate to new places. We didn't discuss cultural appropriation or how enslaved people developed important variations on traditions that maintained what was important to them, but that masked the African influence of the practices to prevent traditions from being taken from them, and to literally save their lives. I know during those food celebrations we didn't celebrate the beautiful ways that families and communities around the world, and in even our own city, bonded and loved each other differently. I think we had fun. I know we ate delicious food. But I don't know that kids from different experiences in my class felt seen. And I know for sure that not everyone's experience was celebrated.

Fernando's reading request was different. He saw something special from his family potentially highlighted in a special community practice of his classroom. He anticipated that his experience would be featured in the most loving way, because in our classroom everyone loves picture books. People get excited when we're reading. They shout out comments or ask questions freely. Fernando was so excited that his experience was going to be a part of that community engagement. And when it seemed I might pass up this book, he knew all he had to do was bring me the book and ask me to read it to everyone, and I would.

I have always been careful to populate my picture book bins with stories of so many different ways that humans live and love in the world. And as I've shifted our read-aloud habits to include picture books on a regular basis, I've been careful to choose books I thought would represent the kids and families in our classroom community, and also those quite different from our community. Fernando reminded me that our picture book read-alouds are a perfect place to include what matters most to the people in our class about how they live and love in the world.

Shifting Who's on Your Shelves

When Mechelle walked into my eighth-grade class, she was dressed in her school uniform, but the male version. Mechelle hung out with the boys and was treated as boyish by all the kids in our class. No one objected to her or made fun of her. She was just Mechelle, who kinda looked like a girl, and kinda acted like a boy, and was everyone's friend. The first time she asked me to help her find a book to read, I took her over to the realistic fiction/high school bins, pulled a big stack, and tucked in a few Julie Anne Peters books, an author of several books about queer teen girls. Guess what she chose.

A few summers ago, there was a fairly heated, lengthy debate on the Facebook page of the Notice & Note Book Club. This is an active Facebook group of 30,000+ members created and hosted by teachers Alison Jackson and Shannon Clark. The group is dedicated to talking about the professional books written by Kylene Beers and Robert Probst—including *Notice & Note: Strategies for Close Reading, Reading Nonfiction,* and *Disrupting Thinking*—although it has morphed into a space where ELA teachers of all levels come together to discuss reading with kids. During this discussion, a middle school teacher asked if anyone else had read Scholastic's upcoming August release, *George,* by Alex Gino (2015). This middle grade novel is about a transgender middle school kid. The teacher's post asked what people thought about having this book in their classroom libraries as a choice for kids to read.

Many teachers vehemently objected. Those teachers cited parental rights about what kids could be taught in school, and argued that it wasn't a teacher's job to discuss sexuality with kids (those teachers were also clearly confused about the differences between gender expression and sexual orientation). Others, myself included, countered with a need for all children to be present in the texts of classroom life.

The original question morphed into a discussion of classroom ideologies about which texts and what kinds of texts teachers should make available to kids in their classrooms. The conversation was ultimately about which teacher choices constitute censorship, and whether teachers should censor the books on their classroom library shelves. This is big, hard work for a literacy teacher to grapple with. Or maybe it's not. Maybe it's very simple.

For me, the question is this: How do we decide which "kinds of people" make it onto our classroom shelves, and what do we do when we've left out a particular kind of person and then that kind of person actually shows up in our classroom as a student? In Rudine Sims Bishop's piece mentioned earlier, she lauds the work of children's book scholars like Nancy Larrick, who exposed the lack of diversity in children's literature in a 1965 study, but critiques the 1990 status of children's literature. At that point, not much had changed from the late 1960s in terms of the demographics of kid characters; in fact, for some ethnic groups, the numbers had decreased. Bishop famously wrote:

> Books are sometimes windows, offering views of worlds that may be real or imagined, familiar or strange. These windows are also imagination to become part of whatever world has been created or recreated by the author. When lighting conditions are just right, however, a window can also be a mirror. Literature transforms human experience and reflects it back to us, and in that reflection we can see our own lives and experiences as part of the larger human experience. Reading, then, becomes a means of self-affirmation, and readers often seek their mirrors in books. (1990, p. ix)

With this opening sentence, Bishop gave us the metaphor—mirrors, windows, and sliding glass doors—that we have since used to describe the need for stories in children's literature with the varied diversity of human beings.

When a new book like *George* is published, teachers are offered a "mirror, window, door" opportunity. Many of those who chimed in on the Facebook conversation were quite concerned about the conservative communities in which they teach and how a transgender character would be received in those communities. My argument, and the argument of many others including Bishop and Larrick, is that there are so many different ways to be human in the world. In my experience, sometimes communities that are generally homogeneous house some folks who feel as though other ways of being human are worrisome—at the very least, offensive, and at the other end of the spectrum, intolerable. Communities like these occur everywhere, even in the midst of a large urban area like New York City. The seeds of censorship and intolerance can be planted in this fertile, prejudiced, biased soil. However, the reality is that kids of all gender expression and identity and sexual orientation varieties are born into all communities, no matter the acceptance level of human difference within the community.

When you're in hiding from the people who are supposed to love you most, one place you can feel safe is in the pages of a book about people who are like you. When we censor books because they contain otherness, we are also censoring people who contain otherness. I acknowledge that people all over our country are confused by specific kinds of otherness, but that confusion and the subsequent dismissal don't make the otherness cease to exist. And what does that dismissal do to a kid who belongs to an invisible group? These are big questions teachers need to ask as they decide how to structure their classrooms and the time they spend with kids. I worry about helping *all* kids grow up safely to become all of who they naturally are. I'm not challenging the notions of precarious job protection and the difficulties of teaching in conservative communities. But I worry more about the kids who sit in the midst of our classrooms every day. How can we help everyone be safe and whole and loved no matter who they are and where they live? Books help people be visible, even if it's just quietly inside themselves, when being visible out loud is too dangerous in the world.

Conservative parents and teachers who want to censor what kind of people children come into contact with should not get to decide what representations of people come into the classroom by means of news articles, historical study, or literature. But I know that in many places, adults do have that control. What will they do if a transgender child comes into the school? If we've kept certain authors and characters off of our bookshelves, then what do we do when those same kinds of people show up sitting in our school desks? And if we've kept these representations off of our shelves, do students even feel like they can tell us they are sitting at our desks? We teach all the kids, the kids with vocal parents and the kids who are hiding . . . and we should teach them equally. Or perhaps not. Perhaps the hiding kids need us a little more.

Let me share a story to explain what I mean. In my school, the eighth graders wear actual caps and gowns and have a full-on graduation ceremony. The tradition was the girls wore white caps and gowns and the boys wore navy blue. When Mechelle graduated, she had to wear white with all the other girls. Her mom had not accepted Mechelle's identity. At all. Watching Mechelle stand among her friends in a dress, white tights, and that infernal white cap and gown, watching her be so visually separated from who she actually was in the world, was a painful moment in my career. She didn't just look miserable; she looked like small pieces of her self-ness were dying inside. It was cruel. Afterward, as her teachers, we all talked about how horrible the situation must have been for her. We have since lobbied the principal to move to one color of graduation attire so that the diversity of kids' gender expression is protected during this celebration. From now on, everyone will wear blue.

That summer Facebook discussion was about the inclusion of a single title in our classroom libraries, but we wouldn't have had such a lively discussion if those who participated weren't all thinking of the specific individual people we've had sit in our classrooms who needed a book like *George*, or who needed all the graduation robes to be the same color, or who needed, like the small boy in North Carolina several years ago, an observant teacher to read a picture book that celebrates two princes loving each other because that's who you are, even if you're only eight years old (Shaub, 2015). All the kids need us to be on their sides, and a huge part of being a teacher who uses literature in the classroom is including books for *all* the kids.

I recall Mechelle's mom, stuffing her child into tights and a dress because our school highlighted her "girl-ness" through our graduation gown choice. I think about Mechelle standing there, dying slowly. I think about all the pictures Mechelle's mom was snapping of her kid that graduation day, that kid who was so not the kid she had dressed up. And I think about how those pictures will be viewed years from now. And I'm relieved that I had books by Julie Ann Peters and Nancy Garden and David Levithan and so many others to hand to Mechelle all year.

From an Author

Ellen Oh is a prominent middle grade and young adult fantasy author. Her works include the young adult Prophecy *series, the middle grade* Spirit Hunter *series, and an edited anthology,* Flying Lessons. *In recent years, Oh has been at the forefront of the author-created movement* We Need Diverse Books *(WNDB). The movement seeks to change the face and voices of children's literature to include more diversity. The movement also includes #ownvoices, stories about characters who share the same identity as the author, thereby changing the landscape of authorship in children's literature.*

Recently, I was able to interview Oh through an email exchange. She shared with me her own experiences as a middle school reader of color, and I'm happy to share her memories and thinking with you here.

An impactful experience in Ellen's journey toward understanding the importance of identifying, including, and thinking about diverse books goes back to her middle school days. As she explains:

> *My favorite book when I was a middle schooler was* The Count of Monte Cristo *and Alexander Dumas was my favorite author. I had no idea that he was a Black author until I was an adult. And when I think about that, it makes me mad and sad. One of the greatest writers of all time and it was not widely known that he was both a Frenchman and a Black man.*

Her current work in promoting diverse books takes her into many schools as she interacts with both kid audiences and their teachers. In those settings, she tells us,

> *I talk about diversity a lot, not just race but LGBT and disabilities. At every school presentation, at every event I go to, teenagers come up to me to thank me for talking about them. For fighting for them. And I am always deeply moved by their words and the emotion they feel knowing that they are being recognized. That someone is out there fighting for more representation for all of them. It reminds me of just how important this work is.*

Here, Oh shares her thoughts on the development of the We Need Diverse Books *Foundation and its impact on the world of children's literature.*

The Diversity Movement and We Need Diverse Books
Ellen Oh, Children's and YA Author

When Walter Dean Myers was the National Ambassador for Young People's Literature, he said, "Reading is not optional." He went on to explain, "You can't do well in life if you don't read well" (2012). But Myers also knew that reading was harder for many children in this country who don't see themselves reflected in the pages of the books they read.

The idea behind We Need Diverse Books is not a new one. There have been diversity advocates championing the need for diverse books in children's literature for decades. In 1965 the Council on Interracial Books for Children (CIBC) was formed to demand that the publishing industry address the issue of the lack of multicultural representation in children's literature. That same year, Nancy Larrick, founder of the International Reading Association (now the International Literacy Association), wrote an article called "The All-White World of Children's Books" for *The Saturday Review*. In it she said, "Across the country 6,340,000 non-white children are learning to read and to understand the American way of life in books which either omit them entirely or scarcely mention them." When asked by a five-year-old African American girl why the children in books were always white, Larrick began a comprehensive survey of children's publishers and determined that out of 5,206 books published between 1962 and 1964, only 359 included one or more African American characters (Sebesta & Donelson, 1993).

It was clear that the CIBC was necessary. Not only did it harshly criticize the industry, but it also took positive steps to help find talented authors of color by holding contests for unpublished writers. Authors who got their start in children's books as a result of winning these contests included Walter Dean Myers and Mildred D. Taylor (Horning, 2010).

In response to the CIBC's pointed charges and Larrick's jarring statistics, publishers began to publish more books about African Americans. This led to a series of firsts and the landscape began to change. In 1975, for the first time ever, an African American author won the Newbery Medal—Virginia Hamilton won for *M. C. Higgins, the Great*. Two years later, Mildred D. Taylor won the Newbery for *Roll of Thunder, Hear My Cry*. More history was made in 1976 and 1977 when Leo and Diane Dillon won the Caldecott Medals for *Why Mosquitoes Buzz in People's Ears* and *Ashanti to Zulu*, which was the first time the Caldecott Medal had been awarded to an African American artist.

But this multicultural heyday did not last. By 1983 the increase of African American books that had occurred in the 1970s was halved. Once again, we were facing a crisis. On November 9, 1986, Walter Dean Myers wrote the first of his great op-ed pieces on diversity, "Children's Books; I Actually Thought We Would Revolutionize the Industry." In that article, he stated, "If we continue to make black children non-persons by excluding them from books and by degrading the black experience, and if we continue to neglect white children by not exposing them to any aspect of other racial and ethnic experiences in a meaningful way, we will have a next racial crisis."

The movement for more diverse books has risen on the shoulders of advocates like Rudine Sims Bishop, whose groundbreaking article "Mirrors, Windows, and Sliding Glass Doors" has clarified the role of children's books for many educators since it was published thirty ago. In it she stated, "When children cannot find themselves reflected in the books they read, or when the images they see are distorted, negative, or laughable, they learn a powerful lesson about how they are devalued in the society of which they are part" (1990, p. ix).

These were powerful statements by important voices, and yet publishing didn't change. Then the Cooperative Children's Book Center (CCBC), under the leadership of Ginny Moore Kruse and later on K. T. Horning, began documenting the numbers of books written and/or illustrated by African Americans since 1985. In 1994 they began adding statistics for books by Native Americans, Asian Pacific Islander Americans, and Latinx. And in 2012, the CCBC published numbers that were not so different from the ones published forty-six years earlier in Larrick's original survey of children's literature. Out of 3,600 children's book titles published in 2012, CCBC found that only 3.3 percent were about African Americans, 2.1 percent were about Asian Pacific Americans, 1.5 percent were about Latinx, and a mere 0.6 percent were about Native Americans (CCBC, 2020).

On March 15, 2014, a month before the official launch of the We Need Diverse Books campaign, both Walter Dean Myers and his son, Christopher Myers, wrote back-to-back op-eds for the *New York Times*. Christopher Myers's piece was titled "The Apartheid of Children's Literature," in which he stated,

> We adults—parents, authors, illustrators and publishers—give them in each book a world of supposedly boundless imagination that can delineate the most ornate geographies, and yet too often today's books remain blind to the everyday reality of thousands of children. Children of color remain outside the boundaries of imagination. The cartography we create with this literature is flawed.

Myers Senior's op-ed would prove to be his last and most powerful, titled "Where Are All the People of Color in Children's Books?" (2014). He ends his appeal for more diversity with the urgent statement, "There is work to be done."

This became the impetus for the We Need Diverse Books campaign, a rallying cry that brought advocates from all over the country together. And the world responded. The #WeNeedDiverseBooks hashtag went viral all over social media as people shared just how important diversity was to them. It was a loud and collective roar that could not be ignored. No longer was diversity being spoken of only by industry people. The need and the demand had crossed over into a larger audience and into other mediums. Television, film, books, people were demanding more diversity to mirror the reality of the American population.

But it was the response from teachers, librarians, booksellers, and parents that made the We Need Diverse Books movement a resounding success by embracing it wholeheartedly. The American Library Association (ALA) Youth Media Awards have celebrated diversity every year since 2014. The National Book Award for Young People's Literature of 2014 went to Jacqueline Woodson's *Brown Girl Dreaming*. And in 2015, for the first time in the history of the Newbery Awards, three diverse books won the award and honor categories: Kwame Alexander's *The Crossover*, Jacqueline Woodson's *Brown Girl Dreaming*, and Cece Bell's *El Deafo*. The celebration of diversity continued a year later when the 2016 Newbery was awarded for the first time in its ninety-four-year history to a Latinx author. Matt de la Peña won for his beautiful and endearing picture book, *Last Stop on Market Street*. The 2016 National Book Awards were a celebration of diversity, with four out of five finalist books authored by writers of color. The winner of the 2016 National Book Award for Young People's Literature went to the brilliant graphic novel *March, Book 3* by US Congressman John Lewis, Andrew Aydin, and Nate Powell. *March* then went on in 2017 to sweep the ALA awards and take home the prestigious Michael L. Printz Award for excellence in young adult literature.

Not only in awards, but even on the *New York Times* bestselling list, books by writers of color would dominate the list. Nicola Yoon, Jason Reynolds, and Angie Thomas proved that books by and about people of color were bestsellers.

WNDB has been able to provide grants for new writers and illustrators, as well as internship grants for college students interested in working in children's publishing, send free books to thousands of students across the country, and provide awards for outstanding books by diverse authors in the name of the great Walter Dean Myers. None of this would have been possible without the support of all the advocates who work tirelessly to make reading accessible to all of our children. Children's publishing has made great strides in the last few years. But there is still work to be done.

From an Advocate

Kristin McIlhagga is a children's literature scholar and assistant professor at Oakland University in Rochester, Michigan. A social justice approach (Adams et al., 2013) informs all of the work she does with both children's literature and teacher education. Her work examines the ways that K–12 teachers and teacher candidates choose, respond to, and use children's and young adult literature to disrupt schools as a place of inequity and oppression. She has long been an advocate for deeply examining children's literature for nonbiased, antiracist representation. In this piece, she builds on the classroom experiences I shared in this section as well as the information about We Need Diverse Books from Ellen Oh to support you in shifting your own shelves.

Now What? Shifting Your Shelves
Kristin McIlhagga, Assistant Professor, Reading and Language Arts, Oakland University

The first time I taught a university children's literature course, I was preparing to teach a class that focused on having diverse representations in the books we select for our classrooms. As a former classroom teacher, I had a considerable library of books at home to select from. I was confident that I had diverse books on the shelf. My master's project was focused on teaching elementary students about jazz music, and a large number of the books on my shelves had been selected to support that project.

As I went to my shelves to select books to bring in for class the next day, my excitement diminished with every book I looked at. I realized that my collection was not in fact diverse, not even a little bit. I had books with people of color characters, yes, but almost all of them were historical. The books about African Americans were almost entirely about slavery, a few about the Civil Rights Movement, and the rest biographies of people no longer living. The few books I had about other ethnicities and cultures were all folktales. My bookshelves relegated Indigenous and people of color to either "overcoming struggle" or folklore. I was shocked. I considered myself someone who actively worked to promote diversity; I thought I was an aware, socially conscious white teacher. Those shelves filled with historical stories about the struggles of African American people reflected that I was not promoting diversity. I was promoting a single story. I knew if I looked through my shelves for books with characters who represented any race or ethnicity other than straight white European American, such as those who identified as gay, lesbian, or bisexual; spoke English as a second language; or had a dis/ability, the results would be abysmal.

Fast-forward ten years. I realize that the books I selected were based on my extremely limited perception of people whose identities did not match my own. I realized that as an educator, simply adding books to my shelves with characters who had brown or black skin was not only not enough, but it was also likely harmful to all the students in my classes. I was perpetuating stereotypes that came from my own biases as a white, straight, cisgendered, married, college educated, able-bodied, and middle-class person. If I were truly going to support all students (those visible in my classes, as well as those not), I needed to make changes. I also needed to figure out how to help teachers and teacher candidates learn to change their own thinking—something that I continue to work on as an assistant professor and researcher of children's literature. I share my story to illustrate that even the best of intentions can result in unintended consequences. I want you to know that the work of shifting our shelves, and our thinking, takes time and work.

To support you in shifting your own shelves, I compiled a list of commonly asked questions and responses as a quick reference and starting place. I've also included a list of resources that can extend your thinking when you finish this book. Starting is the most important step in shifting your thinking, teaching, and shelves. The responses and resources I share are a place for you to start; I hope that you will collaborate with colleagues to grow and extend beyond the ideas listed here.

What if I share a book that has problematic representations? What do I do if the book I normally use for a whole class I now realize is problematic?

- Acknowledge it to your students and teaching colleagues. So many teachers I've worked with share that they are afraid to admit they "messed up" or don't know something. But there is immense power in being real with your students and colleagues about the work of critically selecting and sharing books. Share how you learned about the problematic representations and any resources that you've used for support.

- Find and share alternative titles. There are resources to help you in the recommended resources at the end of my section and in the annotated bibliography at the end of the book.

- Locate additional texts with authentic representations to read alongside the problematic book. Compare the representations together as a class.

Our mandated curriculum includes book(s) with problematic representations. What should I do?

- Big picture/longer term: Find out who is responsible for text selections—is it a department chair decision or district curriculum coordinator decision? Compile documentation to support your new understandings about problematic representations in that book. Seek out alternative books to suggest as replacements that you can share. If replacing the text is outright rejected, don't give up. In the meantime, offer to work on creating revised lesson plans to go with the text.

- Short term: Reframe your lesson plans to include analysis and discussion of the problematic aspects of the mandated book. Seek out supplemental texts to provide accurate, authentic, and nuanced portrayals of the problematic representations. Consider other books, articles, reviews, blog posts, videos, movies, music, artwork, and poetry written by #ownvoices represented in the book.

- Be a model for students and colleagues by being transparent about your own experiences. Share how you became aware of the problematic aspects of the book and that you are working to become a more critical reader of representations outside of your own identities.

What do I do if I discover problematic representations in a book that I love to share with students?

- Do the personal work of identifying why you love to share that particular book. Ask yourself: Why do I love this book? Why am I invested in sharing it with students? Be honest with yourself and be as specific as possible. Identify your own personal feelings associated with the book and reasons for sharing. It's important to separate those feelings from pedagogy. Regardless of how much we love a book, sharing those problematic representations is perpetuating stereotypes and single stories.

- What other books and texts do you use that contain authentic representations that aren't problematic? If you don't have anything else, you need to find other texts to add to the collection.

What if I upset someone?

- You probably will and you may not always know it. I know that isn't a comfortable answer, but I found that once I admitted this to myself it became easier and "less scary" to do this work.

- If someone chooses to share what upset them and why, listen. Apologize without explanation. This is *especially* true if the person shares a marginalized identity with a character in the book, one that you do not share.

I've seen #ownvoices. What does that mean and should I be using it as I choose books?

This hashtag was originated on Twitter by Corinne Duyvis on September 6, 2015, as a way "to recommend kidlit about diverse characters written by authors from that same diverse group." Some key points that Duyvis makes on her website are:

- "'Author,' as in the actual author has this identity, not their relative or student."

- "'Identity,' as in at least somewhat specific. Aim for: 'character and author are both blind' and 'character and author are both African-American,' rather than: 'character is blind and author is autistic, thus both are disabled' and 'character is African-American and author is Korean-American, thus both are people of color.'"

- "And 'a' marginalized identity, not 'all.' Sometimes a character will be part of a group the author isn't. For example: a straight Cuban author writing a lesbian Cuban protagonist. As long as there's another marginalized aspect of their identity they *do* share, it's #ownvoices."

- These quotes and more information can be found on Duyvis's website: http://www.corinneduyvis.net/ownvoices/.

I teach in a conservative area/district/school; there is no way I can use LGBTQ+ books. I realize the importance of having those representations in my classroom, so what can I do?

- Do the work of articulating why it is important to include LGBTQ+ in your classroom library. This is a time when it is crucial to use professional, pedagogical language as a way to make an argument.

- Consider including books with LGBTQ+ and various gender representations in your classroom library for student choice.

- Read anything published by Caitlyn L. Ryan and Jill M. Herman-Willmarth, in particular their book *Reading the Rainbow: LGBTQ-Inclusive Literacy Instruction in the Elementary Classroom* (2018). Although their research and work are situated in elementary classrooms, the frameworks and ways of thinking can be applied across grade levels.

I have Christopher Paul Curtis and Mildred D. Taylor in my library; isn't that enough?

- If the only representations of African Americans (or any marginalized group) found in a classroom or school library are historical, that is a problem because it reduces them as a marginalized group to a single story.

- Much like the story I shared, having only Curtis's and Taylor's books on your shelf relegates African American experiences to very narrow, and historical, single stories (see Chimimanda Ngozi Adiche's 2009 TED Talk, "The Danger of the Single Story").

I've never thought about any of this before, but I want to make changes; where do I start?

There are two aspects to this work and both are equally important. One aspect is inward, individual work to consider your own identities.

- Educate yourself about the connections between identity and bias. TeachingTolerance.org has some excellent resources, including "Test Yourself for Hidden Bias" and "Unpacking Identity."

- If you are white, I highly recommend reading or listening to the book *White Fragility* by Robin DiAngelo.

The other aspect is to expand the resources to identify, review, and select literature. I've provided a wide range of websites and social media suggestions as resources. One place to start is to look for books and reviews written by people who share the same marginalized identity as the main character(s) in the book.

Recommended Resources

Adams, Maurianne, and Warren J. Blumenfeld, editors. *Readings for Diversity and Social Justice* (4th ed.). Routledge, 2018.

Ahmed, Sara K. *Being the Change: Lessons and Strategies to Teach Social Comprehension.* Heinemann, 2018.

Banaji, Mahzarin R., and Anthony G. Greenwald. *Blindspot: Hidden Biases of Good People.* Delacorte Press, 2013.

Diangelo, Robin. *White Fragility: Why It's So Hard for White People to Talk about Racism.* Beacon Press, 2018.

Garcia, Antero, and Cindy O'Donnell-Allen. *Pose, Wobble, Flow: A Culturally Proactive Approach to Literacy Instruction.* Teachers College Press, 2015.

Love, Bettina L. *We Want to Do More Than Survive: Abolitionist Teaching and the Pursuit of Educational Freedom.* Beacon Press, 2019.

Morrison, Toni. *Playing in the Dark: Whiteness and the Literary Imagination.* Harvard University Press, 1992.

Muhammad, Gholdy. *Cultivating Genius: An Equity Framework for Culturally and Historically Responsive Literacy.* Scholastic, 2019.

Paris, Django, and H. Samy Alim, eds. *Culturally Sustaining Pedagogies: Teaching and Learning for Justice in a Changing World.* Teachers College Press, 2017.

Ryan, Caitlyn L., and Jill M. Hermann-Willmarth. *Reading the Rainbow: LGBTQ-Inclusive Literacy Instruction in the Elementary Classroom.* Teachers College Press, 2018.

Thomas, Ebony Elizabeth. *The Dark Fantastic: Race and the Imagination from Harry Potter to the Hunger Games.* New York University Press, 2019.

A Final Thought from Jen

Shifting our classrooms shelves is big work. It's personal work. It requires teachers to move beyond personal biases they may or may not have previously identified to read more widely and share more openly with the kids they teach. It requires teachers to include in their classrooms stories that reflect the full range of human existence, despite possible objections by school leaders and community members. It's uncomfortable work. But it's necessary work. In homogeneous communities, especially those that are more conservative in political and ethical views, I fear that many teachers may make attempts at this work, such as adding stories that offer problematic historical representations of people of color, but leave out stories that feature characters of varied gender, sexual orientation, and disability, among other representations. I fear that at the first hint of challenge, narrow literary choices will be reinstated. I fear that in communities that include large populations of color, teachers will include only mirror books, assuming that kids need only see themselves and not the wide diversity of human representation.

When NCTE offered us *The Students' Right to Read*, first in 1981, revised in 2009, and revised again in 2018, the writers of the policy brief spoke to these fears. The opening lines of the current statement place us directly in this situation:

> For many years, American schools have been pressured to restrict or deny students access to texts deemed objectionable by some individual or group. These pressures have mounted in recent years, and English teachers have no reason to believe they will diminish. The fight against censorship is a continuing series of skirmishes, not a pitched battle leading to a final victory over censorship. (p. xiii)

But this policy also offers us the community of teachers doing this hard work and the support of our professional organization. If you are a teacher attempting to shift the shelves of your classroom, your school curriculum, or your school library, honing in on the latter portion of this policy statement will be helpful. This section, "A Program of Action," contains excellent suggestions for moving your community toward title inclusion, and what to do when a title you've shared is challenged. In addition, you can utilize the resources on NCTE's website housed under the Intellectual Freedom Center. In this space on the website are invaluable resources available to teachers as they move to shifting their shelves, as well as support for situations in which those shifts result in controversy. Later in this book, Millie Davis, former director of NCTE's Intellectual Freedom Center, shares practical advice that can guide you through making curricular shifts that cause controversy. But first, just as deeply interrogating the books you share with kids is one step toward honoring all the varied readers in your classroom, a careful examination of the composing practices you employ with kids can help you honor the diversity of writers you teach. In the next section, I invite you to consider how you currently ask kids to compose, and what kinds of changes you might make so that students face a minimum of barriers in your classroom to what and how they write.

Part IV
Reconsidering Composition: Analyzing Standard School Composing Practices to Honor Students' Right to Write

Jennifer Ochoa

So much gets in the way of writers writing in school. A person's natural composing process is at the whim of graphic organizers and prompts and rubrics. Teachers are beholden to grade-level writing standards, which drive decisions about units of study and the student products that are born of those units. And in many classrooms, the writing flexibility of being able to work on a draft, come back to it, and work more as you think more can't happen because a yearlong curricular map imposes deadlines that rush all the writers to the same time of completion, whether or not they are ready to be done with the piece. What really gets in the way of writing in school is, well, school.

In my classroom, we just finished making poetry chapbooks. Because of several unplanned school events, bad weather, and people's disgruntled January behavior in class, our time for writing poetry for our books was cut extremely short. We had to be done by a certain day so that we could start our TED Talk unit, which we had to perform by another specific date so that we could start test prep. I just finished responding to the chapbooks. Some were quite good, with poetry that is interesting and offers important ideas the poets have about the world and their identities in the world. Most also incorporated some aspects of our "What Makes a Good Poem?" list of craft moves we developed as a class (see Figure IV.1). I love the lists students drew up as guidelines for writing poems. Don't you? These lists were created after a study of mentor poems and also trying out their own poetry writing skills in quick poem drafts. It seemed as though the kids had what they needed to craft good poems.

However, I noticed that several kids, kids with whom I worked while they were revising poetry for this chapbook, had not turned in the assignment. Some of the students without chapbooks are kids who often have trouble turning in final projects when they are due. But some were kids who generally get projects completed. In each of my classes, maybe three or four people didn't have a chapbook. Because of the quick timing in our curricular schedule, during our writing workshop days of revising and editing my co-teachers and I were hyperaware of timing. We kept saying things like, "We're publishing by Thursday. If you don't

FIGURE IV.1. Student-generated lists of poetic merit.

What Makes a Good Poem? From Class 804	What Makes a Good Poem? From Class 801
What it's about: • It makes you feel deeply • You can connect to what it says • It makes sense and it's easy for us to understand • It's relatable, even if it's not familiar • It teaches a good lesson **Structure:** • It sounds good when you say it out loud, it "rolls off your tongue" • The rhyming makes sense AND sounds smooth • It looks good/interesting on the page • The poet makes good choices with italics and stanzas and lines **Writing:** • The way it's written sounds professional • Written using interesting words and language • Has golden lines people want to remember • Includes figurative language that's original and doesn't sound boring • Has good imagery • The title is memorable	• Shares good information • Has golden lines and golden details • The images are easy to relate to and help you make pictures in your mind • Good and interesting rhymes • Creates empathy • Has a clear theme • Tone and mood are intense or inspiring • It has a good story, even though it's a poem • Has negative and positive examples of how people might feel • The writing lives in your imagination • It might be about the poet • It might contain facts, but they sound beautiful

start revising, you won't have anything to publish on Thursday." Yep, we were THOSE teachers, more worried about our school timing than the time it takes to be satisfied with the poetry you've written. Kids had created guidelines for what they needed to write good poems. But we didn't give them the time they needed to write good poems. With all the harassing we did, I probably would have stopped writing too. School, and I as an agent of the school system, got in the way of poets writing poetry that they felt was ready to publish. Ugh. I hate when I realize that I've used my agency to be oppressive to the kids in my classes. But once that real-ization occurs, I always feel that I need to find my way back toward kids reading and writing, and away from schooling. The deep, often uncomfortable reflection of my practice always leads me to figure out a way to reposition our classroom work so that it is student centered and student driven, rather than system centered and curriculum driven. The reflection reminds me it's my job to figure out how to get out of the way and facilitate writing, rather than dictate it.

Looking through the bullet-pointed elements that make up *NCTE Beliefs about the Students' Right to Write*, I noticed aspects of students' rights that teachers might read and think, "Well, I can't do that!" or "They would never allow me to . . ." Teachers are overwhelmed by having to constantly consider outside agents that are impacting, shaping, and directing the writing instruction in their class-rooms. If you're reading this position statement and thinking you won't be able to fit this kind of writing instruction into your curriculum, perhaps some of the ideas offered here might feel doable to you. In this section, I examine some fairly standard classroom composing practices in middle school, and then think about ways we all might reconsider those practices to ensure they are more aligned with students' rights as writers, despite mandates that might insist otherwise.

What Is the Composing Process?

The composing process or writing process in most middle schools is fairly stan-dard. Generally, in an ELA middle school classroom, a piece of writing is produced as the centerpiece for a unit of study on a particular genre or format, such as the memoir unit, the poetry unit, the argument unit. In these units, the teacher shares several mentor texts, often professionally published examples of what the teacher hopes the students will produce. The mentor texts are carefully studied in terms of elements so that the students can model their own pieces after the mentor texts using those same elements in their own pieces. The other standard writing product that middle school kids create is a piece in response to something the whole class has read. Literature response pieces might be standard thematic essays or argu-ments about some aspect of the text, or the writing might be something creative, based on the piece of literature. In such cases, the product students craft could be an imagined alternative chapter, or a retelling from another character's point of view. Some teachers might ask kids to *restory*, as Ebony Elizabeth Thomas suggests, a piece of literature they've just read. Restorying asks the reader to reshape a piece to include perspectives that are "missing or silenced," as Lin-Manuel Miranda did in the musical *Hamilton* (Thomas, 2018). Literature response pieces are often used as the final assessment for a whole-class novel unit. Whether a try at a particular genre or form or a response to a piece of literature, once the purpose of a piece is determined, the process begins.

At some point in our school career, we've all been asked to engage in "the writing process." The process goes like this:

- Students are first given a prompt to write to. Sometimes it's just one question, and students need to base their entire piece of writing around that question. Sometimes there is flexibility, and students have a choice between several prompts.

- Students are then asked to gather ideas. This is the planning/prewriting/brainstorming phase. Often the whole class engages in activities to help do this "before writing" work. Usually the teacher organizes and manages these planning opportunities so that the whole class is brainstorming and planning in much the same way.

- Once the class has brainstormed and organized, students are asked to engage in several days' worth of drafting. This is when they actually write. The writing happens in school, and as homework, as well. During this time, the teacher might be conferencing with students as they write to help move the piece forward. Turning in various stages of drafting to the teacher for assessment is also common. For instance, the whole class might be writing the introduction today, and by the end of the class period, all students need to give their teacher a draft of their introduction for feedback. Tomorrow, the class will revise their introductions and begin composing body paragraphs.

- Once students have a draft, they revise and edit. Students might be asked as a group to revise to make sure their pieces contain certain elements. For instance, if students are writing short stories, the teacher might give a lesson on dialogue and then ask students to revise to include dialogue. Sometimes the revising is just "adding details" or "explaining the evidence." Revising generally includes sharing a draft with others, either a partner or a writing group. These peer writers are meant to read the work and give suggestions about how to make the piece—somehow—better. Then writers take the suggestions and go back into the draft to do the work that will make the draft a stronger, more coherent, more interesting piece of writing. When revising is done, students edit for mechanical correctness.

- Finally, students share the writing in some way with an audience. We publish. The publishing could simply be trading final drafts with others for compliments and feedback. Publishing might actually involve including each piece in a collective publication that goes out to a wider audience. Publication might entail posting a draft on a bulletin board or reading a piece aloud in front of the class. Making work public is the final stage of the writing process.

All the parts of this process are fine. In fact, composers in the world engage in all aspects of this process in some way. But too often in school, teachers behave as though this process is linear and the same for all composers. School is a generally standard place, so parts of school get standardized, like the writing process. I do this too in my own classroom. If I introduce a particular graphic organizer to plan an essay, I might expect all the writers in our classroom to use that graphic organizer to plan their essays. I do this even though I know it's not the most inclusive practice, because school sometimes gets in the way of my teaching.

The problem is that writers aren't standard. Writers use a composing process of some sort when they are writing, but that process is rarely linear, nor does it exactly match the process of other writers. If someone imposes a particular format on part of the process that doesn't complement how the writer's brain composes, the writer can feel stifled or become stuck. As teachers, we see this happen in our classrooms, and as writers ourselves, we may have had this happen to us at some point as we engaged in school writing. My goal is to recognize when I'm teaching in an overly structured manner and to reflect on how I might change that practice to be more inclusive of the different ways people compose. What follows asks us to reconsider different aspects of the composing process so that we might open them up a bit. I suggest strategies that honor the rights of the writers in our classrooms so that they have the most autonomy and control over a very personal process in a very standardized setting.

The Prompt—What Are We Writing?

The prompt, of course, is what students are asked to write—the question kids need to answer in their writing or the ideas they should explore. The prompt might also require specifics of topic, form, genre, as well as certain craft elements such as dialogue in a narrative or a counterclaim in an argument essay. *NCTE Beliefs about the Students' Right to Write* actually offers some suggestions for how teachers can prompt student writing. The position statement reminds teachers that "students should, as much as possible, have choice and control over topics, forms, language, themes, and other aspects of their own writing while meeting course requirements" (2014, p. xxv).

Because there are so many potential parts to a prompt, opening up the prompt for more student choice and autonomy is possible. To reconsider crafting prompts that will direct the writers in your class, first consider aspects of the prompt that do need to be dictated—what are the nonnegotiables that the curriculum mandates, and what decisions could the writers make for themselves?

A Reconsideration from Room A205

For several years, my co-teacher and I asked kids to write a thematic essay based on Jerry Spinelli's novel *Stargirl*. We used "The Most Important Word" strategy from Kylene Beers's *When Kids Can't Read, What Teachers Can Do* to help kids think about thematic concepts, and then had them build a theme around one of five

thematic words we picked as teachers (2002, pp. 173–75). Each student decided which word was the Most Important Word (MIW) to connect to the novel, and then each developed an argument to claim that *that* word, and a subsequent theme they developed, fit the book best. The whole argument piece was heavily scaffolded. There was choice in the MIW each kid picked, but as teachers we preselected the five thematic word choices. Students loved arguing aloud for their chosen words in a Socratic seminar, and they loved helping one another write a theme for the book that sounded like a lesson. This was a solid literary argumentative essay unit. But their essays were boring. The process offered no real space for students' voices as readers. And when they met with other writers in class to share their drafts as revising partners, those meetings were over in three to four minutes, the time it took for them to skim each other's essays and say, "Yeah, yours is good."

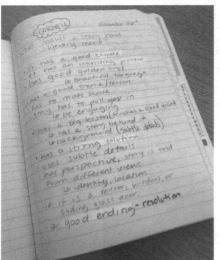

As teachers, we were bored, and the kids were definitely bored. We considered how to revise this prompt and remembered that different pieces of literature affect readers differently (Rosenblatt, 1983, p. 42). We decided to teach the concept of literary merit, defining *literary merit* as "Awesome Author Craft Moves" and "Excellent Ways a Piece of Literature Teaches Us Lessons," and working together to create a piece of literature worthy of our literary study. The kids in small groups crafted lists of elements they felt best exemplified each aspect of literary merit (see Figure IV.2). Then we compiled the small-group lists into a large class master list. Because they'd written the literary merit lists, students felt ownership over those lists as an assessment tool to establish the level of merit each short story and the novel, still *Stargirl*, held. Now

---

FIGURE IV.2. Students' lists of elements that constitute literary merit.

The Merits of a Piece of Literature
(as told by Class 801 and Class 804)

Awesome Author Craft Moves
- Exciting plot twists/cliff-hangers
- The theme is clear
- Good action and relatable scenes
- Important background info—flashbacks, character histories, setting explanations
- Showing us how a character feels and does things/thorough characterization
- Makes us care about the characters
- Debatable actions . . . conflict makes us think . . . conflict that's hard to decide right/wrong
- Mysterious questions for us to think about and build theories about
- Lots of internal thinking of the character
- Dialogue that reveals something/tells us something important to the story
- Realistic situations
- Golden lines and golden facts that make us think or we can see are "good writing"
- By the end of the story, all the pieces come together, even the pieces that don't seem to fit or are unexpected

Excellent Ways a Piece of Literature Teaches Us Lessons
- Shows characters making the right decision
- Shows characters making the wrong decision
- Applies to the real world; helps us connect to the story; conflicts are realistic
- Shows the consequences of the characters' actions and choices
- Makes you feel like you are walking in the characters' shoes
- Makes you react all throughout the book; plot twists teach a lesson
- Shows multiple ways to solve a problem
- Characters listen to other characters, get advice from others
- Golden lines give us lessons and the theme
- Showing how one character's actions affect others in the story
- When we see characters act in unexpected ways
- The story makes you rethink YOUR OWN actions
- The solution to the conflict teaches a lesson

the literary argument essay offered much more choice. The kids could pick from several pieces of literature. We included independent reading books and picture books as possibilities for kids who hadn't connected to any of the pieces we'd read together. They could also decide—from the big list they had created—which elements of merit each piece displayed. Kids worked together and individually to analyze the stories, and each person decided, based on these assessments, which piece of literature, in their opinion, had the most literary merit. Because the New

York State standards (the Common Core State Standards at the time) required eighth graders to also master writing a counterclaim, the structure of the literary merit essay offered the perfect opportunity to practice this skill. Each kid simply interviewed another student who was arguing that a different piece of literature had the most merit. The interviews involved each kid explaining to the other why they had chosen that particular story as worthy of continued study. The resulting counterclaim paragraphs told of readers who had been affected differently than the essay writer had by the same pieces of literature.

Revising the prompt for this essay strengthened our teaching around what makes a piece of literature worthy of reading—in other words, what it offers us as readers. Students' literary conversations were lively, and their essays, written in the form of letters to us, their teachers, about why we should keep THIS STORY in the curriculum for next year's eighth graders, were passionate and well written. The first year we made this revision, there was a story that no one argued for, and we promised that we would jettison that story from the curriculum the next year. And we did. Revising the prompt offered writers a real opportunity to effect change in their school, even a small change like which stories those who came after them would read. Had we not reconsidered the prompt for the literary argumentative essay, kids would have missed an opportunity to write about a topic that mattered to them, to an audience who was really interested and listening.

Getting Started—Prewriting/Planning/Gathering Ideas/Brainstorming

This is the part of the composing process during which all ideas are welcome. This part looks messy. This part is all about possibilities. This part is scribbles and lines or sketches and jots or Roman numerals and bullets. This part is thinking. For people composing in the real world, the getting started part of the process looks many different ways. Getting started might even just look like walking around thinking. For me, much of my getting started process happens in my head. I think and rethink form and organization. I compose whole sentences and paragraphs before ever getting myself to a blank page. When I was in school, this kind of prewriting was unacceptable to my teachers. They did not appreciate my thinking, most calling it procrastination (as did my mom). At that time, we were always expected to have a traditional outline for each piece of academic school writing. I usually planned my own way, wrote a draft, and then created an outline afterward for a grade. I'm sure that isn't what my teachers had in mind when they required an outline. And the outlines certainly didn't help me write my essays.

In the middle school classrooms I'm familiar with, the getting started part of the composing process varies greatly, both between classrooms and within the same classroom depending on the piece of writing students are composing. However, in many classrooms, getting started often involves every student meeting standard expectations. For instance, everyone might be expected to make a planning web or sketch a storyboard. All writers might need to use the same graphic organizer that clearly lays out an introduction with suggestions; several body paragraphs with sentence starters; and a conclusion with suggestions. Conformity in planning might be helpful for some kids and the teacher, but for other kids, planning using a standard structure is confining and results in feeling stuck.

The blank page intimidates and taunts. In my classes, kids frequently get stuck at this stage of the process, lamenting, "I don't know what to write!" with whiney exasperation. I have tried sharing many possible getting-started strategies for one piece of writing, and then asked kids to pick the strategy they thought might help them get a strong start on a plan. For instance, I might show what a web plan for the piece could look like, in addition to what someone else's plan might look like if they worked best with a bulleted list. I also often have a structured graphic organizer available for kids who feel that strategy is helpful. With multiple doors into the writing project, most kids can find some planning strategy that feels comfortable and productive.

A Reconsideration from Room A205

For many years, the getting started part of writing was the biggest hurdle most kids in my class faced. I often teach classes of kids traditionally considered not great ELA students, generally grouchy readers and sparse writers. The kids who often populate the classes I teach have had long histories filled with strong evidence that ELA class is not a place where they will feel successful. My goal, always, is to put into practice structures and strategies that will help them begin to change their identities as literacy students. Knowing that getting started felt overwhelming to many kids, and also knowing that people have different kinds of planning techniques to help them begin composing, I developed a strategy called "writing relays" that helps kids manage their writing anxiety.

Writing relays are short, prompted bursts of writing that quickly fill up a page or two, thereby overcoming the blank page fear kids sometimes face. By the end of a writing relay session, writers have many short starts to choose from, and sometimes, throughout the session, one good idea takes hold and the writer has launched into a piece.

Writing relays work like this:

- I create a few specific prompts that might help someone begin a piece on a particular topic, generally five to six prompts.
- I organize the prompts into a series of quick writing bursts—relays—that are targeted, either in time, space, or form.

- Throughout each relay, I continue to coach from the sidelines, giving other possible entry points to the prompt.

- As each new relay begins, I always say, "You can begin the next relay, or keep writing on a past relay if you've got more to say."

We used this strategy to help us get started when we began our Becoming Literate essays at the beginning of the school year. In their Becoming Literate essays, students write an argumentative personal narrative describing their identities as readers and writers at the beginning of eighth grade. The idea is to develop an essay that furthers the prompts "I'm the kind of reader who . . ." or "As a writer I . . ." Kids use memories from their lives as evidence to show that the statements they've claimed about themselves as literate people are true. Writing relays always help with getting started on this piece of writing.

As you can see from the writing relay prompts in Figure IV.3, a relay might be a short amount of time, perhaps three to four minutes, or a short amount of space, maybe four notebook lines. A relay might also take on a specific form: a sentence, a paragraph, a sketch, a web. In this way, varied brainstorming strategies are honored. And always, I suggest that if that format isn't working for an individual kid, they can try something else.

Coaching into the writing relays might sound like this:

For the first relay today, we're going to write for three minutes about your most favorite or least favorite place to read. Think about a place you really love to read, a place you can fall deep into the story world. Where is that place? What does it look like? Or you could think about a place you hate to read. Maybe you get motion sickness, so reading in the car or on the bus or the subway makes you feel terrible. Where do you love or hate to read? Okay, three minutes—on your mark, get set, go! Write about your perfect or worst reading place. [pause for thirty seconds] When you're reading in this perfect place, what does it look like? Describe the setting. What's around you? What makes this place so perfect for reading? [pause for thirty seconds] If you're writing about a place you hate to read, what is it about this place that makes concentrating difficult? What interrupts you from being deep in your story? Is it noisy? Is it uncomfortable? Describe the ways this place is terrible for reading.

The variety of prompts and formats and the constant suggesting all help kids move from intimidating blank pages to pages full of ideas after only a brief bit of time. This strategy takes fifteen or twenty minutes and kids always have several ideas to write about when we are done. As we finish writing relays, I ask if people have some good ideas they would like to expand on, and the answer is usually a resounding "Yes!" After completing writing relays, continuing to plan for a piece or launching into drafting feels more manageable for even the most stuck writers.

FIGURE IV.3. Writing relay questions: Becoming Literate essay.

---

1. Describe your favorite place (or least favorite place) to read. Why is that place the best (or worst) for you? [3 minutes]
2. What's your favorite topic to write about? Friendship? Equality? Love stories? Poems? Self-struggles? [4 notebook lines]
3. If you could create your own bins for the library, what would you call them and what kinds of books would be in them? [List of 3 bullets]
4. If you were going to read an exciting book, would you rather read it alone? Out loud in a small group? With a class? A friend? Why? [4-sentence paragraph describing the setting]
5. If your teacher assigned you a topic, would you rather write about it in a story? Poem? Diary/Journal? Essay? Comic? Something else? Why? [Web with the forms of writing you like; you can include topics too!]
6. How do you like to plan for writing? Drafting? Drawing scenes? Thinking about it in your head? Talking it through with a partner? [6-word memoir]
7. What is your least favorite thing to do in literacy/English class? [1 drawing or symbol and 1 sentence]

Drafting—Writing, Writing, Writing, and Some Sharing

While we're in the drafting stage, I would love for my classroom to seem like a great coffee shop. I imagine people sitting quietly with open laptops or notebooks in front of them, some furiously concentrating on writing, fingers or pens flying as they draft their ideas into pieces they love, others staring into space as they think about what they'd like to write next. Perhaps a few people chat quietly over drafts they've shared with each other, their conversations purposeful and filled with thoughtful suggestions. Maybe the scene I've described is similar to your writing classroom, but it's far from the often chaotic writing zone in my middle school classroom when we are actively drafting. Even though drafting time should be quiet and productive, it is also the time when worried writers are fearful of going solo. The kids in my classes, no matter how well they are set up with a rich writing plan, often feel insecure about drafting, wanting sentence-by-sentence reassurance that what they've written "sounds okay." As I move from kid to kid trying to quietly check in and provide brief conferences, invariably there is a short line of three or four other kids following me, notebook in hand,

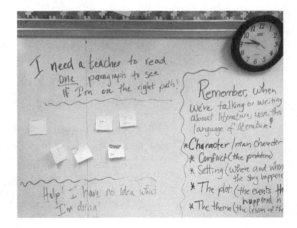

pleading, "Will you read this, please?" Sharing my experiences during drafting with other middle school teachers assures me that this scene is a usual one for a group of middle school writers. But as I've moved to encouraging the fairly simple feedback process of asking questions of a writer's draft during writing groups, partnerships, and conferences, and then offering a menu of working options for kids to choose from on drafting days, writers have more opportunity to feel supported and autonomous while they write.

A Reconsideration from Room A205

Drafting is such a personal process. Some people need a notebook and a special pen. Some people like yellow legal pads and pencils. Some people draft only on Google Docs so that they have access to their drafts everywhere, all the time. Some people need music and others like quiet. Some people like to write without interruption and then go back and reread what they've written to do a bit of early revising. Some people revise by the sentence as they go. Some people like to share their drafting often for cheering feedback, and others don't want anyone to look at what they've written until the piece is nearly ready for publication. Accommodating all of these drafting needs in a middle school classroom is hard.

When we're in the middle of a drafting time, I try to offer as much flexibility and support as I can so that all the writers get what they need. I start by asking the kids three questions:

- What did you get done on your piece while you were away from our classroom?
- What are your drafting plans today?
- What do you need to accomplish those plans?

These questions come in the form of an entrance slip, which I quickly collect and use to decide which kids I need to check in with first.

Alternatively, I've used another quick self-selecting system to make a plan for a drafting session. On the board, I have posted the following charts:

- Today, I just need to write.
- Today, I need to research something to add to my draft.

- Today, I'd like to have teacher feedback on one part of my draft.
- Today, I'd like to get the feedback of a colleague writer.
- Help! I'm really stuck and I need emergency assistance!

Kids take sticky notes and write their names on them. Then they add their notes to whichever charts seem to fit their drafting needs for the day. This is an easy visual way to sort kids by conferencing need, and also to see if people are being productive in the way they've planned to be. Using this strategy, I can quickly move to whoever needs to work with me immediately. And, because the stickies are movable, if a writer needs to change their plan, they can easily move their name to whichever new chart fits their needs. Once we started using this system during drafting, our classroom *did* begin to resemble a coffee shop of writers, each working away at their own pieces in the way that suited them best.

Publication—Finding an Audience beyond the Teacher

When I first began teaching in Lansing, Michigan, in the 1990s, I was a ninth-grade teacher. At that time, the Lansing School District had a printing shop in the technical/trade high school. For a minimal fee, I could, as a teacher, take a publication there, and the print shop would duplicate many copies with tagboard covers, stapled like a book. Many times every school year I took our class books over to that shop, where they printed professional-looking booklets with our writing inside. At the end of an identity unit, we published *More Than Just a Teenager*. When we read *Neighborhood Odes* by Gary Soto, we published *My Neighborhood: Portraits of Lansing*. And every year we published a poetry book after a unit on writing poetry. When I moved to New York, I continued the tradition, only on a slightly humbler scale. Our "books" were simply our finished drafts, carefully revised, edited, and typed into a single document with a kid-designed cover. I just made copies on the copy machine so everyone had one to read and keep. Those books also became part of our classroom library to read during independent reading. Many teachers I know have used this same practice of self-publishing student work. The day the kids come into the room and see their books ready to be passed out for everyone to read, well, the thrill is palpable. Having an audience to read your words is important to all writers.

When I moved to teaching middle school years ago, I was introduced to "publishing parties." We didn't have those in high school. The publishing party is a very middle school entity. When the time came for our first publishing party my first year of teaching seventh grade, I was told that the "party" part of the publishing party was most important. . . . I was to bring treats. I brought the treats, but I didn't turn students' pieces into a book. Instead, they politely did a gallery walk of reading. Kids left great comments on one another's pieces, but the cupcakes were the star that day, not the writing.

A few years later, we debuted our TED Talk unit, the culmination of which was each student writing and performing their own TED Talk modeled after professional TEDs, which are personal narrative in style. The drafting, editing, and revising of their talks was intense and passionate. They wrote and drafted and rehearsed and drafted and revised more. We almost didn't need to encourage revision; it happened throughout the process naturally. And their talks were beautiful pieces of writing, beautifully performed. When we reflected on teaching this unit, we realized that the writing was so good and the revising was so natural because this piece had an actual audience of their peers, and it would be performed. The second year of the TED unit, the same intense writing and revising occurred. At that point, we knew we needed to find wide, authentic audiences for as many of students' pieces throughout the year as we could. I remembered Lansing and those early books. The writing was really good, and the writers took the process seriously because I was not their primary audience—other kids were. I encourage you too to find ways to broaden the audiences for the writing your students do in your classroom beyond yourself or a cupcake party. The more you can do this, the more you will be helping kids meet one of the main goals of writers—to have readers.

A Reconsideration from Room A205

Since we realized that TED Talks made for excellent writing from kids, we decided to try to expand publishing opportunities across the school year. Some of our recent publishing has included the following:

- Their "Becoming Literate" essay, which tells the story of who they are as readers and writers and the events, books, or people that accompanied them along their journeys, becomes their "About Me" piece on the profile page of their Goodreads account.

- Their narrative fiction becomes part of a big online Google page just for our school's eighth graders. Each story is published in a class folder, and all eighth graders have access. We ask everyone to read several stories from other classes and comment on those stories, writing peer reviews of eighth-grade fiction.

- Their poetry chapbooks become the performance pieces for class poetry slams shortly before our TED unit as a means of trying out performing their own writing.

- Their "Literary Merit" essay becomes a letter to the eighth-grade ELA teachers, trying to convince us that the story they feel has the highest literary merit should be kept in the curriculum the following year. We actually use the results of these letters to make curricular decisions.

Publishing kids' writing is not a new or fresh idea. In fact, the idea of authentic publication has always been a mainstay of a workshop classroom. But as teachers become busy with writing curriculum, planning lessons, attending department and staff meetings, grading papers, and so on, like so many good pedagogical ideas, authentic publication takes a back burner to covering what's expected to be covered. Or perhaps you have one great unit of writing that gets published to outside audiences, but the rest of the writing has only you for a primary audience. I'm suggesting that the more outside audiences you can develop, the more seriously middle school kids take school writing.

A Final Thought . . .

Nothing posed in this chapter is especially new to writing pedagogy in the middle level classroom. However, this chapter could remind us all about how good writing instruction is filled with opportunities for writers to own their own process as much as possible. And really good writing instruction generally leads to really good writing, writing ready to share with audiences beyond our classroom walls. In the last several years, testing and standardized writing tasks stemming from narrow writing standards have caused more than a few classrooms to narrow writing instruction. I hope the suggestions here are reminders of ways to broaden the writing that's happening in your classroom. Two points in *NCTE Beliefs about the Students' Right to Write* guided my thinking in this chapter:

> Teachers should engage students fully in a writing process that allows them the necessary freedom to formulate and evaluate ideas, develop voice, experiment with syntax and language, express creativity, elaborate on viewpoints, and refine arguments. (2014, p. xxv)

And

> Teachers should foster in students an understanding and appreciation of the responsibilities inherent in writing and publication by encouraging students to assume ownership of both the writing process and the final product. (2014, p. xxv)

As I revise units and plan new ones in our curriculum, I'm going to keep these two ideas close by and use them to shape the writing work we do in our classroom. Maybe you'll keep these notions close to you as well as you plan writing with the kids in your classrooms.

The work of revising our curriculum and our teaching practices requires careful study and thoughtful reflection, but it also requires community. When

I'm planning new instruction, whether it's a strategy or a full unit, or when I'm building up the underpinning philosophical pillars that define my teaching life, I do better work when I do it with others. The conversations that I've had with my co-teachers, grade-team planning partners, literacy coaches, teacher colleagues outside of my school, and teacher friends I've met throughout my years of involvement with NCTE have been invaluable to my growth as a teacher. I can't do it alone. I suspect none of us can, really. And while reading professional books and attending official professional development is necessary for my teacher growth, for me the day-to-day work of teaching needs more interpersonal connection. As you move to reflecting on and including the elements of *The Students' Rights to Read* and *NCTE Beliefs about the Students' Right to Write* into your own teaching, I suspect you'll want a community to learn with and bounce ideas off of, a community of other educators doing similar work. Perhaps you have good support in your school and local teacher groups. But maybe you'll want to seek connections with those outside of your immediate circles. In the next section, Millie Davis, former director of NCTE's Intellectual Freedom Center, shares ways NCTE can support your work if you meet any resistance or negativity as you include more diverse books and practices in your classroom. And then I'll share ways I've built my own virtual professional community through various social media platforms. In all, by the end of the next section, you will know about the many avenues of support available to teachers who honor the already active and varied readers and writers in their middle school classrooms.

Part V
Shoulders to Lean On and Arms to Link With: Seeking Support and Connection as We Do This Work

From an Advocate

As the former director of NCTE's Intellectual Freedom Center, Millie Davis often helped NCTE support teachers who were facing complications in their work to include more diversity in the texts students read in class and the choices they had for crafting pieces of writing. Here, she shares with you ideas to help protect yourself as you work to honor your students' rights to read and write.

Protecting Your Students' Rights to Read and Write and Yours to Teach
Millie Davis, Former Director of NCTE's Intellectual Freedom Center

So, students' rights to write and read serve as a catalyst to think about . . . our teaching—not just curriculum, not just pedagogy, but the thinking, talking, and listening that we as ELA teachers do together with our students.
                                          —Jonna Perrillo, "More Than the Right to Read"

As Jonna Perrillo suggests, do plan your curriculum and make your text choices to foster reading, writing, thinking, and talk. *Then* take proactive steps to protect these most important activities for your students and their learning. But know where to turn if you're challenged. While basing your curricular choices and classroom activities on *The Students' Right to Read* and *NCTE Beliefs about the Students' Right to Write*—the Golden Rules of Reading and Writing, as editor Jennifer Ochoa calls them earlier in this book—you should at the same time be aware of and consider the rules and procedures school districts have in place and that, as an employee, you need to follow.

Know and Follow Your School Policies

In a 2016 survey of NCTE INBOX readers, 41 percent of respondents stated that their selection of materials was guided by an informal policy, 29 percent stated that decisions were guided by a formal policy, and the rest stated that their school district had no policy or they didn't know whether there was a policy. Don't be among those who don't know about your district's policies.

Most school districts do have school board policies governing how curriculum and texts are chosen. While the board has to approve these selections, they often cede the selection process to teachers or administrative committees. And usually there are also provisions for supplemental texts. In addition, most school districts have policies on teaching controversial materials and on reconsidering texts, and they have a mission statement about educating the students in their schools. Only a few districts have policies concerning student writing.

You'll usually find district policies on the district website under "school board" and "school board policies" and then under "curriculum" or "instruction" and sometimes under "parent/community relations." You may have to dig a bit, but do know those policies—for two reasons. First, know the policy so you can follow it in the selection of materials and methods for your classroom. Second, know the policy so you can at least notice where and when it's not being followed—for example, if a parent goes straight to a school board meeting to complain about a text or method you're using in your class instead of coming to you first. (See the model procedure spelled out in *The Students' Right to Read* under "Defending the Texts" [2018, pp. xx–xxiii].)

Keeping People Informed and Building Buy-In

Beyond knowing the district policies, make sure to keep others in the loop about how you are teaching reading and writing—especially if you're including activities and texts that may seem controversial. Open your door and share with your colleagues, the principal, and parents about *what you're doing in your class and why*. You don't need to be super specific. Something important to remember, as Emily Knox's *Book Banning in 21st-Century America* (2015) points out, is that challengers often just want to be heard, and they don't really understand the reading process as we do. So help them understand. Jennifer Buehler offers suggestions for making colleagues and parents your allies in Chapter 7 of her book *Teaching Reading with YA Literature: Complex Texts, Complex Lives* (2016). One example is to start reading groups for parents or colleagues to familiarize them with YA novels and the depth these stories provide for student learning. James S. Chisholm and Kathryn F. Whitmore, in *Reading Challenging Texts* (2018), talk about how important it is for our students to be exposed to difficult texts, even if those texts have the potential to draw challenges. Penny Kittle has a great way of notifying parents about what she's doing in her class and explains a bit about how she teaches reading and writing in her "Letter to Parents about Reading and Writing" (n.d.). She begins her letter by saying, "A central goal of Writing is to establish a reading habit in the busy lives of seniors in high school." (Kittle, n.d.). She goes on to detail all the methods she'll use to help students develop that reading habit. Get buy-in from stakeholders, or ask yourself what you're willing to risk without it. Jeff Kaplan, former chair of the NCTE Standing Committee against Censorship, spells out how to do this in his blog (2016), listing all the people in the school and community whom we should let know what we're teaching, how, and why. What you say depends on who you're talking to—sometimes you'll be explaining a method, as Kittle does, and sometimes you'll be talking about specific texts.

But even the best laid plans do occasionally go awry.

What to Do When Challenges Arise

If the challenge comes and you need help, contact NCTE through the Intellectual Freedom Center (http://www2.ncte.org/resources/ncte-intellectual-freedom-center/): use the Report a Censorship Challenge form (https://secure.ncte.org/forms/reportcensorship) or email intellectualfreedom@ncte.org.

Although many organizations deal with challenges to reading and writing in schools, they are not all equal in terms of the help and insight they can provide, their methods for doing so, and their understanding of reading and writing in terms of English language arts curriculum and instruction. Many resource books about censorship provide lists of organizations that work with challenges, but they don't do any more than that—leaving a person who needs help with a list to pick from at random.

Chutzpa or not, we at NCTE are the best door for people to walk through when they have a problem. We understand reading and writing in terms of ELA curriculum and instruction. We know and regularly work with all the other First Amendment organizations. We rarely try to solve the problem alone, but work instead with those organizations whose expertise can help.

NCTE bases its responses to challenges on

- procedures—what the district policies say about curriculum, texts, and instruction;
- whether the procedures have been followed;
- the value of the text—we have ready-made, adaptable rationales for hundreds of books and a form to create your own rationale; and most important,
- NCTE beliefs about good curriculum and instruction in English language arts.

We keep private our interactions with teachers who have been challenged unless the challenge is already public knowledge because it's been broadcast in the media. Two examples of public challenges NCTE has worked on are the following:

- When Sissy Lacks was fired from the Ferguson-Florissant School District for letting her students use profanity in their prewriting in her creative writing class, NCTE wrote letters and gave testimony to defend Lacks and the freedom of students to write. Lacks, who continues as an advocate for students' right to write and for teachers, was recognized with many awards, including the NCTE National Intellectual Freedom Award.

- When the state of Virginia tried to insist that teachers label the texts they were teaching with ratings according to sexual content, NCTE wrote statements on the state school board's public comment website and letters to legislators and to the governor. We worked with NCTE's Virginia affiliate to have members send letters of protest to their legislators on more than one occasion. NCTE and Virginia Association of Teachers of English members visited gubernatorial staff. Newspaper op-eds, interviews, and public statements were written and given, and the proposed rating scheme failed.

Many other challenges have remained private because the challenge was between the teacher and the school district.

It would be great if our discussions with parents could all be managed as Heather Anderson describes in her vignette in the "Intervisitations" section earlier in this book, without the text we're teaching being banned. We could listen to parents carefully and attentively; offer them information about the text and why we're teaching it; ask them to think a moment, to back away to take the high view; and after that, state their feelings about the text and about letting their student read it. No promises here, but it is worth a try. And if parents still believe they must challenge the text, we could offer their child an alternative text. Better yet, we might have all students work in groups, each with a different text, with some texts being safer than others from potential challenges.

Often challengers react to parts of a text (e.g., an incident on a certain page of the book, such as the boy-on-boy rape scene early in *The Kite Runner*); to something they don't approve of and don't want their child or any child to read about (such as sexuality in *A Bad Boy Can Be Good for a Girl*, *Beloved*, or *Looking for Alaska*, or magic in the Harry Potter books); or to something they've seen in a movie about the book (Atticus Finch as white savior in the film version of *To Kill a Mockingbird* versus Scout as questioner of the adult behaviors she sees in the book version); or to language in the text (like the use of the *N*-word in *Adventures of Huckleberry Finn* or Lenny's talk in *Of Mice and Men*). It's important to remind challengers that we teach whole texts and not bowdlerized parts, that their children are likely much stronger and wiser than they give them credit for, and that kids need and benefit from books that parents often object to (such as *Eleanor & Park* and *The Hate U Give*). In addition, we often teach controversial materials. In fact, the Supreme Court case *Island Trees Union Free School District v. Pico* (1982), which NCTE joined in amicus curiae, established that minors do have First Amendment rights in schools, including the right to receive information, even controversial information. This means that the philosophy, ideology, or beliefs presented in a text used in class need not agree with the challenger's beliefs (think, for example, of *Persepolis*, *Mexican WhiteBoy*, *Two Boys Kissing*, *The New Jim Crow*) and that students can write on and discuss a wide variety of issues on which there is disagreement. Note the

Monteiro v. Tempe Union High School District decision recognizing the First Amendment right of students to read books selected for their "legitimate educational value" (1988), even if offensive to some parents and students. The blog post *"The Post, the First Amendment, and the Student Press"* (Davis, 2018) focuses on an earlier US Supreme Court decision governing student publications (*Hazelwood v. Kuhlmeier*, 1988) that gives principals the right to censor those publications if they fear the publication will cause disruption in the school or community. NCTE has joined student press organizations in the New Voices Initiative to get states to remove the restrictions of *Hazelwood*. The body of law pertaining to student writing is much less defined than that pertaining to students' right to information. Although the *Hazelwood* ruling speaks to student publications, there are no established rulings on student writing in class. Most states and districts do have rules requiring teachers to report students whose writing is disturbing or threatening.

Despite our efforts, challenges happen. The first step is to keep your head. Then contact the NCTE Intellectual Freedom Center, where you can explain the situation and be heard, ask questions, receive resources, and walk through some possibilities for handling the challenge.

Sometimes we'll want to involve other organizations, including the following:

- **National Coalition Against Censorship (NCAC)** (http://ncac.org/report-censorship-page). NCTE is a member of the coalition. According to its mission statement, NCAC supports the "freedom to explore, the freedom to think, the freedom to create," and through the Kids' Right to Read Project deals with a wide variety of challenges to classroom materials and to student rights. Most challenges result in a letter to the school board—NCTE is often a signatory on these. NCAC also deals with other sorts of challenges, such as the display of artwork in a wide variety of venues and more, and has staff with legal expertise.

- **American Library Association (ALA)** (http://www.ala.org/aboutala/offices/oif). ALA's Office of Intellectual Freedom focuses on challenges to libraries in schools or communities. It produces the annual list of most challenged books and was the initiator of Banned Books Week (http://www.bannedbooksweek.org/ where you can also find resources). It has staff with legal expertise and a nationwide network of librarians who report on challenges in their areas. NCTE works with ALA on library challenges, and ALA occasionally signs onto NCAC letters.

- **Comic Book Legal Defense Fund (CBLDF)** (http://cbldf.org/resources/). CBLDF supports intellectual freedom by making various resources available, specifically working with challenges to comics or graphic novels, and by signing onto letters produced by NCAC. CBLDF is a great resource for information about graphic novels.

- Your local **teachers' union** can help you should the challenge result in a personnel issue such as suspension or accusation of insubordination.

- **American Civil Liberties Union (ACLU)** (https://www.aclu.org/defending-our-rights). The ACLU is a great organization to have on your side if you think your civil liberties have been tampered with. NCTE and NCAC have worked with ACLU in challenge cases that have become political. ACLU staff are quite knowledgeable about personal freedoms and local and state education politics.

- **American Booksellers Foundation for Free Expression** (http://www .bookweb.org/abfe) is a great supporter of free expression in books. They are often signatories on the letters NCAC sends.

- **Authors Guild** (https://www.authorsguild.org/) supports working writers and their works. Authors Guild writes letters in defense of authors' books and often signs onto letters that NCAC sends.

- **Society of Children's Book Writers and Illustrators (SCBWI)** (https:// www.scbwi.org/) supports those individuals writing and illustrating for children and young adults in the fields of children's literature, magazines, film, television, and multimedia. SCBWI writes letters in support of children's book writers and illustrators, and is often a signatory on letters from NCAC.

- **PEN America Children's/ Young Adult Book Authors Committee** (https://pen.org/childrensyoung-adult-book-authors-committee/) supports writers and librarians whose books have been banned or challenged. The committee writes its own letters and commentaries and often signs onto letters from NCAC.

Helpful NCTE Position Statements and Resources

- *The Students' Right to Read* (http://www2.ncte.org/statement/righttoread guideline/)

- *NCTE Beliefs about the Students' Right to Write* (http://www2.ncte.org/state ment/students-right-to-write/)

- *Guidelines for Selection of Materials in English Language Arts Programs* (http:// www2.ncte.org/statement/material-selection-ela/)

- *Resolution on Collecting Rationales for Defending Challenged Works* (https:// ncte.org/statement/rationalesfordefend/)

- *Guidelines for Dealing with Censorship of Instructional Materials* (http://www 2.ncte.org/statement/censorshipofnonprint/)

- *Statement on Classroom Libraries* (http://www2.ncte.org/statement/classroom-libraries/)

- *NCTE Position Statement Regarding Rating or "Red-Flagging" Books* (http:// www2.ncte.org/statement/rating-books/)

- *Statement on Academic Freedom (Revised)* (https://ncte.org/statement/academic-freedom-copy/)

- *Statement on Censorship and Professional Guidelines* (http://www2.ncte.org/ statement/censorshipprofguide/)

A Final Thought from Jen

I love the way that Millie explains so clearly for us the steps we can take to know our district's guidelines for the books we share with students and the writing students share with us. It's also helpful to know where to turn if an issue does arise, especially knowing that NCTE can be a support as we defend students' literacy rights. I'd like to share with you another way you can build a support system for your teaching life. Next I show you how to build and maintain a personal learning network that will give you a community of other educators and organizations also doing the work of supporting students' literacy rights.

From an Experienced Teacher

Developing a PLN That Supports Your Work
Jennifer Ochoa, MS 324, The Patria Mirabel School, New York City

Sitting on my couch, sobbing, I finished reading *The Poet X* by Elizabeth Acevedo (2018). The story, the writing, the humanity in this book got right into my heart. Sitting there, wiping tears and nose, I texted a teacher/sister/reader friend and encouraged her to download the book for her flight to Paris that night. I texted a picture of the cover to a recently graduated eighth grader who loves to read, is Dominican American, and lives in Harlem, just like the main character of the book. I told her she must go to the library today and get the book, and that she should pass it on to several of her classmates, whom I named. Then I thought about how I would shout this book out to my personal learning network (PLN), my online group of teacher and author colleagues. I logged into Goodreads and posted the book to my yearly reading challenge. Because this novel is one of the 2017–2018 Project LIT books, I checked the #ProjectLIT community to see how others were incorporating the novel into their book club plans. I tweeted to the #DisruptTexts community and the #WNDB community and the author explaining that this book was the mirror I had been looking for on my classroom shelves. As I finished this book that my online community had been telling me to read, I could immediately interact in multiple ways with other readers who'd read the book. That reading afterglow I have when I've finished a "heartprint book" (McCarthy, 2013) moved beyond my couch, my living room, and texting my friends, and was shared with people who would understand across the country. That's my PLN in action.

I contrast this kind of in-the-moment-when-it's-needed professional learning to the more structured professional development at my school, a school that—unlike many—has strong and powerful PD. Our after-school PD is focused on restorative justice practices, and our during-school PD, presented through department meetings, guides us through research and readings that we can implement to meet our school-wide instructional focuses. The PD is developed in our school, by our staff, and when we use outside resources, we invite organizations like our local National Writing Project site. We have good PD. We have quality, interesting PD. But we still have PD. We still need to sit, participate, and do what we're asked. We still have to meet in a specific room, at a specific time, for a specific length of time. And like most school-based PD, many of us feel contrary during that time. This is especially true for teachers whose school setting and approaches to PD contradict their own stances and practices as teachers.

If you teach in an environment that does not respect students' rights to read and write, and does not respect your right to teach from your place of truth, how do you support yourself and your own learning? When you want to engage with authors and other educators to share your practice or your reading life, how do you manage those connections? One possible direction is to develop a PLN of people and organizations that support you, your teaching, and your own learning.

A PLN or a PLC?

In education we are famous for throwing around acronyms, a practice that often leaves people who aren't in the know out of the conversation. When I first began developing my own PLN, I also saw the acronym "PLC" in online conversations. I didn't know which I was supposed to use. I'll share with you what I learned about the difference between the two.

As you keep reading this section, you might realize you belong to a professional learning community, or PLC. A professional learning community is an organized community that comes together to do specific work around a specific topic or set of practices. Often a PLC is created by an organization to do work for that organization. Generally, you are invited to be part of a PLC because of your work within the group. Usually, PLCs are created so that a large group of people can engage in specific work across distances. For instance, a few years ago I was asked by my local National Writing Project site to head our site's work with an NWP argument writing initiative called the College-Ready Writers Program (CRWP). As a part of this group, which included teachers from across the country, we met in person a few times but did most of our collective work in a Google+ community designed specifically for this group. Announcements about deadlines and new strategies would go out to the Google group, and project participants shared the work they were doing with the teachers at their NWP sites. This is an example of a PLC. I would not have been a part of this virtual conversation if I hadn't been an invited member of this working group. As a member, I was expected to be present in the group, both as a contributor and as a person using the site to meet deadlines and disseminate information to the local teachers I was leading. Once my participation with this initiative ended, even though the Google+ site is still used and active, I was no longer responsible for continuing to contribute. I still peruse the site, especially if I get notification of a post that piques my interest in terms of my own classroom work, but I'm essentially not utilizing this PLC in my teacher life anymore.

A personal learning network is a much different entity. A PLN is a networked collection of people, places, and spaces that you gather together to fit your own personal professional needs and interests. Mostly, people create a PLN from online sources, especially social media. For people who aren't social media savvy or interested, the concept of developing a strong, supportive network using tools such as Twitter, Facebook, and Instagram might seem overwhelming and unnecessary. However, I'm hoping to help folks who don't have an active PLN think about creating a network that will support you in your own efforts to help kids as readers and writers.

There are a few main components of a typical teacher PLN: Twitter, Facebook, edublogs, and online education information sources like Edutopia and *Education Week*. If you've not joined Twitter, or use Facebook only for personal interactions, thinking about creating and maintaining a PLN can be daunting. The strength of this kind of professional development, though, is that you create and maintain PD as it works for your schedule, needs, and interests. In the next few sections, I introduce some of the possible ways you could begin to develop or add to your PLN so that it reflects the kinds of teaching stances we find in *The Students' Right to Read* and *NCTE Beliefs about the Students' Right to Write* and will give you a supportive community to do this work within, even if you don't find that community in your own school.

Getting Started Building Your PLN

Transitioning or beginning to use your social media spaces as tools in your PLN is actually not complicated. It just takes sitting down at your computer and starting to build and shape your spaces. People mostly use Twitter and Facebook groups as PLN spaces, so building your PLN by following people and groups on Twitter, or sending friend requests or following groups on Facebook, is a good place to begin.

Here are a few suggestions if you're just starting to build your own PLN:

1. Find other educators and teacher leaders you may have interacted with in live spaces like district PD sessions or summer workshops. If you had a connection in person, you might be interested in their educational social media sharing.

2. Check to see if the organizations that you look to the most in your teaching life have an active Twitter account or host a group or page on Facebook. Often, organizations use these spaces to share work being done within the organization, such as face-to-face conferences, online polls, initiatives, and interactive conversations like Twitter chats. Most organizations with active social media accounts also share articles and blogs thought to be of interest to members. For instance, NCTE, ILA, ALA, and NWP all have active Twitter and Facebook accounts that are used to share information and thinking with the public.

3. Find the literacy leaders whose books or articles you've read that really impacted how you think about reading and writing and teaching. Folks who

lead, curate, write about, and shape our literacy landscape are often active or semiactive on social media. Many literacy leaders share their thoughts on the latest developments and conversations in the literacy world, as well as ideas and research they are working on. Also, these are folks who are great at sharing in the form of retweeting and reposting articles and blog posts they come across as they do their own work.

4. Look for authors you love online. In addition to literacy leaders, many children's, middle grade, and young adult literature authors and illustrators are active on social media. While they may not have space to accept more friends on Facebook (this platform limits friends to 5,000), you can certainly like or follow them on Facebook. On Twitter, many authors and illustrators share what they are working on and their thoughts on big issues in the publishing and kidlit communities. Just today on Twitter, at least three authors I follow were hosting giveaways of their latest books to the first ten to twenty-five teachers who responded. Most authors on social media are generous in their interactions with teachers and kids, and following their social media lives is a good way to interact with them. However, understand that expecting authors to do extended, uncompensated work, like a Skype event, with your classes is unreasonable. Remember, writing and working as a writer in educational spaces is their livelihood. You should expect to compensate authors for formal interactions with your classes, as it's part of their job.

5. Think about the publishing companies that publish great professional teacher books and great children's and YA literature. These companies often have active social media accounts that allow teachers to have access to their authors and special events through, for example, sales and giveaways or Facebook Live or Twitter chats with authors. Publishers often advertise new books that are coming out, so you can be current on your own reading lists.

6. Finally, once you've followed several people or organizations (starting with a group of twenty-five to fifty is a good number), check to see who your favorite people themselves follow. In this way, you are expanding your network to folks you might never have known about who will engage you in new thinking.

Shaping your PLN by following people you think might enhance your learning and help you grow as a teacher is not a commitment to actually doing anything other than read what the people you follow post, when you have time and when you're interested. That's the beauty of a PLN: it's a network cultivated by you and used by you when you'd like to use it, nothing more. In fact, there have been months at a time when I take a PLN break, either from busyness or because I want to be more tech-free. At first I felt guilty about this, but then I realized that was ridiculous. My PLN is by me and for me, and if I need a break, I can just pick back up when I'm ready to be active again.

Twitter as Professional Development? Really?

I just scrolled through my Twitter feed from the last ten minutes. Penguin Classroom tweeted out that a picture book I've been waiting for has a book birthday today, and they tagged #classroombookaday, an initiative I follow and a practice I use in my classroom every day. I'll be heading to the bookstore later! NCTE tweeted a blog post by David Kirkland called "Letter to a Young English Teacher" (2013), which I've saved under my bookmarks to use with my first-year teacher graduate students this semester. It will be a good read for them as they begin their teaching careers. My friend Shanay retweeted a tweet in which someone shared a blog post called "8 Black Children's Authors You Should Know" (Boswell, 2012), and I've already read the blog and made notes on my Goodreads page to check out books that I haven't read but need in my classroom library. I also scrolled through past posts on this blog, and several of them will inform my practice. It's called *Black Moms Blog*, moms writing about parenting healthy, fulfilled Black children, the same children who sit in the desks of my classroom. I already signed up to receive posts from this blog so that I can stay connected to ways that the children I teach are flourishing at home. And finally, three people I follow retweeted a link to the *Washington Post* article "Do Children Have a Right to Literacy?" (Balingit, 2018). I also retweeted it, both so I can go back to read it later and because the article's title directly speaks to work I'm doing in my own teaching life. In just a few minutes and a few tweets, I am already a richer and more knowledgeable teacher, and my classroom has been physically and pedagogically impacted. A few minutes on Twitter, and I've already had a good day of PD.

Twitter is sometimes the butt of cultural jokes, has been known to be a space where celebri-

What does it mean to be a lurker?

The term *lurker* doesn't sound favorable, but in the social media sense, it basically means you participate on social media primarily by consuming, not producing. As teachers, we're trained to contribute and constantly help build community. However, on social media, it's perfectly acceptable to simply be a consumer—to lurk—on sites. This means you may read your Facebook or Twitter feed several times during the day, and maybe you even follow links that are interesting, but you don't often post. As you become more familiar and more comfortable in these virtual spaces, sometimes you might feel like sharing your practice with your PLN, but posting is not necessary to have an active life with your PLN. I've had Twitter for nine years, for example, and benefit often from scrolling through my timeline, but as of this morning, I have a mere 1,001 tweets to my name, and that includes times I've retweeted someone else's smart thinking. In the social media sense, being a user who benefits from others' virtual contributions without making many of your own is one way to participate in your PLN. As much as I might not actively post online, however, I do actively use what I learn online in my real life. I might learn a strategy online and try it out in my classroom soon thereafter. I keep a notebook filled with all the book recommendations of my PLN that I want to read, and then I seek out those books from my local bookstore or library. And because I have been learning from so many wise antiracist, antibias educators online, I am actively working to change my way of living in the world.

What is #EduTwitter?

#EduTwitter is the collective network of the educational world sharing and collaborating on Twitter, specifically, and more widely on social media as a whole. It's really just a general hashtag that points to education work being done via social media. Just a quick search on Twitter using the hashtag will show that it's all-inclusive in terms of the kinds of information shared. #EduTwitter is often thrown into a series of hashtags to indicate that a tweet is part of the teaching and learning networks of the Twitter universe. If you begin to cultivate a PLN based on literacy leaders and literature for young people, you will automatically be involved in #EduTwitter.

What is #kidlit?

#Kidlit is the social media community involved with the writing, illustrating, publishing, reading, and sharing of children's, middle grade, and young adult literature. This hashtag is more commonly used than #EduTwitter to tag tweets and other social media posts. A quick search of the hashtag will garner many relevant current posts pertaining to books and kids. Children's authors and illustrators regularly post using this hashtag, but teachers and librarians do too. If you are looking for ways to increase your book knowledge for your classroom library, or you're trying to read more widely for diversity on your shelves, searching this hashtag is a good place to begin.

ties share pithy opinions and bits of their lives, and has been used controversially as a political soapbox by the highest-level officials. And despite all this, Twitter remains a mainstay in the education community as a means of interesting, thoughtful, timely professional development as a part of teachers' PLNs. If you ask an educator with an active PLN if they use Twitter often, they most likely will answer resoundingly, "YES!" You might be skeptical about beginning to use Twitter as a means of professional development because of its negative associations and because tweets are confined by character limitations, making it feel impossible to say all you have to say. However, if you're beginning a PLN, Twitter is an excellent starting point, mostly because you don't have to request friends, you just follow folks, and because Twitter also offers a good amount of rich professional development within the #EduTwitter and #kidlit communities.

How Does Twitter Work? A Primer

Basically, Twitter requires that you create an account, which includes creating a Twitter handle. Your Twitter handle is designated with @ and then whatever handle you choose. (For instance, mine is @ochoajen.) Your Twitter handle is how your tweets are announced to others, and is also used to "tweet at" or tag someone else on Twitter. For example, when I wanted to tag the author of *The Poet X*, Elizabeth Acevedo, in a tweet after reading her book, I started my tweet with @AcevedoWrites, her Twitter handle, so that she would see the tweet.

Tweets used to be limited to 140 characters, which also includes the spaces and any Twitter handles or hashtags you use (more on hashtags in the next section). But in late 2017, the company expanded the tweet limitation to 280 characters, offering people more space to say what's on their minds.

Gathering a PLN on Twitter is quite simple: just search for the person, organization, or business you want to follow, and then follow them. If you begin following twenty-five to fifty Twitter handles, you'll quickly see interesting and informative content in your Twitter feed. Often your feed brings you to more interesting handles to follow, broadening your PLN and the professional learning Twitter offers you. If you see something on your feed you like, simply click the heart button to like the tweet. You can pass the tweet along to others by clicking on the retweet button. In this way, you can start to add your voice to the #EduTwitter community, even if you don't feel comfortable tweeting your own thoughts.

How Can You Make Twitter Work for You?

Nine years ago, when my friends Franki Sibberson and Shelbie Witte encouraged me to join Twitter, I laughed. What a ridiculous notion! What's ironic about me encouraging *you* to use social media as a means of professional development is that I am terrible with technology. I'm not a techie at all. I need the kids to help me turn on the Smartboard, and if I want to switch from the document camera to the internet on the computer linked to the Smartboard, I panic and text my teaching partner for assistance. So Franki and Shelbie saying I would love Twitter was more than humorous. But the two convinced me that I could craft my Twitter account to work for me and I would end up loving it. In the ensuing years, I have actually developed a Twitter account that feeds my teaching and learning life. I don't follow celebrities, with the exception of a few who tweet about politics, such as George Takei and Ava Duvernay. I just scrolled through those I do follow, and the majority are fellow teachers and librarians, publishing companies and authors, and organizations associated with the literacy education field, especially those engaging in antibias-antiracist teaching and learning practices. In this way, what comes across my Twitter feed is already curated to support me as a learner in the areas I'm most interested in. I use Twitter in very specific ways that feel manageable and engaging, and you might use Twitter in these ways too:

1. *Curating online reading.* I don't have time to do deep delves into news media and educational blogs that may help me grow as a teacher. I use Twitter specifically for that. When the state of New York was in the middle of a huge standardized testing fight, and the whole country was reeling while trying to align with the Common Core State Standards, I was happy that I followed Diane Ravitch. Ravitch daily tweeted out links to articles that kept me informed on the debates affecting my teaching. I also follow many political activists who tweet out articles as well as videos I'm interested in learning from so I can take current events into my classroom to discuss with students. Using Twitter as my curation system narrows down what I'll be interested in reading without me having to do that searching myself.

2. *Educational debates.* Twitter is a place where people throw questions into the wind for folks to pick up and run with. It is a place where many in our field engage in rigorous debates about important topics. These debates often end up changing practices in classrooms, making our classrooms places where kids can read and write more freely. Recently, for example, the debate about choosing books for kids to read that are not just representing diverse experiences of humanity, but also written by authors who share the same background as their characters cropped up on Twitter. This debate, gathered around the hashtag #ownvoices, is an entire network of teachers, librarians, and writers engaged in talking about representation and authenticity in the literature we share with children. Within this debate, many people share titles and authors who represent a point of view in their writing coming from their own experiences. From following these Twitter conversations for a few months, I am now able to stock the shelves in my classroom with books that are true mirrors for the kids I teach. I've even been able to pull up a Twitter thread from an author, allowing kids to hear an author's perspective directly.

3. *Excellent graphics.* Twitter is the go-to place for graphics I can share to enhance my classroom work. I've shared with my classes graphics that include information about how many minutes of reading a day helps readers increase their vocabulary. With the restorative justice team at my school, I shared a Google Doc that one of the authors of *Kids First from Day One*, Christine Hertz, tweeted about the common practices teachers use in the classroom and what those practices might be saying about what teachers believe. And finally, I will be using the ideas in a graphic tweeted by Alex Corbitt that he found from @4OClockFaculty titled "5 Ways to Incorporate Movement in the Classroom."

4. *Live tweeting from events.* I do love going to conferences and other in-person professional development events, but many people find the travel and conference fee costs prohibitive, making attendance to more than one or more events a year unlikely. Others aren't able to travel to conferences because schools won't pay for substitute teachers, or because they have obligations to be home, or because their busy schedules make travel difficult. If there's an in-person event I'm really interested in attending but can't for any number of reasons, I immediately know I need to find out the hashtag the event is using and begin following that hashtag. Nowadays, lots of people live tweet from events like conferences. Those events create a unique hashtag so that attendees can share their experiences and learning with folks who couldn't attend. People tweet quotes from presenters, pictures of presenters' slides and links to slideshows and other materials that presenters share. Presenters are aware that this is happening and often live tweet themselves when they are attending other sessions. While following an event via Twitter is not the same as attending, you will gain loads of good information from what other people share.

5. *Twitter chats.* You may have heard someone say they participated in a Twitter chat and wondered what that is and how people could chat with such limited

character space. A Twitter chat is a live event, happening in real time using Twitter as the platform. A Twitter chat is organized around a unique hashtag and is often scheduled on a recurring day and time. This kind of recurring Twitter chat is generally associated with a bigger idea, like #TitleTalk, which has been hosted by Donalyn Miller and Colby Sharp, focused around independent reading with kids and children's literature. Sometimes a recurring Twitter chat is hosted by an organization, like #NCTEchat, which has a different focus every time but is ELA teaching related. Other Twitter chats are one-time events, often associated with a new professional book. For instance, Kylene Beers and Bob Probst have hosted Twitter chats about *Notice and Note*, *Reading Nonfiction*, and *Disrupting Thinking*. The author of the book is not always the host of the chat; sometimes one or two really interested teachers who've loved reading the book host the chat and invite the authors to participate. Twitter chats are generally fast moving and can feel frustrating for those of us who need more time to think and faster fingers to type; however, most hosts archive the chat on another platform and share the link. In this way, you can go back to read people's comments at your leisure. In my experience, Twitter chats contain a gold mine of good ideas, and even if I read only a handful of participant comments, I always come away with strategies and resources I can use in my classroom.

How does a Twitter chat work?

- Twitter chats are usually organized in a Q&A format. The hosts welcome people at the beginning of the chat and then tweet out Q1, which is the first question.

- Participants then tweet out answers by labeling their tweets A1, to correspond to the question they are answering.

- You always need to include the unique hashtag belonging to that chat with each of your answers so that your tweets are collected with all the others in the chat.

- A new question comes about every six minutes. Twitter chats are generally an hour long, with six to ten questions.

- You can keep answering previous questions all through the chat, as long as you label them with the correct answer number.

- You can participate by lurking only, especially if you don't feel comfortable answering questions. You'll still have a rich experience if you do this.

- There are platforms such as Twubs, TweetChat, and TweetDeck that help you more easily participate in the Twitter chat by allowing you to follow and respond only to that unique hashtag.

- Twitter chats are not for everyone. They are fast moving, and you might feel as though you're missing something—and in all likelihood, you are. But they are also an excellent form of PD, and with the ability to reread the conversation later, you might be willing to try one. It took me several Twitter chats to really feel comfortable in the format, but now I look forward to them.

From Alex Corbitt: Using Twitter as PD

I was at NCTE's 2014 Annual Convention when I first learned the importance of Twitter. I noticed educators tweeting their thoughts about sessions, posting resources they gathered, and offering peers advice. If session panelists ran low on time, they would tweet a link to their entire presentation so audiences wouldn't miss out. Twitter seemed like a teacher's lounge of the internet: a place for educators to connect, inform, and support one another.

I went through some postconvention "withdrawal" when I returned home. I felt like I still had so much more to learn and discuss. Turning to Twitter again, I saw that the conversations started at the convention had only just begun! Ideas, resources, and suggestions are shared and refined on Twitter 365 days a year. I began participating in Twitter chats, and I was endlessly inspired by the optimism, determination, and innovation of my colleagues around the world. There are many times throughout the school year when I'm tired and frustrated, almost defeated by the challenges that teaching poses. In these moments, I lean heavily on the Twitter community, finding strength in everyone's deep knowledge and support of other educators.

Over the years, Twitter has helped me forge many friendships and collaborations with educators around the world. For example, I connected with a teacher in Norway and codeveloped a digital project that allowed our students to write and revise narratives together. It was a powerful learning experience for everyone involved. I also use my Twitter feed to curate helpful resources and ideas for educators. Curating resources allows me to shout out the brilliant thinking of my colleagues while humbly adding a few practices of my own.

Twitter continues to shape my teaching practice. It will always be a space where I find camaraderie, support, and inspiration.

Even though jumping into Twitter if you've been a resister might seem overwhelming, I can't stress enough how much I learn from my PLN on Twitter. My Twitter PD has changed my pedagogy and has helped me critique the equity and decolonization work I do with kids in my classroom, as well as in my own life outside of school. When I think about immersing myself in the work of helping students fully realize their rights to read and write, I think of Twitter as the place to find resources to do that work most intentionally.

Hashtags: How Social Media Collects Ideas

In the Twitter section above, we talked a bit about hashtags (#) and a few hashtags you might follow as you build your PLN. When I was new to building my PLN, I knew that hashtags were about ideas, but I didn't really understand the difference between a made-up hashtag to prove a point—for instance, today, texting about our eighth-grade classes with my teaching partner, I used #justsitdown sarcastically because weirder than normal wandering is happening often during class—and an official hashtag everyone uses to indicate that the comment should be collected with other comments in the same conversation. Basically, in the social media world, hashtags are a means of sorting people's posts around specific ideas, concepts, or communities. People generally include a hashtag on their social media posts to show that this post should be included in a bigger virtual conversation. Hashtags are used on all forms of social media, and often they cross-reference posts.

In the education PLN sphere, hashtags tend to collect in a few specific ways: around concepts and communities; around particular practices or movements; and around specific events, such as conferences or PD activities. I explain in the following sections a few examples of active social media hashtags you might encounter and follow.

Hashtags for Concepts and Communities

Many times folks develop a hashtag around a concept that's currently being discussed or shared. We've already heard about a couple so far in this book that will help you curate your library so that kids can read more freely and more diversely. People use #ownvoices to indicate that the author of a book is part of the community the book is written about. This hashtag was actually suggested by a young adult author, Corinne Duyvis, in a tweet in 2015, to delineate books written by authors who identified as part of a particular community. Ellen Oh, from the organization We Need Diverse Books, shared with us earlier that #WNDB indicates conversations emphasizing the idea that books and authors need to be written by and about people from marginalized communities.

Likewise, many professional communities use their own hashtags to follow ideas from that community. Teachers College Reading and Writing Project uses #TCRWP, NCTE uses #NCTE, International Literacy Association uses #ILA, and the National Writing Project uses #NWP. Often within these groups, other hashtags are used; for instance, my own Writing Project site uses #NYCWP.

Other kinds of organized communities also use hashtags to share ideas. The community of children's literature, from authors and illustrators to publishers to teachers and librarians, uses #kidlit to channel posts within this literature community. José Luis Vilson, a New York City teacher, founded EduColor, a collective of educators and scholars of color doing important antiracist activist work within education. Like other communities, members of EduColor use a unique hashtag to collect posts about the work they're doing. They can be found at #EduColor, and following this hashtag will help you think deeply about ways you can truly teach literacy within students' rights as literate people. While the #EduColor movement has its own formal Twitter handle and website, people in the #EduTwitter community posting about issues of race and equity in education often use #EduColor as well to link ideas and people and writing that support or connect to the movement.

Hashtags for Particular Practices and Movements

The #MeToo movement is perhaps one of the most famous hashtags recently developed around a movement, but in the #EduTwitter world, similar movement hashtags abound. The authors who created #WNDB took their frustration about the lack of diversity in the publishing of children's literature and created a hashtag to voice that frustration. The hashtag turned into an organization and a movement that is changing the face of children's literature. Often, though, hashtags used in the education realm around a movement or a practice have more immediate impacts on classrooms. One such hashtag is #AmWriting. Many folks in my PLN who are working on their own writing practices use this hashtag to indicate they have their butts in chairs and they are composing, even if it feels difficult. I've shared this hashtag with the kids in my classroom, and now we use it on days where the work we're doing is developing our writing practices. Another hashtag I follow that has had an impact on my classroom is #classroombookaday. This practice and its subsequent hashtag were developed by Jillian Heise, a teacher-librarian in Wisconsin. Several years ago, as a middle school teacher, Heise made it her goal to read a picture book every school day in her eighth-grade classes. To keep herself honest, she began posting the daily picture books in her classroom on a bulletin board with spaces for 180 book covers. She also shared her daily classroom read-alouds on Twitter and on her blog, *Heise Reads & Recommends*. She now writes and presents on the practice, and she hosts a Facebook group specifically geared for teachers who are using the practice of reading a picture book a day in their own classrooms. As a teacher who follows the practice and is a member of the Facebook group, I actively search for #classroombookaday posts on social media looking for picture books I may have missed that I want to share in my classroom.

I've also recently joined a movement started by teacher Jared Amato in Nashville, Tennessee. Amato began a grassroots movement with his high school students focused on getting more diverse, highly engaging books into middle and high school classrooms around the country. The idea was that a teacher would start a ProjectLIT chapter in their school and then connect with other ProjectLIT leaders around the country using #ProjectLITBookClub. Teachers who are leading a ProjectLIT chapter host book events in their schools and communities around a yearly set of current book titles that fit the #ownvoices and #WNDB categories. If you are just beginning to shift your shelves to include more diverse stories, following this hashtag will give you an immediate set of titles to include in your library, as well as a community of several hundred teachers doing this work in their own classrooms.

Unique Hashtags for Specific Events and Conferences

As I mentioned above, because many people can't attend professional conferences, these events generally develop a unique hashtag that folks can use to post from the event or to follow the event in real time. Often that hashtag is the acronym of the organization and the year. For instance, last year's NCTE convention used #NCTE19, and last summer, ILA used #ILA19 for their conference. In fact, most education PD has a unique hashtag you can follow. Scholastic is a good example of this: they asked people to use #ReadingSummit and then tweet @Scholastic so that folks could follow all the Reading Summits during the summer months. Likewise, smaller events might have a unique hashtag. Heinemann's Boothbay Literacy Retreat, which takes place every summer in Boothbay, Maine, and features Bob Probst, Kylene Beers, and other Heinemann authors such as Penny Kittle and Linda Rief, always uses #boothbayliteracy and adds the year. It's well known, but very small, so teachers who can't attend love to follow participants' posts.

While people use unique hashtags for live events, virtual events also host hashtags that participants can follow over social media. In September, children's author Peter H. Reynolds hosts International Dot Day, which celebrates creativity and courage by asking kids around the world to "make their mark," like the characters in his picture book *The Dot.* The event asks people to share their creative dot efforts at #dotday or #makeyourmark. Scholastic and LitWorld host World Read Aloud Day every winter and ask people to share their global celebrations of reading at #WorldReadAloudDay or #WRAD. And on October 20 every year, NCTE hosts the National Day on Writing and asks people to post using #WhyIWrite. All of these efforts, and so many more, are ways that you can connect with other teachers and authors, and will provide your students with a wide audience to share their writing and creating and reading and thinking. A hashtag not only connects you to like-minded teachers, but it also gives the writers and readers in your classes audiences beyond your classroom, helping them authentically interact with other readers and writers around the country and across the globe.

Facebook Can Be More Than Just Vacation Photos and Funny Memes

I love Facebook for checking out the people I went to high school with, tracking their triumphs and daily lives. I love connecting with my cousins who live far from me, and my greatest Facebook joy is connecting with people who were my students years and years ago, now adults with children of their own. But I also use Facebook regularly as part of my PLN.

First, I have become Facebook friends with many people I know only from my PLN. While I may have "met" them on Twitter, I am happy to know them on Facebook, a space where people can share with more depth than the space limitations of Twitter allow. I adore sharing the excitement and sometimes misery of being a teacher in our country right now. But I also use Facebook as a PLN space much more pointedly through Facebook groups. Facebook groups can be created by anyone and always have one or more moderators monitoring the group's inter-actions. Many Facebook groups are closed and require you to request joining the group. Generally, requests are quickly and easily granted by the moderators.

As part of your PLN, you might consider joining a few specific groups that will support the work you do in your classroom promoting students' rights to read and write.

First, as mentioned above, if you are interested in learning more about #classroombookaday from Jillian Heise and those who use this practice in their classrooms, request to join this group. To join the group, you need to answer a few simple questions, mostly about how you intend to use the practice in your classroom. Heise asks potential group members to answer these questions because she'd like to keep the content of the page fully focused on this particular prac-tice. Another group you might consider joining is the Notice and Note Facebook group. Started several years ago by teachers Allison Jackson and Shannon Dean Clark, this group began as a focus on the reading strategies Kylene Beers and Bob Probst present in *Notice and Note: Strategies for Close Reading* (2013). The group has since grown to more than 30,000 members who share a plethora of literacy-based questions and strategies with one another. Just reading the posts and comments on this page for an hour is a good day of professional development for any level of literacy educator.

In addition to joining literacy-based education groups, many people follow or request to friend literacy leaders and children's book authors on Facebook. These folks often post about aspects of their work or research and their thinking on education subjects. They are also generally happy to answer questions from teachers. And, in a classroom, being able to share a bit about the personal life of favorite authors with kids is a big hit. Once, as we were reading *Brown Girl Dream-ing* together, the kids in my class got very worried about Jacqueline Woodson's younger brother, who is described in the book as having lead poisoning. With issues of lead poisoning in the news, the kids knew it was a dangerous condition. I told them I was Facebook friends with Woodson, and I earned instant eighth-grade credibility. They asked me to look up her brother, and we did. We were happy and relieved to know that he looks like a healthy, successful businessman. Facebook comes in handy in the middle school classroom! One point to remember, however, as I mentioned earlier, is that Facebook limits friends to 5,000. Recently, several literacy leaders and authors were lamenting that they couldn't accept any more friend requests because they had reached their limits. If you request a literacy favorite as a friend and they don't accept, don't despair—they may not be able to. You can simply follow that person, and you'll be able to view their public posts.

Following people is, of course, interesting and informative, but following our main professional organizations is helpful for learning important information about the organizations' upcoming events and work in progress. In this way, I closely follow the NCTE, NWP, and ILA Facebook pages. All are informative and helpful as I plan conferences and Twitter chats and look forward to the journals and blog posts each organization produces.

Finally, as you follow our literacy leaders, many have begun using Facebook Live as a way to do a quick in-person PD event. I've "attended" Facebook Live events with Kylene Beers and Bob Probst, Cornelius Minor, Donalyn Miller, Gholdy Muhammad, and the Education for Liberation Network. Some were quick, fifteen to twenty minutes, but some were full hour-long learning sessions.

Even though most of my PLN professional development work occurs on Twitter, I don't discount my Facebook connections for supporting my teaching work and helping me grow in my classroom.

A Few More Adds to Your PLN

While Twitter and Facebook make up much of my PLN activity, I do have a few other spaces that fill out my network. First, I follow a few select blogs that keep me in the children's literature loop. If you haven't yet followed the *Nerdy Book Club* blog, do so immediately. It's a collective blog started by teachers Donalyn Miller, Colby Sharp, Katherine Sokolowski, and Cindy Minnich in 2011. Focused on reading with kids and reading books written for kids, this space is the ultimate #kidlit bookfest. The blog comes out several times a week, and the moderators invite authors, illustrators, teachers, librarians, and parents to be bloggers on the site. Every December the Nerdy Book Club site hosts its own community awards program called the Nerdy Book Awards, or the Nerdies. Nerdy book lovers in the community look forward to adding their favorite books from the year as possible contenders. The Nerdies provide excellent lists of current books at all levels that kidlit readers adore. The Nerdy Book Club has also blossomed into a Twitter chat, a podcast, and an in-person celebration of children's literature every summer called nErDcamp. This event originated in Colby Sharp's school district, and now there are many nErDcamp events around the country. I encourage you to look for one near you to share in the book joy.

In the last few years, I have been inspired by the work of my PLN to deeply examine my practice toward always teaching from an antiracist, antibias stance. As I work to learn and grow in my knowledge and the revision of the knowledge base I previously held, I count on the work and writing, often in the form of blogs and Twitter threads, of the folks in my PLN. I am especially grateful to the work of educators and scholars of color who are using social media as one vehicle through which to have important and challenging conversations and share their own work and the work of others. By following not only #EduColor, but also the #DisruptTexts community, created and sustained by teachers Tricia Ebarvia, Lorena Germán, Kim Parker, and Julia E. Torres, I have been able to carefully critique my classroom practice with the support of others who are also doing the work and leading with examples from their own classrooms. The way in which I think about the books I share with kids and the structures I maintain in my lesson planning, classroom management, and writing work have all changed due to the work many teachers share as they too teach from a stance of equity and justice.

I receive daily posts from many of these blogs and on Twitter that help me both curate my classroom shelves and connect with authors and other adults who love reading with kids. And I'm in connection with people who teach me to revise and transform my practice so that the reading and writing we do in my classroom not only honors the rights of all the kids I teach, but also honors all the kids I teach as human beings. My PLN is the place that has truly supported my continued growth as an educator who seeks to dismantle the systems of oppression on which school has been built. If you also are seeking to do this work, please reread the resource suggestions Kristin McIlhagga offers on page 106, and check out resources I include in my PLN that I suggest in the annotated bibliography on pages 158–60.

A Final Word . . .

Developing a PLN that supports the work you do in your classroom helps you feel more connected, even when the work you're doing is outside of the PD focus of your school. Your PLN can support your growth as you try new strategies to help the kids in your classroom develop as writers and have wider audiences to share their work. Your PLN can give you incredible ideas for books to share in your classroom and connect you with other kid reading communities reading the same books, as well as authors you or your students might want to chat with. As you shape your classroom around students' explicit rights to be seen and treated as authentic readers and writers, your PLN can help inform that philosophy, and also connect you with other teachers who are doing this same work. Throughout writing this book, as I perused my PLN, I daily found teachers asking and answering questions, giving recommendations, engaging in debates, offering learning opportunities for other teachers and for kids, sharing practices, collaborating between classrooms, forming working groups, publishing kids' real writing, and responding to books. Every day I encountered multiple examples of teachers living out the stances advocated in NCTE's policy statements, and then sharing their work and their inquiry for others to experience and join. As you work to shape your classroom around *The Students' Right to Read* and *NCTE Beliefs about the Students' Right to Write*, the social media spaces you might include in your own PLN can support your growth.

Afterword:
A Call to Action

Please remember that the kids in our middle school classrooms are already readers and writers. They are thinkers and idea followers. They are composers and creators and makers. They are poets and book critics and analyzers and try-outters and start-overers. They abandon and revise and redo when what they've imagined isn't working. They fall deeply into stories, both those written for them and those they write themselves. They passionately argue for their beliefs, and they are interested in learning new ideas. They question and, yes, they sometimes get stuck on one way of doing or thinking. They are humorists, both in writing and in speaking. They are loyalists to their causes, and to the series, characters, and authors they love. In general, middle schoolers are interesting, creative, thoughtful people. And they are students.

Unfortunately, the systems of school often don't honor all that our students are as people in the world. And often, school makes students feel as though all they are *is* students. I'm thinking back to the 1939 seventh-grade day in my father-in-law's classroom that I shared at the beginning of this book. That day, the substitute teacher treated the kids in Stan's class not as students, but as

reporters and newspaper editors. That teacher broke away from the typical structure of school by asking the kids to act as the writers and readers they already were.
As English language arts teachers, thank goodness we have *The Students' Right
to Read* and *NCTE Beliefs about the Students' Right to Write* to guide us, especially
when these rights are being challenged or ignored by the systems of school. When
we are worried that we have to change how we've always taught writing to fit new
standards or mandates, we can remember how Shelly Unsicker-Durham revised
the requirement to teach text-based modes of writing to include the essence of
honoring student voice and interest, something she had always done as a writing
teacher. When we are asked to incorporate reading workshop into our classroom
structures, but we have kids in our classes who don't choose to read, say they hate
reading, have language processing structures in their brains that make reading feel
difficult, or who have just moved to the United States and don't yet fluently read
in English, we can remember Carole Mashamesh and Chad Everett and Ellen Oh.
We can revisit their classrooms and literary work to think about how to organize
our classroom libraries, our classroom reading time, and our classroom reading
conversations so that we have authentic spaces and rich chats with kids as they
grow their reading lives. If we're wondering how to plan a whole-class novel unit
that honors students' rights to read and think deeply about the ideas in books, and
then take those ideas into the world to change the world for the better, we just
need to use April Fulstone and Heather Anderson as mentors to guide our unit
planning. If we know that our kids are writing important ideas about important
aspects of the world they live in, understanding that those ideas should be shared
beyond our classroom walls, we can remember Alex Corbitt and imagine his Teen
Activism students running through the hallways before school, stuffing lockers
with their anonymous writing, knowing that as journalists, their words would be
taken seriously by their readers. And if we have a reliable classroom practice that
suddenly stops motivating the writers and readers in our classroom, we can turn to
Linda Rief to help us think about how to reflect on our practice and change those
practices so that they meet the students and tools in our classrooms. As we do all
of this work, we can continue to be supported by the sharing of those in our PLN.
We can add their suggestions to our own to-be-read piles, and we can use the ideas
they share in Twitter chats in our own classrooms. We can ask for suggestions
about how to revise our teaching to incorporate our new knowledge as we work to
make our classrooms spaces of antiracist, antibias thinking, systems, and behaviors.
We can reach out across virtual space and feel like we are not alone in the ELA
work we do that most honors students' rights as readers and writers.

    In June 2015, I attended the Boothbay Literacy Institute in Boothbay, Maine,
facilitated by Kylene Beers and Bob Probst. For many ELA teachers, this opportu-

nity is a goal and a dream. For me, driving to the beautiful conference center right on the water of Boothbay Harbor felt like a true gift to my teaching career. The first night, Bob and Kylene asked us all to engage in a table project that examined our areas of influence. They asked each table to draw on giant chart paper a huge dart board–like shape consisting of three concentric rings and a bull's-eye. For the outermost ring, Bob and Kylene asked us to brainstorm together and to fill it up with all the most pressing influences on our classroom work that were "way out there." Things like federal educational policy, which at the time included Race to the Top and Common Core State Standards; standardized state tests; and historical structures of race and poverty that influenced our teaching filled up the ring at my table. For the next ring, they asked that we name the influences from our homes, our students' homes, and communities that impacted our daily work as teachers. My table listed the socioeconomic statuses that prevailed in our teaching communities, as well as levels of liberal or conservative thinking that shaped community practices and behaviors. In the third ring, Bob and Kylene asked us to describe school policies, structures, and personnel that either shaped or hindered our teaching lives. You can probably imagine what went into that venting conversation and the subsequent notes that we added to our chart. In good form, Bob and Kylene had saved the best, and probably the hardest, for last. In the bull's-eye, they asked us each to list what we actually had the influence, ability, autonomy, and agency to fix.

Whew. Right. In our classrooms, we are the gatekeepers. We make daily huge and tiny decisions that either move forward outside agendas, mitigate outside agendas, or protect kids from outside agendas. Thinking about that bull's-eye, I imagined myself standing in front of my classroom door with my arms outstretched, protecting all the kids behind the door I stood in front of who were inside waiting to see what we would read and write and talk about together. What do I let through the door of my classroom? How do I take directives that might be harmful to students' literacy development and bat them away, or at the very least revise and shape them enough that the "way out there" or "right in our school" influences don't become toxic to authentic reading and writing? How do I amplify and share the reading and writing that the middle schooolers in my classroom do so that outside audiences take them seriously? How do I protect the rights my students have as readers and writers and literate beings so that they can fully flourish in all these areas of humanity?

I'm glad that as an organization, NCTE has given all of us these two policy statements to help guide and support classroom work when it may be challenged. The teachers whose classrooms we've visited in this book provide examples of ways you too can ensure that literacy rights are honored in your classroom. And as parting words, I encourage you, as you talk with and listen to, analyze and compose with, plan for and plan with the students in your classrooms, to always remember that they are all already readers and writers. Imagine your own bull's-eye and fill it with all the ways you can think of to honor and support those rights. And then go teach with your bull's-eye in mind.

Annotated Bibliography

Throughout my career, I have sought the support of professional resources in the form of books and journals, websites, social media, blogs, and personal interactions with other teachers and literacy leaders. I love talking with other teachers and gathering lists of titles and online spaces that they find valuable. In that spirit of teacher sharing, below I offer some of the resources I've found helpful in my own teaching life. Some of these resources are well-known classics and some are more recently published and might be new to you. The subjects of workshop classrooms, choice reading, and students as writers are all hefty topics, with shelves of professional texts available for teachers to turn to as guides. These are pieces I've found especially helpful, fully acknowledging there are so many more resources I've left off this list that are also rich and supportive of teachers' classroom work.

Favorite Titles from Reading-Writing Workshop Leaders

Atwell, Nancie
In the Middle: A Lifetime of Learning about Writing, Reading and Adolescents
3rd ed. Heinemann, 2015

Since the purchase of my first copy of *In the Middle* for an undergrad ELA teaching methods class in 1990, Atwell's work has been a touchstone for me. In 2015, she issued the third edition of this book, which has been deeply revised for teaching in the twenty-first century. Her practical writing style helps teachers seeking to set up a traditional reading-writing workshop. She offers examples of her procedures and provides the documents that accompany those procedures. The book is also filled with examples from her own work as a middle school teacher.

Other titles by Atwell I've found useful include the following:

- *Lessons That Change Writers*. Heinemann, 2002.
- *Naming the World: A Year of Poems and Lessons*. Heinemann, 2005.
- *The Reading Zone: How to Help Kids Become Passionate, Skilled, Habitual, Critical Readers*. 2nd ed. (with Anne Atwell Merkel), Scholastic, 2016.

Minor, Cornelius
We Got This.: Equity, Access, and the Quest to Be Who Our Students Need Us to Be
Heinemann, 2018

While this book is not specifically about workshop teaching, it has been a book I've turned to continually since its publication. Because I am actively trying to teach in the most equitable and just way and to provide a classroom space that is constantly dismantling systemic oppression, I have used this book repeatedly to revise common practices I use. Minor gives us thoughtful ways to interrogate our own classrooms and then provides language and strategies to rebuild what needs to change after examination. If you are trying to teach with equity and justice, you need this book.

Rief, Linda
Read, Write, Teach: Choice and Challenge in the Reading-Writing Workshop
Heinemann, 2014

When I think about books to hand to teachers new to workshop teaching, this is one of them. Rief offers us all the ways to get started with creating a reading-writing workshop classroom. She begins by building the kind of classroom community that encourages middle school kids to work deeply and seriously on becoming passionate readers and thoughtful writers. I use *Read, Write, Teach* in my own Methods of Teaching Secondary English course. The new and preservice teachers taking the course often cite Rief's book as their starting point for imagining their own classrooms. I was grateful that she offered to write a vignette from her teaching life in this book. For a fuller picture of Linda's classroom reading, *Read, Write, Teach* will be immensely helpful.

Other titles by Rief I've found useful include the following:

- *The Quickwrite Handbook: 100 Mentor Texts to Jumpstart Your Students' Thinking and Writing.* Heinemann, 2018.
- *Inside the Writer's-Reader's Notebook: A Workshop Essential.* Heinemann, 2007.
- *Adolescent Literacy: From Promise to Practice.* (Edited with Kylene G. Beers and Robert E. Probst), Heinemann, 2007.
- *Seeking Diversity: Language Arts with Adolescents.* Heinemann, 1991.

Favorite Titles That Support Shifting Your Shelves and Choice Reading

Beers, Kylene G., and Robert E. Probst
Disrupting Thinking: Why How We Read Matters
Scholastic, 2017

In this age of misinformation and often a lack of empathy for those different from ourselves, Beers and Probst offer us this book that gives us a way to help kids become responsive, responsible, and compassionate readers. They posit a framework called "Book, Head, Heart" that moves kids from reading closely simply to critique and answer questions toward reading to understand the story, feel compassion for the people in the story, and then think about how they might move beyond the story to create change in the world.

Cherry-Paul, Sonja, and Dana Johansen
Breathing New Life into Book Clubs: A Practical Guide for Teachers
Heinemann, 2019

As a middle school teacher who had not implemented book clubs in many years because the

chaos and tracking of roles and scheduling was too overwhelming, I was delighted with this new handbook. Cherry-Paul and Johansen offer a structure for classroom book clubs that not only honors the exuberance of middle schoolers, but also mirrors more closely the authentic reading communities of adult book clubs. At the end of each chapter, the authors give us several mini-lessons that support the aspects of book clubs discussed in that chapter. This school year, we have restarted book clubs using this book as our guide, and we have a buzzing classroom filled with passionate eighth-grade readers.

Crowder, S. Travis
Reflective Readers: The Power of Reader's Notebooks
Benchmark Education, 2020

When I think of choice reading, I don't immediately think about how I'd like kids to respond to what they've read. In fact, I think about all the ways I *don't* want them to respond to what they read for pleasure. Crowder gives us beautiful and authentic ways the readers in his middle school classroom reflect on the books they are reading. He explains the structures in his reading workshop, explores the differences between asking kids to reflect on instead of just responding to what they are reading, and then moves us into helping kids create and keep reflective reading notebooks. The book is filled with excellent tips for management and strategies immediately useful in your classroom. I love that Crowder also asks the teachers reading his book to stop to reflect and take notes as they think about implementing these ideas.

Miller, Donalyn, and Susan Kelley
Reading in the Wild: The Book Whisperer's Keys to Cultivating Lifelong Reading Habits
Jossy-Bass, 2014

This is the follow-up to Miller's wildly popular 2009 *The Book Whisperer* and is based on the five key habits self-reported "wild readers" do to cultivate their reading lives. Miller and Kelley surveyed several hundred people who consider themselves avid readers. Survey results showed that respondents had several habits in common, and those habits form the structure of the rest of the book. The authors explain how to use those wild-reader habits to form the basis of a reading workshop. The book is practical and engaging and is a must-read for any teacher who wants to begin reading workshops or revise current workshop structures.

Miller, Donalyn and Colby Sharp
Game Changer! Book Access for ALL Kids
Scholastic, 2018

All kids need books in their lives. Lots of books. Books everywhere. And people who love to read and share books with them. And time to read those books and fall in love with reading. It's basic. But this isn't a certainty for many kids in our country. This book discusses the inequities in book access for kids in US schools and suggests what we can do about attacking the inequities at their roots. *Game Changer!* is a lively call to action and a practical handbook for acquiring books that kids want to read—those that mirror their identities and their daily lives. I love the interactive nature of the book; reading it felt like being at a book party with some of my favorite educators in attendance.

Favorite Titles That Support Reconsidering Composition

Anderson, Carl
How's it Going? A Practical Guide to Conferring with Student Writers
Heinemann, 2000

I am great at conferencing with kids about reading, but for many years I was not great at leading writing conferences. When this book first came out, I read it quickly and put into practice Anderson's very practical guides for conferencing with kids about their writing. His simple question— "How's it going?"—is only the beginning of writing conferences that move kids to write pieces they are pleased to share with others. I realized that a missing link for me was not only teaching kids how to be in a writing conference and what they should be doing while we were chatting, but also how I could incorporate the mini-lessons I was teaching into our writing conferences.

Fletcher, Ralph
Joyful Write: Cultivating High-Impact, Low-Stakes Writing
Heinemann, 2017

I bought this book because of its title. Who doesn't want to read a book about writing and joy? *Joyful Write* had a recalibrating effect on my classroom writing. Fletcher begins by reminding us about good, old-fashioned writing workshops, and how well that structure works to create happy, confident writers. He then considers how the writing classroom changed when standardized testing became the focus. My favorite notion is that of "greenbelt writing," a concept he takes from urban planning. A greenbelt, or protected space, is designated to remain natural, raw, untamed. Fletcher suggests that we have kids do writing that matches that description regularly in our classrooms. If you want to encourage greenbelt writing in your classroom to bring back the joy of writing and being writers, this is a book you need on your shelf.

Heard, Georgia
The Revision Toolbox: Teaching Techniques that Work
2nd ed. Heinemann, 2014

Middle school writers are notorious for getting to the end of their pieces, exuberantly placing a forceful period at the end of the last sentence they've written, and loudly announcing, "I'm done!" Asking them to go back into a piece, reconsider, and revise takes cajoling. Heard gives teachers clear, simple, yet productive tools to teach kids to excitedly go back into drafts as revisers eager to make their pieces writing they want to share with others. I love that she gives us many tools so that kids can pick the revision technique that works for their personal composing style and purpose of their writing.

Linder, Rozlyn
The Big Book of Details: 46 Moves for Teaching Writers to Elaborate
Heinemann, 2016

When I used to structure writing mini-lessons, I focused on how to begin, how to organize, and how to punctuate tricky structures like dialogue. But the kids' writing was still often uninspired. When the literacy coach at my school brought us this book, I realized what the mini-lessons had been missing: actual strategies for adding details that can spice up students' writing and help them give readers something interesting to read. Linder divides the book into five different ways in which details impact writing, and then offers mini-lessons to help you teach those uses of details. Linder won the 2018 Richard W. Halle Award from NCTE for her impact on middle school classrooms, and I will say that this book has greatly impacted my middle school classroom.

Short Story Collections from We Need Diverse Books

Giles, Lamar, editor
Fresh Ink: An Anthology
Random House, 2018

In this collection, WNDB invited young adult authors of color to write original stories that focus on racial identity.

Oh, Ellen
Flying Lessons & Other Stories
Random House, 2017

In this first collection from WNDB, middle grade authors of color were invited to write original stories that focus on kids' diversity.

Rhuday-Perkovich, Olugbemisola, editor
The Hero Next Door
Random House, 2019

In this third collection from WNDB, middle grade authors of color were invited to write stories about ordinary kids in heroic situations.

Social Media Spaces to Follow as You Build Your PLN

In Part V, I suggest how building a personal learning network on social media can enhance and grow your classroom practice. Below is a starter list of organizations, hashtags, and educators to follow on Twitter, as well as blogs and organization websites I find helpful. This is just a starter list—as you begin to follow people and organizations, you will shape your PLN to fit your own needs. This starter list was built using spaces I love as well as those suggested by Kristin McIlhagga.

- *American Indians in Children's Literature* **(blog)**—This scholarly blog run by Debbie Reese of Nambé Pueblo critically analyzes representations of Indigenous people in children's, middle grade (MG), and young adult (YA) literature. Follow her on Twitter using @debreese and visit www.americanindians inchildrensliterature.blogspot.com.

- **Anti-Oppression Guide, Simmons University Library**—This online guide thoroughly explores issues of antiracism, antibias, privilege, and oppression, and the guide provides multimedia resources that are easy to access for classroom and professional uses. Visit https://simmons.libguides.com/anti-oppression#Welcome.

- *Booktoss* **(blog)**—This scholarly blog run by Laura M. Jimenez critically analyzes children's literature, especially graphic novels, for issues of racism, sexism, homophobia, gender bias, and other forms of oppression. You can follow Jimenez on Twitter using @booktoss. Visit https://booktoss.blog.

- **#BuildYourStack**—As part of a books and reading initiative begun by NCTE in 2018, teachers write and share short blog posts on the NCTE website's Build Your Stack page, featuring short stacks of books they recommend. Most entries have a specific focus or topic. Teachers also share on social media book stacks that fit this kind of sharing using #BuildYourStack. Finally, at the NCTE Annual Convention for the last few years, there has been a lineup of #BuildYourStack thirty-minute presentations in the Exhibit Hall. For more information, visit https://ncte.org/build-your-stack/.
- **#classroombookaday**—Follow this daily picture book reading practice created by Jillian Heise on Twitter using #classroombookaday; www.classroombookaday.com provides a full description of the practice. Heise also hosts a Facebook group for teachers using this practice in their classrooms.
- **Clear the Air**—This group/space/movement of educators dedicated to their own education and growth as they engage in reading and discussion around social justice and dismantling systemic oppression was founded by Valeria Brown in December 2016. Brown develops a syllabus in the fall and spring and then folks join in reading and discussing on Twitter chats. You can tune into Clear the Air discussions by following #ClearTheAir and @cleartheairedu on Twitter. For more information, visit cleartheaireducation.wordpress.com.
- **The Conscious Kid**—This organization dedicated to helping parents, schools, and other organizations includes books featuring stories often underrepresented in children's literature. Follow them at @consciouskidlib and visit www.theconsciouskid.org for more information.

- **Cooperative Children's Book Center (CCBC)**—CCBC is a children's literature research center housed at the University of Wisconsin–Madison. CCBC is known for collecting the statistics on diversity in children's book publishing each year. Visit their website at ccbc.education.wisc.edu.
- *CrazyQuiltEdi* (blog)—This is the blog of librarian and literacy activist Edith Campbell. Campbell is a part of the Diversity Jedi, working to improve representation in children's and YA literature. Follow her on Twitter at @CrazyQuilts and visit her blog at https://crazyquiltedi.blog/.
- *Cynsations* (blog)—This is the blog of children's author Cynthia Leitich Smith of the Muscogee Creek Nation. Follow her on Twitter at @CynLeitichSmith and visit her blog at https://cynthialeitichsmith.com/.
- **Disability in Kidlit**—This group is dedicated to examining the representation and portrayal of disability in children's, MG, and YA literature. Follow them on Twitter at @DisabilityInLit and visit their website at http://disabilityinkidlit.com/.
- **Disrupt Texts**—As described earlier in the book, this is the literature movement founded by educators Tricia Ebarvia, Kim Parker, Lorena Germán, and Julia E. Torres. The movement asks teachers to critically disrupt their own practices and the texts they share with kids in their classes. Follow them by using #DisruptTexts and for more information visit www.disrupttexts.org.
- **Diversity Jedi**—This collective of children's literature activists is committed to critiquing representation in children's, MG, and YA literature. Look for #DiversityJedi (alsc.ala.org/blog/2018/06/diversity-jedi) to follow the activist work they do on social media.
- **EduColor**—To check out this collective of educators of color founded by José Luis Vilson, follow #EduColor and @EducolorMVMT on Twitter and visit www.educolor.org for more information.

- **Hijabi Librarians**—This collective of librarians who are critically examining Muslim representation in children's, MG, and YA literature can be followed on Twitter using @hijabilibrarian and by visiting the blog at https://hijabilibrarians.com/.
- **Indigo's Bookshelf: Voices of Native Youth**—This is a group of Indigenous kid readers who blog and tweet about the books they're reading. Follow them on Twitter using @ofglade; visit their blog at https://indigosbookshelf.blogspot.com/.
- **International Literacy Association (ILA)**—To follow ILA on social media, use #ILA and @ilatoday and visit www.literacyworldwide.org.
- **Latinxs in Kid Lit**—This collective of authors and children's literature experts offers a space to examine Latinx representation in children's, MG, and YA literature. Follow them on Twitter using @LatinosInKidLit and visit them at https://latinosinkidlit.com/.
- **MG Book Village**—This is a collective dedicated to middle grade books. Follow them on Twitter using @MGBookVillage. Participate in the Twitter chat using #MGBookChat and visit them at www.mgbookvillage.org.
- **National Council of Teachers of English (NCTE)**—To follow NCTE on social media, use #NCTE and @ncte and visit www.ncte.org.
- **National Writing Project**—To follow the National Writing Project on social media, use #NWP and follow @writingproject.
- **NCTE's Twitter Chat**—The hashtag used to follow the weekly Twitter chat hosted by NCTE is #NCTEchat.
- **Project LIT**—This is the diverse book program developed by high school teacher Jarred Amato. Teachers around the country have joined this reading initiative and use the diverse book lists to host book clubs in their schools and communities and to populate their classroom libraries. Follow on Twitter using #ProjectLitBookClub and @projectLITcomm.

Find out more by visiting https://jarredamato.wordpress.com/.
- **Reading Without Walls Challenge**—This is the national reading challenge that graphic novelist Gene Luen Yang made his platform when he was the National Ambassador for Young People's Literature. For more information on joining the challenge with the kids in your classes, visit https://geneyang.com/the-reading-without-walls-challenge.
- **Teachers College Reading and Writing Project (TCRWP)**—To follow TCRWP and all of the literacy work the organization does to promote workshop teaching in middle schools, use #tcrwp and @tcrwp on Twitter. Visit them at https://readingandwritingproject.org/.
- **Teaching for Change**—This organization helps educators and parents promote antibias, antiracist teaching in schools. The packed website offers tons of resources to use in your classroom. Visit them at https://www.teachingforchange.org/.
- **Teaching Tolerance**—This has long been one of my favorite organizations working to dismantle systems of oppression in education and helping teachers to create spaces of antiracist, antibias learning in their classrooms. The website has hundreds of resources, and you can sign up to receive their excellent magazine for free. Also helpful are the Social Justice Standards, which you can use to help plan lessons and units. Visit them at www.tolerance.org.
- **We Are Kid Lit Collective**—This collective of children's literature experts begun by Edith Campbell works to create children's book lists and materials that feature excellent representations of Black and Indigenous/People of Color (BIPOC). Follow them on Twitter using @WeAreKidLit and visit to view their booklists at https://wtpsite.wordpress.com/.
- **We Need Diverse Books**—As mentioned earlier, this is the organization founded by kidlit authors of color and led by Ellen Oh. Follow them on Twitter using #WNDB and visit at https://diversebooks.org/.

References

Adams, M., Blumenfeld, W. J., Castañeda, C. (R.), Hackman, H. W., Peters, M. L., & Zúñiga, X. (Eds.). (2013). *Readings for diversity and social justice* (3rd ed.). Routledge.

Ahmed, S., & Daniels, H. (2015). *Upstanders: How to engage middle school hearts and minds with inquiry.* Heinemann.

Anderson, C. (2000). *How's it going? A practical guide to conferring with student writers.* Heinemann.

Atwell, N. (2007). *The reading zone: How to help kids become skilled, passionate, habitual, critical readers.* Scholastic.

Atwell, N. (1987). *In the middle: A lifetime of learning about writing, reading, and adolescents.* Heinemann.

Atwell, N. (2015). *In the middle: A lifetime of learning about writing, reading, and adolescents* (3rd ed.). Heinemann.

Balingit, M. (2018, August 13). Do children have a right to literacy? Attorneys are testing that question. The *Washington Post.* https://www.washingtonpost.com/local/education/do-children-have-a-right-to-literacy-attorneys-are-testing-that-question/2018/08/13/926d0016-9042-11e8-8322-b5482bf5e0f5_story.html

Beers, K. (2002). *When kids can't read, what teachers can do: A guide for teachers 6–12.* Heinemann.

Beers, K., & Probst, R. E. (2013). *Notice and note: Strategies for close reading.* Heinemann.

Bishop, R. S. (1990). Mirrors, windows, and sliding glass doors. *Perspectives, 6*(3), ix–xi.

Boswell, S. 8 black children's authors you should know [blog post]. *Black Moms Blog.* https://blackmomsblog.com/11-black-childrens-authors-you-should-know/

Buehler, J. (2016). Being proactive: Helping others understand YA lit and YA pedagogy. In J. Buehler, *Teaching reading with YA literature: Complex texts, complex lives* (pp. 121–54). National Council of Teachers of English.

Calkins, L., Ehrenworth., M., & Lehman, C. (2012). *Pathways to the common core: Accelerating achievement.* Heinemann.

Chisholm, J. S., & Whitmore, K. F. (2018). *Reading challenging texts: Layering literacies through the arts* (pp. 1–17). Routledge and the National Council of Teachers of English.

Christenbury, L. (2010). NCTE and the shaping of American literacy education. In E. Lindemann (Ed.), *Reading the past, writing the future: A century of American literacy education and the National Council of Teachers of English* (pp.1–52). National Council of Teachers of English.

Cooperative Children's Book Center. (2020). Books by and/or about Black, Indigenous and People of Color 2002–2018. https://ccbc.education.wisc.edu/literature-resources/ccbc-diversity-statistics/books-by-and-about-poc-2002-2018/

Daniels, H., & Ahmed, S. K. (2015). *Upstanders: How to engage middle school hearts and minds with inquiry.* Heinemann.

Davis, M. (2018, Feb. 14). The post, the first amendment, and the student press [Blog post]. http://www2.ncte.org/blog/2018/02/post-first-amendment-press/

Duyvis, C. (n.d.). #ownvoices [Blog post]. www.corinneduyvis.net/ownvoices/

Graves, D. H. (1994). *A fresh look at writing.* Heinemann.

Graves, D. (2013). Conditions for effective writing. In T. Newkirk & P. Kittle (Eds.), *Children want to write: Don Graves and the revolution in children's writing* (pp. 57–68). Heinemann.

Hazelwood School District v. Kuhlmeier, 484 U.S. 260 (1988). https://supreme.justia.com/cases/federal/us/484/260/

Heise, J. (n.d.). What is #classroombookaday? [Blog post]. https://sites.google.com/view/cbad

Horning, K. T. (2010). *Can children's books save the world? Advocates for diversity in children's books and libraries* (May Hill Arbuthnot Honor Lecture).

Horning, K. T., Lindgren, M. V., & Schliesman, M. (2013). *A few observations on publishing in 2012.* University of Madison–Wisconsin, Cooperative Children's Book Center. https://ccbc.education.wisc.edu/books/choiceintro13.asp

Island Trees Union Free School District v. Pico, 457 U.S. 853 (1982). https://supreme.justia.com/cases/federal/us/457/853/

Kaplan, J. (2016, Oct. 26). The censors are coming: What you need to know [Blog post]. National Council of Teachers of English. http://www2.ncte.org/blog/2016/10/censors-coming-need-know/

Kirkland, D. (2013, January 29). Letter to a young English teacher. *A Will to Love.* https://davidekirkland.wordpress.com/2013/01/29/letter-to-a-young-english-teacher/

Kittle, P. (n.d.). *Letter to parents about reading and writing.* https://pennykittle.net/uploads/images/PDFs/Workshop_Handouts/ReadingLetter.pdf

Knox, E. (2015). *Book banning in 21st-century America.* Rowman & Littlefield.

Lane, B. (1999). *The reviser's toolbox.* Discovery Writing Press.

Larrick, N. (1965, Sep. 11). The all-white world of children's books. *Saturday Review, 48*(11), 63–65, 84–85. https://www.unz.org/Pub/SaturdayRev-1965sep11-00063

Lehman, C., & Roberts, K. (2013). *Falling in love with close reading: Lessons for analyzing texts and life.* Heinemann.

Lesesne, T. S. (2010). *Reading ladders: Leading students from where they are to where we'd like them to be.* Heinemann.

Lesesne, T. S., & Chance, R. (2002). *Hit list for young adults 2: Frequently challenged books.* ALA Editions.

Lindemann, E. (Ed.). (2010). *Reading the past, writing the future: A century of American literacy education and the National Council of Teachers of English.* National Council of Teachers of English.

McCarthy, J. (2013, Sep. 6). Heartprints [Blog post]. https://nerdybookclub.wordpress.com/2013/09/06/heartprints-by-joellen-mccarthy

Miller, D., with Kelley, S. (2014). *Reading in the wild: The book whisperer's keys to cultivating lifelong reading habits.* Jossey-Bass.

Monteiro v. Tempe Union High School District (9th Cir. 1998). https://caselaw.findlaw.com/us-9th-circuit/1281281.html

Myers, C. (2014, Mar. 15). The apartheid of children's literature. *The New York Times.* https://www.nytimes.com/2014/03/16/opinion/sunday/the-apartheid-of-childrens-literature.html

Myers, W. D. (1986, Nov. 9). Children's books; I actually thought we would revolutionize the industry. *The New York Times.* https://www.nytimes.com/1986/11/09/books/children-s-books-i-actually-thought-we-would-revolutionize-the-industry.html

Myers, W. D. (2012, Mar. 19). *Reading is not optional: An interview with Walter Dean Myers.* https://pen.org/reading-is-not-optional-an-interview-with-walter-dean-myers/

Myers, W. D. (2014, Mar. 15). Where are the people of color in children's books? *The New York Times.* https://www.nytimes.com/2014/03/16/opinion/sunday/where-are-the-people-of-color-in-childrens-books.html

National Council of Teachers of English. (2014). *NCTE beliefs about the students' right to write* [Position statement]. http://www2.ncte.org/statement/students-right-to-write/

National Council of Teachers of English. (2018). *The students' right to read* [Position statement]. http://www2.ncte.org/statement/righttoreadguideline/

Newkirk, T., & Kittle, P. (2013). *Children want to write: Donald Graves and the revolution in children's writing.* Heinemann.

Perrillo, J. (2018, Sep. 29). More than the right to read [Blog post]. http://www2.ncte.org/blog/2018/09/more-than-the-right-to-read-2/

Petrone, R. (2015, Nov.). *Learning as loss: Examining the affective dimensions to learning critical literacy.* Paper presented at the NCTE Annual Convention, Minneapolis, MN.

Rosenblatt, L. M. (1983). *Literature as exploration* (4th ed.). Modern Language Association.

Ryan, C. L., & Herman-Willmarth, J. M. (2018). *Reading the rainbow: LGBTQ-inclusive literacy instruction in the elementary classroom.* Teachers College Press.

Sebesta, S. L., & Donelson, K. L. (Eds.). (1993). *Inspiring literacy: Literature for children and young adults.* Transaction Publishers.

Shaub, M. (2015, May 18). Gay-themed children's book challenged in North Carolina school. *Los Angeles Times.* https://www.latimes.com/books/

jacketcopy/la-et-jc-gay-themed-childrens-book-challenged-20150518-story.html

Thomas, E. E. (2018, Dec.). Critical engagement with middle grade reads: Who lives? Who thrives? Who tells your story? *Voices from the Middle*, *26*(2), 13–16. https://secure.ncte.org/library/NCTE Files/Resources/Journals/VM/0262-dec2018/VM0262Dec18Critical.pdf

We Need Diverse Books. (2017). Our story. http://www.diversebooks.org/ourstory/

We Need Diverse Books. (2019). https://diverse books.org/

Text and Media Resources Mentioned in Teachers' Classrooms

Acevedo, E. *The Poet X*.

Adichie, C. N. "The Danger of a Single Story."

Alexander, M. *The New Jim Crow: Mass Incarceration in the Age of Colorblindness*.

Applegate, K. *The One and Only Ivan*.

Barnett, M. *Leo: A Ghost Story*.

Bobic, I. "Wearing a Hoodie in Oklahoma Could Soon Cost You a $500 Fine."

Bradbury, R. "All Summer in a Day."

Bradbury, R. "The Veldt."

Cisneros, S. "Eleven."

Coates, T. *The Beautiful Struggle*.

Coville, B. "Am I Blue?"

de la Peña, M. *Mexican WhiteBoy*.

DiCamillo, K. *The Miraculous Journey of Edward Tulane*.

DuVernay, A. *13th*.

Garden, N. *Annie on My Mind*.

Gino, A. *George*.

Green, J. *Looking for Alaska*.

Hinton, S. E. *The Outsiders*.

Hoose, P. *Claudette Colvin: Twice toward Justice*.

Hosseini, K. *The Kite Runner*.

Kinney, J. *Diary of a Wimpy Kid*.

Lee, H. *To Kill a Mockingbird*.

Lee, S. *2 Fists Up*.

Levine, K. *Lions of Little Rock*.

Levithan, D. *Two Boys Kissing*.

Lowry, L. *The Giver*.

Martin, M. "OKC Pastor to Wear Hoodie during Sunday Service."

McDonnell, P. *The Monsters' Monster*.

Miele, T. "Meet a Muslim."

Morrison, T. *Beloved*.

Myers, W. D. *The Greatest: Muhammad Ali*.

O'Connor, G. Olympians series.

Palos, A. *Precious Knowledge*.

Patterson, J. & Grabenstein, C. I, Funny series.

Reynolds, J., & Kiely, B. *All American Boys*.

Reynolds, P. H. *The Dot*.

Rowell, R. *Eleanore & Park*.

Rowling, J. K. The Harry Potter series.

Satrapi, M. *Persepolis*.

Shabazz, I., & Magoon, K. *X: A Novel*.

Shabazz, I., with Watson, R. *Betty before X*.

Shan, D. Cirque du Freak series.

Smith, J. Bone series.

Snicket, L. *The Dark*.

Spiegelman, A. *Maus I: A Survivor's Tale: My Father Bleeds History*.

Spinelli, J. *Stargirl*.

Steinbeck, J. *Of Mice and Men*.

Stone, T. L. *A Bad Boy Can Be Good for a Girl*.

Tan, A. "Fish Cheeks."

Thomas, A. *The Hate U Give*.

Thong, R. G. *Día de los Muertos*.

Twain, M. *Adventures of Huckleberry Finn*.

Watson, R. *Piecing Me Together*.

Woodson, J. *Each Kindness*.

Wright, R. "The Ethics of Living Jim Crow."

Index

Editor

Jennifer Ochoa began teaching high school in Lansing, Michigan, in 1992, moving to New York City in 2000, where she continued teaching high school. In 2009, she transitioned from high school to middle school. She continues teaching middle school in NYC and looks forward to a long career in the middle school classroom. In addition to her secondary classroom teaching, she has been an adjunct professor at CUNY's Lehman College campus since 2006, working with preservice and alternative certification teachers in the English education program. Ochoa has also worked closely with the National Writing Project at sites in Michigan and New York City, as well as serving on various committees and in various roles within the NCTE community. Her deep passion is teaching and learning and working with adolescents and teachers.

Contributors

Heather Anderson has been a middle level educator for nine years, also serving as a teacher consultant for the Oklahoma State Writing Project and with the College, Career, and Community Writer's Program. Heather teaches preservice teachers at Oklahoma State University, with an emphasis on curriculum design and educational technology. Currently she is working as an Advanced Placement English language arts eleventh- and twelfth-grade teacher for a home-schooling cooperative in Stillwater, as a curriculum designer for Oklahoma teachers, and as an ACT test-prep consultant.

Alex Corbitt (@Alex_Corbitt) taught middle school literacy for five years in the Bronx, New York. He is an active member of the National Council of Teachers of English, the National Writing Project, the Literacy Research Association, and the American Educational Research Association. Currently, he is enrolled at Boston College and pursuing a PhD in curriculum and instruction. You can learn more about Alex's work at alexcorbitt.com.

Millie Davis is the former director of the Intellectual Freedom Center of NCTE, which supports literacy teachers across the country to ensure their students' rights to know and learn, to read and write.

Chad Everett has served in a variety of roles in his time as an educator, but his home is in middle school where he currently serves as assistant principal. Prior to this role, he worked as a classroom teacher, literacy coach, and basketball coach. He is active in community literacy initiatives, believing the change needed to transform education extends beyond school walls. You can read more about Chad's work at ImagineLit.com.

April Fulstone has been a middle school history and literacy teacher for sixteen years in St. Louis, Missouri. She designs and facilitates professional development at the building and district levels on topics of equity, inclusion, antiracism and antibias. She was pronounced the 2013 Missouri History Teacher of the Year by the Gilder Lehrman Institute, and the 2018 Courageous Educator of the Year from Educators for Social Justice in St. Louis.

Carole Mashamesh teaches eighth-grade humanities at Tompkins Square Middle School in New York City. She has been a middle school teacher for fifteen years. Her school works closely with the Teachers College Reading and Writing Project, where she has participated in think tanks on argument writing and nonfiction reading. Carole's classroom has more than 8,000 books squeezed in to make sure that every student has a perfect book to read.

Kristin McIlhagga is an assistant professor at Oakland University in Rochester, Michigan, where she teaches courses in children's and young adult literature, equity and social justice, and language arts. A social justice approach informs her scholarship, teaching, and service. Kristin's work examines the ways that K–12 teachers and teacher candidates choose, respond to, and use children's and young adult literature with the goal of disrupting schools as a place of inequity and oppression.

Ellen Oh is the author of multiple middle grade and young adult fantasy books, including the middle grade Spirit Hunters series and the young adult Prophecy series. She has also edited two short story collections. She is a cofounder of the nonprofit organization We Need Diverse Books, with a mission to add diversity and equity to the field of children's literature.

Linda Rief left the classroom (reluctantly) in June 2019 after forty years of teaching grade 8 language arts. She misses their energy, their curiosity, and their desire to read and write. She has file folders filled with the thinking of these adolescents and will continue to share all she has learned from them through writing and speaking. She is currently an instructor with the University of New Hampshire's Summer Literacy Institute and a national and international presenter on issues of adolescent literacy. Linda is a former coeditor of NCTE's middle level journal, *Voices from the Middle*. A recipient of NCTE's Edwin A. Hoey Award for Outstanding

Middle School Educator in the English Language Arts, her classroom was featured in the series *Making Meaning in Literature* produced by Maryland Public Television for Annenberg/CPB.

Shelly K. Unsicker-Durham, a National Board Certified Teacher, spent twenty-three years as an ELA teacher, mostly in middle school and mostly in service to Moore Public Schools in Oklahoma. She continues to work closely with the Oklahoma Writing Project. Currently, she is a full-time graduate student and research assistant at the University of Oklahoma. Shelly was the 2018 recipient of NCTE's Linda Rief *Voices from the Middle* Award for her article "Some Things a Poet Does: Sharing the Process."

This book was typeset in Janson Text and BotonBQ by
Barbara Frazier.

Typefaces used on the cover include American Typewriter,
Frutiger, and Formata.

The book was printed on 50-lb. White Offset paper by
Seaway Printing Company, Inc.